Mastering Linux

From Basics to Expert Proficiency

Contents

1 Introduction to Linux **11**

1.1 History and Evolution of Linux 11

1.2 Linux Distributions 14

1.3 The Open Source Philosophy 16

1.4 Linux Kernel Architecture 19

1.5 Benefits of Using Linux 21

1.6 Installing Linux 24

1.7 First Time Boot and Using the Graphical User Interface (GUI) 26

1.8 Basic Command Line Interface (CLI) Operations 29

1.9 Navigating the File System 34

1.10 Understanding the Linux Directory Structure 37

1.11 Accessing Help and Documentation 40

2 Linux Filesystem and Directory Structure **45**

2.1 Overview of the Linux Filesystem 45

2.2 Filesystem Hierarchy Standard (FHS) 47

2.3 Common Directories and Their Purposes 49

2.4 File Types and Extensions 53

2.5 Mounting and Unmounting Filesystems 55

2.6 Creating and Managing Partitions 57

2.7 Using Filesystem Utilities 60
2.8 Understanding Inodes 62
2.9 File System Permissions and Ownership 65
2.10 Symbolic and Hard Links 67
2.11 Introduction to File System Tuning 69
2.12 Backup and Restore Operations 71

3 Basic Linux Commands **75**
3.1 Introduction to the Command Line Interface (CLI) 75
3.2 Navigating the File System with CD, LS, and PWD Commands 78
3.3 Viewing and Editing Files with CAT, LESS, and NANO . 80
3.4 File Manipulation: CP, MV, RM, and TOUCH 82
3.5 Directory Management: MKDIR, RMDIR, and RM -R . . 84
3.6 Finding Files and Directories: FIND and LOCATE 86
3.7 Understanding and Using Wildcards 88
3.8 Managing Processes with PS, TOP, KILL, and NICE . . 91
3.9 Handling Text with GREP, SED, and AWK 93
3.10 Redirecting Input and Output: >, », and | 95
3.11 Using the MAN and HELP Commands 97
3.12 Combining Commands: &&, ||, and ; 99

4 User and Group Management **103**
4.1 Introduction to User and Group Management 103
4.2 The /etc/passwd File 105
4.3 The /etc/shadow File 108
4.4 The /etc/group File 110
4.5 Creating and Deleting Users with useradd and userdel . 112
4.6 Modifying Users with usermod 114
4.7 Creating and Deleting Groups with groupadd and groupdel117

4.8 Assigning and Modifying Group Membership with gpasswd and usermod 119
4.9 Understanding and Setting User Passwords with passwd 121
4.10 Managing User Profiles and Environments 124
4.11 Implementing Sudo for Administrative Access 126
4.12 Access Control and Login Management 129

5 File Permissions and Security 133
5.1 Introduction to File Permissions 133
5.2 Understanding Read, Write, and Execute Permissions . 135
5.3 Using the ls and stat Commands to View Permissions . 138
5.4 Changing Permissions with chmod 140
5.5 Using Symbolic and Numeric Modes in chmod 143
5.6 Understanding File Ownership 144
5.7 Changing Ownership with chown and chgrp 147
5.8 Setting Default Permissions with umask 149
5.9 Special Permissions: SUID, SGID, and Sticky Bit 151
5.10 Access Control Lists (ACLs) 154
5.11 SELinux and AppArmor Basics 156
5.12 File Integrity Monitoring 158

6 Shell Scripting Basics 161
6.1 Introduction to Shell Scripting 161
6.2 Writing and Executing Your First Script 163
6.3 Shebang and Script Execution 166
6.4 Variables and Constants 168
6.5 Basic Input and Output 171
6.6 Using Conditional Statements: if, elif, else 174
6.7 Loop Structures: for, while, until 177
6.8 Functions in Shell Scripts 180
6.9 Debugging and Error Handling 182

6.10 Using Command Line Arguments 185
6.11 Working with Arrays 188
6.12 Scripting Best Practices 190

7 Package Management **195**
7.1 Introduction to Package Management 195
7.2 Package Management Concepts and Terms 198
7.3 Working with DEB Packages in Debian-Based Systems: APT and DPKG 200
7.4 Managing RPM Packages in Red Hat-Based Systems: YUM and DNF 204
7.5 Using tarballs and Source Code Installation 208
7.6 Introduction to Snap Packages 210
7.7 Flatpak and its Ecosystem 213
7.8 Managing Software Repositories 215
7.9 Verifying Package Integrity and Authenticity 218
7.10 Handling Package Dependencies 220
7.11 Upgrading and Removing Packages 223
7.12 Automating Package Management Tasks 226

8 System Monitoring and Performance **229**
8.1 Introduction to System Monitoring 229
8.2 Monitoring System Logs with Journalctl and Log Files . 232
8.3 Real-time System Monitoring with Top and Htop 234
8.4 CPU Usage and Performance Monitoring 237
8.5 Memory Usage and Performance Monitoring 239
8.6 Disk Usage and I/O Monitoring 242
8.7 Network Monitoring and Traffic Analysis 245
8.8 Using vmstat, iostat, and netstat 247
8.9 Monitoring Processes and System Services 250
8.10 Identifying and Resolving Performance Bottlenecks . . . 253

8.11 Setting Up and Using System Monitoring Tools: Nagios, Zabbix, etc. 256
8.12 Automating Performance Monitoring and Alerts 259

9 Networking in Linux 263
9.1 Introduction to Networking in Linux 263
9.2 Understanding Network Interfaces 265
9.3 Configuring Network Interfaces with ifconfig and ip . . . 268
9.4 Managing Network Connections with NetworkManager . 270
9.5 Setting Up Hostnames and DNS 274
9.6 Working with the /etc/network/interfaces File 276
9.7 Understanding and Configuring DHCP 279
9.8 Introduction to Firewalls: Iptables and Firewalld 282
9.9 Network Troubleshooting with Ping, Traceroute, and Netcat 284
9.10 Using SSH for Remote Access and Management 286
9.11 Establishing Secure Connections with SSL/TLS 289
9.12 Setting Up and Managing VPNs 291

10 Advanced Shell Scripting and Automation 297
10.1 Introduction to Advanced Shell Scripting 297
10.2 Working with Advanced Variables and Parameters . . . 301
10.3 Using Advanced Conditional Statements 304
10.4 Looping Constructs and Iteration 306
10.5 Advanced Functions and Modular Scripts 309
10.6 Error Handling and Debugging Techniques 312
10.7 Script Optimization and Performance Tuning 316
10.8 Interacting with System Processes and Daemons 318
10.9 Using Regular Expressions and Pattern Matching 320
10.10 Automating with Cron and Systemd Timers 323
10.11 Creating and Managing Complex Automation Workflows 325

10.12 Best Practices for Writing Maintainable Scripts 329

Introduction

Linux, an open-source operating system first developed by Linus Torvalds in 1991, has become a cornerstone of modern computing. Built upon UNIX, a long-standing, stable, and multiuser operating system, Linux has become known for its robustness, flexibility, and security. This book aims to provide a comprehensive guide to mastering Linux, covering its fundamentals, advanced topics, and practical applications.

Linux's open-source nature means that its source code is freely available for anyone to view, modify, and distribute. This fosters a community-driven development model, resulting in a highly secure and adaptable operating system. Various distributions, such as Ubuntu, CentOS, Fedora, and Debian, cater to different needs and preferences, ensuring that users can find a version of Linux that best fits their requirements.

A foundational understanding of the Linux operating system begins with its history and evolution. Recognizing the milestones in its development provides context for its current capabilities and widespread adoption. Understanding different Linux distributions is crucial for selecting the appropriate one for your needs, whether for desktop use, servers, or specialized applications.

The open-source philosophy underpins Linux and is essential to comprehend. This philosophy promotes transparency, collaboration, and freedom in software development and use. It leads to software that is not only more secure and reliable but also responsive to the needs of its users.

At the core of Linux is its kernel, the heart of the operating system. The kernel manages hardware resources, enables communication between software and hardware, and provides essential services. A deep dive into the Linux kernel architecture reveals the sophistication and elegance underlying this powerful operating system.

The benefits of using Linux are manifold. Its stability and security make it an excellent choice for servers and critical systems. Its flexibility and customizability make it ideal for developers and power users. Additionally, its efficiency and performance often surpass those of other operating systems, especially on older hardware.

Installing Linux is a straightforward process, but it requires some foundational knowledge to ensure a smooth experience. This book will guide you through various installation methods, from creating bootable installation media to configuring essential settings during and after installation.

Once Linux is installed, the first-time boot introduces users to the graphical user interface (GUI) and the command line interface (CLI). Both interfaces have their advantages, and mastering both is crucial for effective use of Linux. The GUI provides a user-friendly environment, while the CLI offers powerful and efficient tools for system management, scripting, and automation.

Navigating the file system and understanding the Linux directory structure are fundamental skills. The hierarchical file system organizes files and directories, making it easier to manage and access data. Familiarity with basic file system navigation commands is essential for effective use of the CLI.

Finally, accessing help and documentation is crucial for ongoing learning and problem-solving. Linux offers extensive documentation and support resources, including man pages, info pages, and online communities. Learning to leverage these resources will empower users to independently troubleshoot issues and deepen their understanding of the operating system.

This book is structured to build your knowledge from the ground up, starting with foundational concepts and progressing to advanced topics. Each chapter is designed to be accessible, engaging, and informative, ensuring a thorough understanding of Linux and its capabilities. By the end of this book, you will have the skills and confidence to utilize Linux effectively for various purposes, from everyday tasks to complex system administration and development.

Chapter 1

Introduction to Linux

Linux, an open-source operating system rooted in UNIX, is renowned for its stability, flexibility, and security. This chapter covers the history and evolution of Linux, explores different distributions, explains the open-source philosophy, and delves into the Linux kernel architecture. Additionally, it outlines the benefits of using Linux, guides through the installation process, highlights both graphical and command-line interfaces, and emphasizes the importance of understanding the file system and directory structure. Accessing Linux documentation and help resources is also discussed to enable ongoing learning and effective problem-solving.

1.1 History and Evolution of Linux

The inception of Linux can be traced back to the early 1990s when Linus Torvalds, a Finnish computer science student at the University of Helsinki, began developing an operating system kernel as a personal project. The primary motivation behind this endeavor was to create a free and open-source alternative to the proprietary UNIX operating systems, which were dominant in academic and professional settings but often required expensive licenses and had restrictions on source code access.

In 1991, Linus Torvalds posted a message to the comp.os.minix news-group, announcing his project and inviting others to contribute. The initial kernel version, 0.01, was released in September 1991 and consisted of roughly 10,000 lines of code. The project quickly garnered attention within the hacker and developer communities, leading to the formation of a collaborative effort to enhance and expand the kernel. By 1992, the Linux kernel was licensed under the GNU General Public License (GPL), a pivotal decision that enabled a vibrant ecosystem of open-source contributions to flourish around it.

The early development of Linux was deeply intertwined with the GNU project spearheaded by Richard Stallman and the Free Software Foundation (FSF). While the GNU project had already developed several crucial components of a free operating system, such as the GNU Compiler Collection (GCC), the GNU C Library (glibc), and various utilities, it lacked a working kernel. The integration of the Linux kernel with GNU components essentially completed the GNU operating system, though it continued to be commonly referred to as Linux.

By the mid-1990s, Linux had matured sufficiently to be used in production environments. Major milestones included the adaptation of the kernel to support a wider range of hardware architectures, expanding its utility beyond Intel x86 processors. The introduction of distributions such as Slackware (1993) and Red Hat Linux (1994) provided packaged versions of the operating system along with essential software and management tools, making it more accessible to users and organizations.

The late 1990s and early 2000s saw an explosive growth in Linux adoption across various sectors. This period witnessed the rise of commercial enterprises like Red Hat, SUSE, and Canonical, which started offering enterprise-grade support and services for their respective Linux distributions. The dot-com boom also played a crucial role, as Internet-based companies leaned heavily on Linux for its robustness, scalability, and cost-effectiveness.

```
# Example of the early installation process using Slackware
fdisk /dev/hda # Create disk partitions
mke2fs /dev/hda1 # Format the partitions with the ext2 filesystem
mount /dev/hda1 /mnt # Mount the partition

# Copy the system files
cp -a /slakware /mnt

# Create necessary system directories
mkdir /mnt/usr /mnt/var /mnt/home
```

At the turn of the millennium, Linux received significant validation from major industry players. IBM's announcement of a $1 billion investment in Linux in 2001 underscored its growing importance in enterprise computing. Additionally, the inclusion of Linux in embedded systems and devices, ranging from networking equipment to smartphones (notably, Android-based devices), expanded its reach beyond traditional desktop and server environments.

The evolution of Linux continued with the advent of modern technologies such as containerization and cloud computing. Projects like Docker, which revolutionized software deployment and scalability, leveraged Linux kernel features like namespaces and cgroups to isolate and manage containers. Concurrently, the rise of cloud service providers such as Amazon Web Services (AWS), Google Cloud Platform (GCP), and Microsoft Azure offered widespread Linux-based virtual machines, further propelling its adoption in various domains.

Community involvement has remained a cornerstone of Linux development, facilitated through platforms like GitHub and GitLab, where developers across the globe contribute to the kernel and associated software. The Linux Foundation, established in 2000, has played a pivotal role in coordinating and advancing the ecosystem through initiatives, funding, and collaborative projects.

```
# Cloning the Linux kernel source from GitHub
git clone https://github.com/torvalds/linux.git

# Building the kernel
cd linux
make menuconfig # Configure the kernel options
make # Compile the kernel
make modules_install
make install
```

The Linux kernel itself has undergone substantial developments, with regular releases introducing performance enhancements, new hardware support, and security improvements. The community-driven model ensures a rapid response to vulnerabilities and technological trends, keeping Linux at the forefront of innovation.

The history and evolution of Linux illustrate a remarkable journey from a hobbyist's project to a dominant force in the technology landscape. Its open-source nature, coupled with the collaborative contributions of a global developer community, continues to drive its advancement and widespread utilization across diverse applications and industries.

1.2 Linux Distributions

Linux distributions, often referred to as "distros," are various versions of the Linux operating system that package the Linux kernel with a set of software applications and tools. These distributions provide users with a complete operating environment, tailored to different needs and preferences. This section aims to provide an understanding of the nature of Linux distributions, their variations, and some of the most prominent examples.

The core of any Linux distribution is the Linux kernel, which serves as the foundation of the system. Beyond the kernel, distributions include various other components: system libraries, user applications, and often a graphical user interface (GUI). The choice of these components can significantly affect the usability, look, and performance of a given distribution, making it crucial for users to select a distro that best fits their requirements.

Classification of Distributions:

Linux distributions can be classified based on several factors, including their purpose, package management systems, and user-friendliness.

- **General-Purpose Distributions**: These distributions are designed for a broad range of users and use cases. Examples include Ubuntu, Fedora, and Debian.

- **Special-Purpose Distributions**: These are tailored for specific tasks such as security (e.g., Kali Linux), multimedia production (e.g., Ubuntu Studio), or lightweight performance (e.g., Puppy Linux).

- **Enterprise Distributions**: Targeted towards businesses and organizations, offering long-term support and stability. Examples are Red Hat Enterprise Linux (RHEL) and SUSE Linux Enterprise Server (SLES).

Package Management Systems:

One of the distinguishing features of Linux distributions is the package management system they employ. Package management systems are responsible for installing, updating, and managing software packages on a system.

- **Debian-based Systems**: These use the *dpkg* package manager and often employ Advanced Packaging Tool (APT) for easier management. Popular Debian-based distributions include Ubuntu, Linux Mint, and Debian itself.
- **Red Hat-based Systems**: Utilizes the *rpm* package manager, with tools like YUM (Yellowdog Updater Modified) or DNF (Dandified YUM) to streamline software management. Fedora, CentOS, and RHEL are part of this family.
- **Arch-based Systems**: Focus on simplicity and flexibility, typically using the *pacman* package manager. Arch Linux and its derivatives like Manjaro are examples.
- **Other Systems**: Some distributions use unique package management systems such as Slackware (using *pkgtool*) and Gentoo (using *Portage*).

Popular Linux Distributions:

Several distributions have gained popularity due to their ease of use, community support, or specific features. Below is an overview of some of the most well-known Linux distributions, each with unique characteristics:

Ubuntu: Known for its user-friendliness, extensive documentation, and strong community support. Ubuntu is ideal for beginners and is based on Debian.

Fedora: Sponsored by Red Hat, Fedora focuses on delivering cutting-edge features and technologies. It serves as a testing ground for Red Hat Enterprise Linux.

Debian: Renowned for its stability and extensive repository of packages. Debian is the basis for many other distributions, including Ubuntu.

CentOS: A free and open-source alternative to RHEL, offering enterprise-level features and stability. Widely used in server environments.

Arch Linux: Targets advanced users who prefer a DIY approach. Arch provides a rolling release model, ensuring users have the latest software updates.

openSUSE: Offers a choice between stable (Leap) and rolling (Tumbleweed) releases. Known for its YaST configuration tool, making system management straightforward.

Choosing a Distribution:
When selecting a Linux distribution, several factors should be considered:

- **Skill Level**: New users might prefer user-friendly distributions such as Ubuntu or Linux Mint, whereas experienced users might opt for Arch Linux or Gentoo for greater control.
- **Support and Community**: Distributions with large communities and active forums (e.g., Ubuntu, Fedora) can provide better support and resources for problem-solving.
- **Purpose and Application**: Distributions like Ubuntu Studio cater specifically to multimedia tasks, while Kali Linux is designed for security professionals.
- **Hardware Requirements**: Lightweight distributions like Puppy Linux or Lubuntu are suitable for older or less powerful hardware.

To install a Linux distribution, users typically download an ISO file from the distribution's official website. This ISO file can be written to a USB drive to create a bootable installation media. The installation process varies slightly between distributions but generally involves booting from the USB drive, partitioning the hard drive if necessary, and following the on-screen instructions to complete the setup.

The diversity of Linux distributions is one of the operating system's greatest strengths, providing flexibility and choice for all types of users and use cases. Whether one requires a robust server environment, a secure penetration testing platform, or a friendly desktop experience, there is a Linux distro that caters to those needs. Understanding the landscape of Linux distributions empowers users to make informed decisions and select the best tools for their specific requirements.

1.3 The Open Source Philosophy

The open-source philosophy, at its core, is defined by a commitment to collaborative development, transparency, and freedom. Originally conceptualized by the free software movement in the 1980s, the philosophy has evolved into a significant cultural and technical force in modern computing. This section elucidates the fundamental principles of open-source development, the distinctions between open source and proprietary software, and the impact of open-source software on the industry and community.

Fundamentally, open source refers to software whose source code is made available to the public to inspect, modify, and enhance. This practice ensures that the software is not only accessible but also malleable, allowing for constant improvements and peer reviews. The definition of open source is formalized by the Open Source Initiative (OSI) which outlines criteria for software to be considered open source.

- The software must be freely redistributable.
- The source code must be included or easily obtainable.
- Derived works and modifications must be allowed.
- The integrity of the author's source code must be maintained.
- The license must not discriminate against any persons or groups.
- The license must not restrict anyone from making use of the program in a specific field of endeavor.
- The rights attached to the program must apply to all to whom the program is redistributed.
- The license must not be specific to a product.
- The license must not restrict other software.
- The license must be technology-neutral.

One of the primary distinctions between open source and proprietary (closed-source) software lies in distribution and modification rights. Proprietary software, controlled by a single entity, generally restricts these rights, withholding source code and strictly regulating the usage, modification, and distribution of the software through licensing agreements.

Open source software thrives on contributions from a diverse community of developers and users. These contributions can range from bug reports, feature requests, patches, documentation improvements, to complete overhauls. The collaborative nature of open source development encourages innovation and rapid iteration cycles, leading to robust and secure software. Projects such as the Linux kernel, Apache HTTP Server, and Mozilla Firefox exemplify the success of this model, serving as cornerstones of modern computing.

Another critical aspect of open source philosophy is transparency. By making source code publicly available, open source projects allow for extensive scrutiny. This transparency leads to higher quality software since developers can identify and fix vulnerabilities and improve performance through peer review processes. Moreover, transparency fosters trust as users can understand exactly how the software works and verify that it does not contain malicious code or backdoors.

The impact of open source on the software industry is profound. It has democratized technology, enabling individuals and organizations to leverage and build upon existing software without incurring prohibitive costs. This inclusiveness has accelerated technological advancement, facilitated education, and empowered under-resourced communities and startups to innovate.

Moreover, open source promotes the principle of autonomy. Users are not bound by vendor lock-in and are free to adapt software to meet their specific needs. This adaptability is particularly important in scientific research, education, and government sectors where customization and transparency are critical.

Linux itself is a paragon of the open source philosophy. Created by Linus Torvalds in 1991, Linux started as a small personal project and has grown into a global phenomenon through contributions from thousands of developers worldwide. The GNU General Public License (GPL), under which Linux is released, ensures that Linux remains free for use, modification, and distribution. The GPL's copyleft provision requires that any derivative works also be open source, fostering an ongoing cycle of improvement and shared knowledge.

The benefits of adopting open-source solutions extend beyond mere access to code. For organizations, it means reduced costs, increased security, and avoidance of dependence on a single vendor. Governments endorse open-source software for its potential to bolster national security through transparency and independence from foreign suppliers. In academia, open source is invaluable for teaching, providing students with real projects to study, contribute to, and learn from.

Despite these advantages, challenges persist in the open-source domain. Project sustainability can be an issue, as many projects rely on voluntary contributions. Ensuring consistent funding to support core developers and infrastructure is crucial for the ongoing success of many open-source projects. Additionally, the onus is on the community to maintain quality standards, documentation, and regulatory compliance.

Continued advocacy and education about the benefits and practices of open source are essential to addressing these challenges and realizing the full potential of open source. Through sustained efforts, the open-source philosophy can continue to foster innovation, collaboration, and technological advancement. As the global community of developers and users grows, so too does the collective capacity to solve complex problems and create software that benefits all.

1.4 Linux Kernel Architecture

The Linux kernel serves as the core interface between a computer's hardware and its processes. The architecture of the Linux kernel is designed to balance the needs for control with performance efficiency. At a high level, it consists of several subsystems, each responsible for distinct functions within the operating system. These subsystems include process management, memory management, file system operations, device drivers, and networking.

The monolithic kernel architecture adopted by Linux integrates all core functions into a single binary. This approach contrasts with microkernel architectures, where the kernel is broken into smaller, interacting components. The monolithic design of Linux provides robust performance benefits as most operations execute within the kernel space without the need to switch contexts between user and kernel spaces.

One of the fundamental components is the process management subsystem, which handles process scheduling and execution. The kernel uses a preemptive multitasking model, meaning the scheduler can interrupt a running process to assign CPU time to another process. The key structures involved in process management are the task_struct, which defines process attributes, and the scheduler, which employs algorithms like Completely Fair Scheduler (CFS) to maintain a balance in CPU resource allocation.

```
#include <linux/sched.h>

struct task_struct {
    volatile long state; /* -1 unrunnable, 0 runnable, >0 stopped */
```

```
    void *stack;
    /* other process information */
};
```

Memory management within the Linux kernel involves the allocation and deallocation of memory, maintaining memory mappings for processes, and handling virtual memory. Linux employs a demand paging mechanism, only loading pages into memory when referenced. This method optimizes the use of RAM by ensuring that only necessary data is loaded and retained. The kmalloc function is a widely used utility for memory allocation within the kernel.

```
void *kmalloc(size_t size, gfp_t flags);
```

The file system interface of the Linux kernel operates through the Virtual File System (VFS) layer, an abstraction layer that supports multiple file system types uniformly. VFS handles system calls related to file operations by translating them into appropriate file system requests. It uses data structures like the inode object that contains metadata about files and the dentry object for directory cache entries.

```
struct inode {
    umode_t i_mode;
    unsigned short i_opflags;
    struct super_block *i_sb;
    struct address_space *i_mapping;
    /* other file information */
};

struct dentry {
    struct dentry *d_parent;
    struct qstr d_name;
    struct inode *d_inode;
    /* other directory information */
};
```

Device drivers in the Linux kernel manage specific hardware peripherals, serving as the interface between the hardware and the kernel. They ensure proper initialization, configuration, and operation of hardware components. Device drivers reside within the kernel space, providing operational APIs to the user space. Linux distinguishes between different types of devices, including character devices, block devices, and network devices, each managed using respective kernel subsystems.

Networking within the Linux kernel is facilitated by the network stack, an extensive suite managing all networking protocols and data transfers. The stack is structured in layers, similar to the OSI model, incorporating layers for socket communication, protocol handling, routing, and interface control. The implementation encompasses functionalities to support protocols like TCP, UDP, and IP, leveraging structures such as sock and sk_buff that handle socket data and packet buffers.

```
struct sock {
    /* socket information */
    struct sk_buff_head sk_receive_queue;
    struct sk_buff_head sk_write_queue;
    /* pointers to functions for protocol operations */
};

struct sk_buff {
    struct sk_buff *next;
    struct sk_buff *prev;
    ktime_t tstamp;
    struct net_device *dev;
    /* data buffer */
};
```

The Linux kernel includes mechanisms for synchronizing processes and protecting data structures via various synchronization primitives like spinlocks, semaphores, and mutexes. These primitives ensure proper sequencing and resource sharing among concurrent processes, thereby preventing race conditions and ensuring consistency within the kernel.

```
spinlock_t my_lock;
spin_lock(&my_lock);
/* critical section code */
spin_unlock(&my_lock);
```

Each component of the Linux kernel architecture works cohesively to manage system resources effectively, ensuring efficient and secure operation. The kernel continuously evolves, integrating newer technologies and techniques to enhance performance and expand its functionalities. As of recent developments, kernel modularization and support for modern hardware interfaces continue to be primary focal points for ongoing kernel improvements.

1.5 Benefits of Using Linux

The adoption of Linux offers multiple advantages, extending from stability to security, efficiency, and flexibility in a wide array of environments. These benefits have made Linux an operating system of choice for various applications, from personal computing to enterprise solutions and embedded systems.

Stability: Linux is well-known for its robust stability. This stability stems from several factors, including its monolithic kernel architecture and the open-source development model. The kernel, the core part of the operating system, is designed to handle many operations without crashing. Additionally, because the Linux community—comprising numerous developers worldwide—diligently maintains and debuggs the system, errors and vulnerabilities are swiftly identified and resolved.

Security: One of the most prominent features of Linux is its strong security. Linux follows a permissions model that restricts access to critical system areas. Root access is required to modify system files, install software, or configure settings. This permission-based system diminishes the risk of unauthorized access and mitigates potential damage. Moreover, the open-source nature of Linux means that security audits can be conducted continuously by users and developers globally, contributing to prompt identification and rectification of security vulnerabilities.

Performance and Efficiency: Linux is optimized for performance and efficiency. Unlike some other operating systems, Linux has minimal background processes, which consume fewer system resources. The modular design allows users to customize their systems by choosing only the necessary components, reducing bloat and leading to better overall performance. This feature is especially important for server environments where resource optimization is crucial.

Flexibility: The flexibility of Linux is evident in its capacity to run on virtually any hardware, from high-end servers to low-end embedded systems. It supports a multitude of filesystems and can interact with diverse types of hardware. Users can select from various distributions tailored to specific needs, such as Ubuntu for general-purpose use, CentOS for enterprise environments, and Yocto for embedded systems. Additionally, the command-line interface provides an unparalleled level of control over system operations.

Cost-Effectiveness: As an open-source operating system, Linux is freely available. This aspect significantly reduces software costs, particularly for startups and small businesses, enabling them to allocate resources to other critical areas. Furthermore, there are no licensing fees, which can be particularly beneficial when deploying multiple systems.

Community Support and Resources: Linux benefits from extensive community support. The collaborative community contributes to a vast repository of resources, including documentation, forums, mailing lists, and tutorials. New users can find a wealth of information to help troubleshoot problems, understand the system, or explore advanced features. This collective knowledge base ensures that assistance is available for virtually any issue one might encounter.

Customizability: The high degree of customizability in Linux allows users to tailor the operating system to their needs. This includes customizing the desktop environment, the choice of window managers, and even the kernel itself. Advanced users have the option to rebuild the kernel to include or exclude specific features, thus optimizing performance for particular tasks.

Compatibility and Interoperability: Linux offers broad compatibility and interoperability with different file formats and network protocols. Its ability to interact seamlessly with other operating systems and devices enhances its utility in mixed environments, such as networks consisting of both Linux and Windows systems. Tools like Samba allow Linux systems to share files and printers with Windows-based machines, ensuring cohesive network operations.

Scalability: Linux's scalability makes it an excellent choice for varying implementations. From servers handling millions of requests per second to small embedded devices, Linux can be scaled to meet performance demands without significant alterations to the core system. This characteristic is valuable for organizations planning to grow their IT infrastructure over time.

Open-Source Philosophy: Embracing Linux means advocating for the open-source philosophy, which emphasizes transparency, collaborative development, and freedom. Users have the ability to inspect the code, contribute enhancements, and share improvements. This model ensures that Linux continuously evolves to meet user needs and adapts to emerging technological trends.

Utilizing Linux provides a multitude of benefits that extend beyond its primary functions as an operating system. Its strengths in stability, security, and performance make it a compelling choice for diverse computing environments. The continuous support from an active community coupled with the advantages of an open-source development model ensures that Linux remains at the forefront of technological advancement.

1.6 Installing Linux

Installing Linux on a computer can be a gratifying experience, providing the user with a versatile and powerful operating system. The process of installing Linux varies slightly between distributions, but there are common steps that can be followed generally. This section will outline these steps in detail, ensuring clarity and ease of execution.

Before starting the installation process, it is paramount to back up any important data on the target machine. Linux installation often involves repartitioning the disk, which can result in data loss if not handled correctly.

Step 1: Choosing a Distribution

Selecting an appropriate Linux distribution is the first step. Popular choices include Ubuntu, Fedora, Debian, and Arch Linux. For beginners, Ubuntu is a highly recommended option due to its user-friendly interface and extensive community support.

Step 2: Downloading the Installation ISO

Once a distribution is selected, download the installation ISO file from the distribution's official website. Verify the integrity of the downloaded file by checking its checksum, which is provided on the download page. This step ensures that the file has not been corrupted during the download.

```
# Example for checking the SHA256 checksum of a downloaded file:
sha256sum ubuntu-20.04.1-desktop-amd64.iso
# Compare the output with the checksum provided on the website.
```

Step 3: Creating a Bootable USB Drive

To create a bootable USB drive, use a tool such as Rufus (for Windows) or 'dd' (for Unix-like systems).

For Windows:

- Download and install Rufus from https://rufus.ie/.
- Open Rufus, select the downloaded ISO file, and choose the target USB drive.
- Click 'Start' to begin the process.

For Unix-like systems:

```
# The following command will overwrite the contents of the USB drive.
# Replace /dev/sdX with the actual device name of the USB drive.
sudo dd if=ubuntu-20.04.1-desktop-amd64.iso of=/dev/sdX bs=4M status=progress
    && sync
```

Step 4: Booting from the USB Drive

Insert the bootable USB drive into the target computer. Restart the system and enter the BIOS/UEFI settings by pressing the appropriate key during the boot process (common keys include 'F2', 'F10', 'DEL', or 'ESC'). Change the boot order to prioritize USB devices over hard drives. Save the changes and exit the BIOS/UEFI settings.

Step 5: Starting the Installation

Upon booting from the USB drive, the Linux installer will start. Follow the on-screen instructions:

- Select the preferred language.
- Choose between trying the distribution (live session) or installing it directly. Opt for the installation option.
- Configure keyboard layout.
- Connect to a Wi-Fi network if necessary.

Step 6: Partitioning the Disk

Partitioning is a critical step during the installation. The installer usually offers several options:

- **Erase disk and install Linux**: This option will delete all existing data on the disk and allocate the entire disk space to Linux.
- **Install alongside existing OS**: This option will resize existing partitions to accommodate Linux. This is suitable for dual-boot setups.
- **Something else**: For advanced users, this option allows manual partitioning.

If manual partitioning is chosen, it is recommended to create the following partitions:

- A root partition ('/') with at least 20GB of space.

- A swap partition, typically equal to the amount of RAM or double the amount if RAM is less than 4GB.
- A home partition ('/home') for user data.

Step 7: User Information and Final Configuration

Enter the required user information such as username, password, and computer name. This user account will have administrative privileges.

The installer may ask for the following configurations:

- Time zone selection.
- Installation of third-party software (e.g., graphics drivers, media codecs).

Step 8: Completing the Installation

Review all configurations and begin the installation process by clicking the 'Install' button. The installation may take some time to complete. Once done, the installer will prompt to remove the installation media and reboot the system.

After rebooting, the system will load the newly installed Linux distribution. Log in with the user account created and proceed with personalized configurations and software installations as needed.

This detailed guide provides a comprehensive walkthrough of installing a Linux distribution, ensuring that both novice and experienced users can achieve a successful installation.

1.7 First Time Boot and Using the Graphical User Interface (GUI)

Upon successfully installing a Linux distribution, the next critical phase is the first-time boot. This section meticulously examines the steps involved and provides an overview of interacting with the Graphical User Interface (GUI).

When the computer is powered on, the Bootloader, usually GRUB (GRand Unified Bootloader), initiates the boot process. GRUB presents a menu of available operating systems or kernels. Should you have multiple operating systems installed, navigate through the menu using the arrow keys and select the Linux operating system by pressing Enter.

Following the selection, the Linux kernel is loaded into memory. During this phase, a series of initialization scripts run, setting up hardware, mounting file systems, and starting essential services. Most distributions display a splash screen with a progress bar; pressing Esc will often reveal verbose messages detailing these processes.

Once initialization completes, the system transitions to the graphical interface if the default target is configured to include a display manager (such as gdm, sddm, or lightdm). If a display manager is properly installed and enabled, you will be presented with the login screen.

At the login screen, you must enter your username and password. Following successful authentication, the display manager will start the default desktop environment (e.g., GNOME, KDE Plasma, XFCE).

Interacting with the GUI

The desktop environment offers a user-friendly interface to interact with the system. Common components include:

- **Desktop Area**: The main screen area where icons for files, applications, and shortcuts may reside.

- **Panel or Taskbar**: Typically located at the top or bottom of the screen, displaying open applications, system tray icons, and the application menu.

- **Application Menu**: Provides access to all installed applications, usually organized into categories.

Consider the GNOME Desktop Environment as an example:

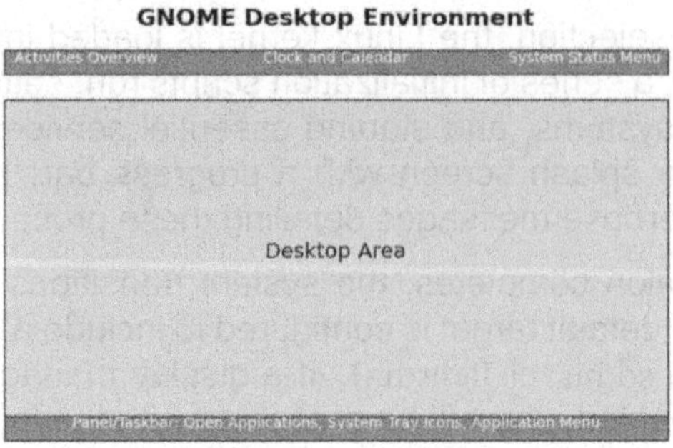

In GNOME the top bar includes:

- **Activities Overview**: Located at the far left, enabling window and workspace management, and access to the Application Menu.
- **Clock and Calendar**: Centrally positioned, displaying the current time and date.
- **System Status Menu**: Found at the top-right corner, providing quick access to system settings like volume, network, and power options.

Launching and Managing Applications

Applications can be launched from the Application Menu or by using the search functionality in the Activities Overview (GNOME). For example, to open the terminal:

1. Click on Activities or press the Super key.
2. Type "Terminal" into the search bar.
3. Select the Terminal application from the results.

Customizing the Desktop Environment

Linux distributions allow significant customization of the desktop environment. Options typically available include:

- **Appearance Settings**: Change themes, icons, fonts, and backgrounds.
- **Keyboard Shortcuts**: Customize keybindings for frequently used actions.
- **Extension Management**: Particularly in GNOME, extensions add functionality like additional panels or workspace management improvements.

These settings are usually accessible from the System Settings application, which provides a centralized interface for managing system preferences.

Managing Windows and Workspaces

Advanced window management features allow users to utilize multiple workspaces and perform various window operations. Common actions include:

- **Tiling**: Arrange windows side by side or in a grid.
- **Switching Workspaces**: Use keybindings like Ctrl+Alt+Up/Down or the Activities Overview.
- **Window Snap**: Drag windows to screen edges to snap them to half-screen size.

Shutting Down and Rebooting

When finished with the session, it is essential to properly shut down or reboot the system via the GUI. Access the System Status Menu in GNOME, and select Power Off / Log Out. You will be given options to log out, restart, or power off the machine.

Integrating these practices ensures efficient usage of the Linux graphical environment, providing a foundation for transitioning to more advanced concepts in later chapters.

1.8 Basic Command Line Interface (CLI) Operations

The Command Line Interface (CLI) is a powerful way to interact with the Linux operating system. Unlike the Graphical User Interface (GUI), which relies on visual representations and point-and-click operations, the CLI enables users to execute commands directly. This offers a higher level of control and flexibility over the system.

Accessing the Command Line

To access the CLI, open a terminal emulator in your Linux distribution. Common terminal emulators include gnome-terminal, konsole, and xterm. The terminal provides a prompt, usually ending with $, indicating that it is ready to accept commands.

Basic Commands

- pwd: Print Working Directory

```
$ pwd
/home/username
```

  This command outputs the full path of the current directory.

- ls: List Directory Contents

```
$ ls
Desktop Documents Downloads Music Pictures Videos
```

  The ls command lists the files and directories within the current directory. Options such as -l for detailed information and -a for hidden files enhance its functionality.

```
$ ls -la
total 40
drwxr-xr-x 6 username username 4096 Oct 27 10:00 .
drwxr-xr-x 3 username username 4096 Oct 27 10:00 ..
-rw-r--r-- 1 username username 220 Oct 27 10:00 .bash_logout
-rw-r--r-- 1 username username 3771 Oct 27 10:00 .bashrc
drwxr-xr-x 2 username username 4096 Oct 27 10:00 Desktop
drwxr-xr-x 2 username username 4096 Oct 27 10:00 Documents
```

- cd: Change Directory

```
$ cd Documents
$ pwd
/home/username/Documents
```

  The cd command changes the current directory. Absolute and relative paths can be used:

```
$ cd /home/username/Music
$ cd ../Downloads
```

  Here, .. denotes the parent directory.

- mkdir: Make Directory

```
$ mkdir new_folder
```

This creates a new directory named new_folder within the current directory.

- rmdir and rm: Remove Directory and Files

```
$ rmdir new_folder
$ rm filename.txt
```

The rmdir command removes empty directories, while rm removes files. Use rm -r for recursive removal of non-empty directories.

```
$ rm -r directory_name
```

- cp: Copy Files and Directories

```
$ cp file1.txt /home/username/backup/
```

The above command copies file1.txt to the backup directory. Use cp -r for directories.

```
$ cp -r source_dir /home/username/backup/
```

- mv: Move or Rename Files and Directories

```
$ mv oldname.txt newname.txt
$ mv file.txt /home/username/Documents/
```

The first command renames oldname.txt to newname.txt, and the second moves file.txt to the Documents directory.

- touch: Create Empty Files

```
$ touch newfile.txt
```

This creates an empty file named newfile.txt. If the file exists, its access and modification timestamps are updated.

File Viewing and Editing

- cat: Concatenate and Display File Content

```
$ cat file.txt
Hello, this is a file content.
```

- less and more: View File Content with Paging

```
$ less file.txt
$ more file.txt
```

- nano and vim: Text Editors

```
$ nano file.txt
$ vim file.txt
```

Redirection and Piping

Commands can be combined using redirection and piping to perform complex operations.

- Output Redirection:

```
$ ls > file_list.txt
```

  This command redirects the output of ls to file_list.txt.

- Input Redirection:

```
$ sort < unsorted_list.txt
```

  It takes the content of unsorted_list.txt as input to the sort command.

- Piping:

```
$ ls | grep "pattern"
```

  This pipes the output of ls to grep which searches for "pattern".

Process Management

- ps: Display Current Processes

```
$ ps
  PID TTY TIME CMD
 1341 pts/0 00:00:00 bash
 1355 pts/0 00:00:00 ps
```

- top: Monitor System Processes in Real-Time

```
$ top
```

- kill: Terminate a Process

```
$ kill 1341
```

Here, the process with PID 1341 is terminated. Use kill -9 for a forceful termination.

Permissions Management

- chmod: Change File Mode (Permissions)

```
$ chmod 755 script.sh
```

This sets read, write, and execute permissions for the owner, and read and execute permissions for the group and others.

- chown: Change File Owner and Group

```
$ chown user:group file.txt
```

Networking Commands

- ping: Check Network Connectivity

```
$ ping www.example.com
```

- ifconfig and ip: Configure a Network Interface

```
$ ifconfig
$ ip addr show
```

- ssh: Secure Shell for Remote Login

```
$ ssh username@remote_host
```

Getting Help

- man: Manual Pages

```
$ man ls
```

This command shows the manual page for ls. Use q to quit.

- –help: Help Option

```
$ ls --help
```

It provides a summary of command usage and options.

Understanding and mastering the CLI is pivotal for efficient system management and navigation. The examples provided offer foundational knowledge, forming a springboard to more advanced UNIX command capabilities. With practice, users will gain proficiency and confidence in leveraging the CLI to its fullest potential.

1.9 Navigating the File System

Navigating the Linux file system efficiently is a fundamental skill for any user, as it enables effective interaction with the operating system. Understanding the structure and commands for file system navigation lays the groundwork for performing a wide range of tasks, from everyday operations to advanced system management.

The Linux file system is organized as a hierarchical structure that starts from the root directory, denoted by a single slash (/). All files and directories are located under this root, forming a tree-like structure. Directories (also known as folders) can contain files or subdirectories.

To navigate this structure, several command line utilities are essential. The following explanations and examples will illustrate their usage.

1. The pwd Command:

The pwd (print working directory) command is used to display the full path of the current directory.

```
pwd
```

/home/user

2. The ls Command:

The ls (list) command is used to list the contents of a directory. Various options can modify its output.

Basic usage:

```
ls
```

Listing files with detailed information:

```
ls -l
```

```
total 8
drwxr-xr-x 2 user user 4096 Jan 01 12:34 Documents
-rw-r--r-- 1 user user  123 Jan 01 12:34 example.txt
```

Including hidden files (files beginning with a dot):

```
ls -a
```

Combined options for long format including hidden files:

```
ls -la
```

3. The cd Command:

The cd (change directory) command changes the current directory. It requires a path as an argument.

To navigate to another directory:

```
cd /path/to/directory
```

To move up one directory level:

```
cd ..
```

To return to the home directory:

```
cd ~
```

4. Absolute vs. Relative Paths:

Paths can be specified as absolute or relative. An absolute path starts from the root directory and specifies the complete location. A relative path is defined in relation to the current directory.

Example of absolute path:

```
cd /home/user/Documents
```

Example of relative path (assuming current directory is /home/user):

```
cd Documents
```

5. Directory Shortcuts:

Certain shortcuts simplify navigation: - : user's home directory - .: current directory - ..: parent directory

For example:

```
cd ~
cd .config
cd ..
```

6. Creating and Removing Directories:

To create a new directory, use the mkdir (make directory) command:

```
mkdir new_directory
```

To create nested directories:

```
mkdir -p parent_directory/child_directory
```

To remove a directory, use the rmdir (remove directory) command. Note that the directory must be empty:

```
rmdir new_directory
```

7. Moving and Renaming Files and Directories:

The mv (move) command is used for moving files or directories, as well as renaming them.

To move a file:

```
mv /path/to/source /path/to/destination
```

To rename a file:

```
mv oldname.txt newname.txt
```

8. Copying Files and Directories:

The cp (copy) command is used to copy files and directories.

To copy a file:

```
cp source_file destination_file
```

To copy an entire directory recursively:

```
cp -r source_directory destination_directory
```

9. Removing Files and Directories:

The rm (remove) command deletes files and directories.

To remove a file:

```
rm filename.txt
```

To remove a non-empty directory recursively:

```
rm -r directory_name
```

10. Viewing File Contents:

Several commands allow viewing the contents of files:

- cat: displays content of small files

```
cat filename.txt
```

- more and less: display large files one page at a time

```
more filename.txt
less filename.txt
```

- head: displays the first few lines

```
head filename.txt
```

- tail: displays the last few lines

```
tail filename.txt
```

Understanding these commands and concepts forms the basis of effective file system navigation in Linux, empowering users to perform tasks with precision and confidence.

1.10 Understanding the Linux Directory Structure

Understanding the Linux directory structure is fundamental for effective system navigation and management. Linux utilizes a hierarchical file system layout, where directories branch from a single root directory. This approach follows the Filesystem Hierarchy Standard (FHS), which ensures that the directory structure is consistent across various distributions, facilitating a predictable organization.

The root directory, denoted as /, is the starting point of the Linux directory tree. All other directories are subdirectories of the root. Each directory serves specific purposes and contains files and further subdirectories. Here, we explore the main directories commonly found in a typical Linux system:

- /bin: Short for "binaries", this directory contains essential command-line binaries necessary for booting and repairing the system.

- /boot: Includes files required for booting the system, such as the Linux kernel and initialization files.
- /dev: Stands for "device", it holds device files representing hardware components. These files provide an interface to hardware devices.
- /etc: Contains system configuration files and scripts. Almost all system-wide configurations are stored here.
- /home: Each user's personal files and directories reside in /home, with each user having a subdirectory labeled with their username.
- /lib: Libraries essential for binaries in /bin and /sbin reside here. It includes shared libraries and kernel modules.
- /media: Temporary mount points for removable media such as USB drives and CDs/DVDs are found in /media.
- /mnt: Used for manually mounting file systems. It is commonly used for temporary mounts.
- /opt: Optional software packages can be installed here by administrators.
- /proc: A virtual filesystem providing an interface to kernel data structures. It is used to obtain system information dynamically.
- /root: The home directory for the root user, the system administrator.
- /run: Contains runtime data utilized since the last boot. It provides data that requires fast reading and writing.
- /sbin: System binaries essential for system administration tasks. Unlike /bin, it primarily targets the superuser.
- /srv: Site-specific data served by the system, such as web server files.
- /tmp: Temporary files created by system and user processes. These files may be deleted without notice.

- /usr: A secondary hierarchy containing user utilities and applications. Subdirectories include /usr/bin, /usr/lib, and /usr/local, which have extensive user applications and libraries.
- /var: Variable files such as logs, caches, and spool files. Subdirectories include /var/log for log files and /var/spool for print queues.

Effective navigation and utilization of these directories depend on understanding the commands and operations associated with the command line interface (CLI). The ls command is fundamental for listing directory contents:

```
ls /home
```

This command will list the contents of the /home directory. To navigate between directories, the cd command is employed:

```
cd /etc
```

This command changes the current working directory to /etc. To confirm the current directory, use the pwd command:

```
pwd
```

The output will display the path of the present working directory. Comprehending these basic commands enriches the user's ability to manage and interact with the file system efficiently.

An advanced understanding also involves file permissions and ownerships, centralized in the FHS directories. The ls -l command provides a detailed list, including permissions, owners, and groups:

```
ls -l /bin
```

Output example:

```
total 936
-rwxr-xr-x 1 root root 938840 Apr  8  2022 bash
-rwxr-xr-x 1 root root  40664 Mar  5  2022 cat
-rwxr-xr-x 1 root root  53224 Mar  5  2022 chgrp
-rwxr-xr-x 1 root root  54256 Mar  5  2022 chmod
...
```

Each line indicates file permissions, the number of links, owner, group, size, modification date, and filename. Understanding these attributes enhances the management of access controls within the system.

Moreover, the find command facilitates locating files within the directory structure based on given criteria:

```
find /usr -name "*gcc*"
```

This command searches for files within the /usr directory that contain "gcc" in their names.

Furthermore, filesystem integrity is often monitored with tools like df to check disk space usage:

```
df -h
```

Output example:

```
Filesystem      Size  Used Avail Use% Mounted on
/dev/sda1        50G   20G   28G  42% /
/dev/sda2       100G   85G   10G  90% /home
...
```

The command df -h provides a human-readable format of disk usage, showing the size, used space, available space, percentage used, and the mount points.

Understanding the Linux directory structure, combined with related commands, forms the bedrock of proficient system navigation and management. This knowledge empowers users to handle tasks efficiently, emphasizing the significance of each directory in maintaining system coherence and functionality.

1.11 Accessing Help and Documentation

Mastering the ability to efficiently access help and documentation is crucial for any Linux user, whether a novice or an expert. Linux provides comprehensive documentation and a variety of help tools that enhance your problem-solving skills and knowledge acquisition.

Man Pages: The manual pages, commonly referred to as "man pages," provide detailed information about commands and programs available on the system. Each man page is divided into sections that contain standardized information, including a description, synopsis, options, and examples. To access the man page for a specific command, use the man command:

```
man <command-name>
```

For instance, to view the manual page for the ls command, execute:

```
man ls
```

You'll see the following format:

```
LS(1)                    User Commands                    LS(1)

NAME
       ls - list directory contents

SYNOPSIS
       ls [OPTION]... [FILE]...

DESCRIPTION
       List information about the FILEs (the current directory by
       default).
       ...
```

The sections of the man pages are typically categorized as follows:

- Section 1: User Commands
- Section 2: System Calls
- Section 3: Library Functions
- Section 4: Special Files
- Section 5: File Formats and Conventions
- Section 6: Games and Screensavers
- Section 7: Miscellaneous
- Section 8: System Administration Commands

To specify a section when accessing a man page, include the section number before the command, as in:

```
man 5 passwd
```

Info Pages: Another valuable resource is the GNU Info system, which supplements man pages by providing hyperlinked documentation. Use the info command to access these documents. For example, to view the info page for the coreutils, use:

```
info coreutils
```

Navigating the info pages involves using the arrow keys or specific commands such as n (next), p (previous), and q (quit).

The –help **Option:** Many commands support the –help option to display a brief summary of their usage and available options. This is useful for quickly looking up command syntax and options without accessing the detailed man page. For example, to get help on the cp command:

```
cp --help
```

The output will be:

```
Usage: cp [OPTION]... [-T] SOURCE DEST
  or:  cp [OPTION]... SOURCE... DIRECTORY
  or:  cp [OPTION]... -t DIRECTORY SOURCE...
Copy SOURCE to DEST, or multiple SOURCE(s) to DIRECTORY.
...
```

The whatis **Command:** The whatis command provides a brief description of a command. This can be useful when you need a quick reminder of what a command does.

```
whatis <command-name>
```

For instance:

```
whatis grep
```

The output will be:

```
grep (1) - print lines that match patterns
```

The apropos **Command:** The apropos command searches the man page descriptions for a keyword. This is useful when you need to find a command related to a particular topic but are unsure of its exact name.

```
apropos <keyword>
```

For example:

```
apropos copy
```

The output might include:

```
cp (1)           - copy files and directories
install (1)      - copy files and set attributes
```

Online Resources: The Linux community offers extensive online documentation, forums, and tutorials. Notable resources include:

- The Linux Documentation Project (LDP): http://www.tldp.org/
- Stack Overflow: https://stackoverflow.com/
- Super User: https://superuser.com/
- Various distribution-specific wikis and forums (e.g., https://wiki.archlinux.org/, https://askubuntu.com/)

These platforms provide a wealth of information, ranging from beginner guides to advanced troubleshooting steps. Engaging with the community via forums and mailing lists can also help address specific queries and contribute to collaborative problem-solving.

Efficiently accessing help and documentation empowers users to tackle challenges and deepen their understanding of Linux. The combination of built-in tools like man pages, info pages, and the –help option, along with external resources, ensures comprehensive support for ongoing learning and proficiency in Linux system usage.

Chapter 2

Linux Filesystem and Directory Structure

This chapter provides a comprehensive overview of the Linux filesystem and directory structure, explaining the Filesystem Hierarchy Standard (FHS) and the purposes of common directories. It details file types and extensions, the processes of mounting and unmounting filesystems, and managing partitions. Additionally, the chapter covers filesystem utilities, inodes, file ownership, and permissions, as well as symbolic and hard links. It introduces filesystem tuning concepts and essential backup and restore operations to ensure data integrity and system reliability.

2.1 Overview of the Linux Filesystem

The Linux filesystem is a vital component of the operating system, dictating how data is stored and retrieved. It is structured hierarchically, starting from a single root directory, denoted by '/', and branching into various subdirectories. This organizational scheme facilitates efficient data management and retrieval, providing a systematic way of organizing files and directories.

In Linux, everything is considered a file, including directories, devices, and even network sockets. This uniformity simplifies the handling of different types of data and devices. The root directory '/' is the top-most directory in the hierarchy and contains all other directories and files. It serves as the foundation of the filesystem, and its proper maintenance is crucial for system stability.

Beneath the root directory are crucial directories such as '/bin', '/boot', '/dev', '/etc', '/home', '/lib', '/media', '/mnt', '/opt', '/root', '/sbin', '/tmp', '/usr', and '/var'. Each of these directories has a specific purpose:

- '**/bin**': Contains essential user command binaries that are fundamental for system operation, such as 'ls', 'cp', and 'mv'. - '**/boot**': Stores static files required for booting the system, including the Linux kernel and bootloader configuration files. - '**/dev**': Holds device files that represent hardware and virtual devices. - '**/etc**': Contains configuration files for the system and installed applications. - '**/home**': The home directories for regular users, providing personal storage space. - '**/lib**': Essential shared libraries and kernel modules. - '**/media**': Mount points for removable media such as CD-ROMs, USB drives. - '**/mnt**': Temporary mount points for filesystems. - '**/opt**': Used for the installation of add-on application software packages. - '**/root**': The home directory for the root user. - '**/sbin**': Contains essential system binaries, typically for use by the root user. - '**/tmp**': Temporary files stored by the system and applications. - '**/usr**': Contains user utilities and applications. - '**/var**': Variable files such as logs, spools, and caches.

Each file and directory in the filesystem is represented by an inode (index node), which stores metadata about the file or directory, such as its size, permissions, and timestamps.

Filesystems in Linux can be of different types, such as ext3, ext4, XFS, and Btrfs. Each type has distinct features and optimizations. The most commonly used types are ext4 and XFS, known for their balance of features, performance, and reliability.

Mounting a filesystem integrates it into the directory tree. The mount command is used to attach a filesystem to a specified directory, known as a mount point.

```
mount /dev/sda1 /mnt/mydrive
```

Unmounting a filesystem detaches it from the directory tree and is accomplished using the 'umount' command.

```
umount /mnt/mydrive
```

The flexibility of the Linux filesystem is further enhanced by its support for symbolic and hard links. Symbolic links are pointers to files, whereas hard links are direct references to the data on the disk. These linking methods provide versatile ways to manage and access files across different parts of the filesystem.

Permissions and ownerships are critical aspects of the Linux filesystem, providing security and control over who can read, write, or execute files. The permission system uses a combination of user, group, and other settings to specify access rights.

Understanding and managing the Linux filesystem requires familiarity with various utilities and commands, such as 'ls' for listing directory contents, 'df' for checking disk space usage, and 'fsck' for filesystem consistency checks. Mastery of these tools is essential for system administration and ensuring the filesystem's integrity.

In-depth knowledge of the Linux filesystem empowers users with the ability to efficiently organize, manage, and secure their data. This understanding is fundamental to proficient and reliable system administration.

2.2 Filesystem Hierarchy Standard (FHS)

The Filesystem Hierarchy Standard (FHS) is a crucial concept to understand when working with Linux operating systems. The FHS provides a standardized directory structure and directory contents that allow users and software developers to know where specific types of files and directories should reside. By adhering to FHS, systems maintain uniformity and predictability, facilitating easier management and navigation within the filesystem.

The FHS defines the directory structure and directory contents in Unix-like operating systems, including Linux. The primary objective of FHS is to ensure consistency across various distributions so that users, system administrators, and software applications have a uniform environment. The commonly used directories under FHS include /bin, /boot, /dev, /etc, /home, /lib, /lib64, /media, /mnt, /opt, /proc, /root, /sbin, /srv, /tmp, /usr, and /var.

/bin: The /bin directory contains essential command binaries needed for single-user mode and for all users. Common utilities such as ls, cp, and mv are located here. These binaries are necessary for the booting process and system repair.

/boot: The /boot directory includes all the files needed to boot the system, such as the kernel (vmlinuz), the initial ramdisk image (initrd), and the bootloader configurations (GRUB or LILO).

/dev: The /dev directory houses device files, allowing the operating system and applications to interact with hardware devices via device files. For example, /dev/sda represents the first hard drive, while /dev/tty denotes terminal interfaces.

/etc: The /etc directory contains all the configuration files for the system. System-wide configuration settings and initialization scripts reside here. Files such as /etc/fstab for filesystem mounting and /etc/passwd for user account information are examples.

/home: The /home directory is allocated for users' personal directories. Each user gets a directory under /home with a name corresponding to their username (e.g., /home/user1). Users typically store their documents, configurations, downloads, and other personal files in their respective home directories.

/lib and **/lib64**: /lib contains essential shared libraries and kernel modules, which are required for booting the system and executing binaries in /bin and /sbin. For 64-bit systems, /lib64 is used for the 64-bit library files.

/media: /media is designated as a mount point for removable media, such as CD-ROMs, USB drives, and other temporary storage devices. When a removable device is connected and mounted, it typically appears under this directory.

/mnt: This directory is reserved for temporarily mounted filesystems. It is often used during the installation process or when manually mounting a filesystem by an administrator for maintenance tasks.

/opt: The /opt directory is used for the installation of additional software packages that are not part of the standard system. Proprietary applications or large software suites are typically placed here (e.g., /opt/VMware for VMware products).

/proc: /proc is a virtual filesystem that provides an interface to kernel data structures. It's dynamically created and resides only in memory. By accessing the /proc directory, users and system administrators can obtain detailed information about system resources and processes (e.g., /proc/cpuinfo for CPU details).

/root: The /root directory serves as the home directory for the root user. It is distinct from /home/root, emphasizing the elevated privileges of the root user.

/sbin: /sbin contains essential system binaries used for system administration. Utilities like fdisk, reboot, and ifconfig are situated here, which are typically only needed by the root user.

/srv: /srv stands for "service" and is used to store data for specific services provided by the system, such as web and FTP servers. For instance, /srv/www could be used for websites served by the Apache or Nginx web servers.

/tmp: The /tmp directory is intended for temporary files created by both the system and users. It is accessible to all users and often cleared upon system reboot, providing a space for temporary data storage during system operations.

/usr: The /usr directory is one of the largest directories, containing user utilities and applications. It houses binaries, libraries, documentation, and source code for second-level programs. Major subdirectories include /usr/bin for non-essential command binaries, /usr/sbin for non-essential system binaries, /usr/lib for non-essential libraries, /usr/share for architecture-independent shared data, and /usr/local for local customization.

/var: The /var directory contains variable data files, such as logs, mail spools, and temporary files maintained by daemons and other services. Important subdirectories include /var/log for system log files, /var/spool for print queues and mail spools, and /var/tmp for persistent temporary files.

By understanding the FHS, users and administrators can navigate the filesystem more efficiently, locate necessary files quickly, and maintain the system in an organized manner. This standardized directory structure ensures consistency and predictability across different Linux distributions, which is crucial for system administrators and developers alike. Adherence to FHS is essential for maintaining a well-organized, functional, and manageable Linux filesystem.

2.3 Common Directories and Their Purposes

The Linux filesystem is organized hierarchically, with directories organized in a tree structure. Each directory has a specific purpose, serving as a logical container for files and subdirectories related to particular system functionalities. Understanding the role and contents of these directories is crucial for effective system administration and usage. This section delineates these directories as standardized by the Filesystem Hierarchy Standard (FHS), providing essential knowledge for navigating and managing a Linux system.

- **/** (Root Directory): The root directory is the top-level directory in the hierarchy. All other directories branch out from the root directory. It contains essential binaries, libraries, and configuration files necessary for system boot and repair.
- **/bin** (Essential User Binaries): Contains essential command-line utilities and executable programs that are required for system boot and operation, even when no other filesystems are mounted. Examples include bash, ls, mkdir.

```
# Example of listing contents of /bin directory
$ ls /bin
bash cat chmod cp mv ls mkdir rm
```

- **/boot** (Boot Loader Files): Stores the kernel and other files needed for the boot process. These include bootloader configuration files and the initial RAM disk image used during the initial boot process.

```
# Checking boot loader files
$ ls /boot
vmlinuz-5.10.0-8-amd64 initrd.img-5.10.0-8-amd64 grub/
```

- **/dev** (Device Files): Contains device nodes that represent hardware and virtual devices. This allows programs to access hardware in a consistent manner. Devices include disks (sda), terminals (tty), and random data sources (random).

```
# Listing device files
$ ls /dev
sda tty random null
```

- **/etc** (Configuration Files): Houses all configuration files and shell scripts required for system management and configuration. This directory is crucial for system administrators, containing files like passwd, fstab, and network configuration scripts.

```
# Example of listing configuration files
$ ls /etc
passwd fstab network/
```

- **/home** (User Home Directories): Each user has a directory within /home, where personal files and directories are stored. For example, user alice would have a home directory /home/alice.

```
# Listing user home directories
$ ls /home
alice bob
```

- **/lib** (Essential Shared Libraries): Holds shared library files, which contain code used by multiple programs. It also includes kernel modules that provide hardware-specific functionality.

```
# Finding essential shared libraries
$ ls /lib
libc.so.6  ld-linux.so.2
```

- **/media** and **/mnt** (Mount Points): /media is used for automatically mounted filesystems such as removable media (CD-ROMs, USB drives), and /mnt is traditionally used for manual mounts. Both directories serve as mount points where filesystems can be attached to the system.

```
$ ls /media /mnt
/media: cdrom usb
/mnt:
```

- **/opt** (Optional Software): Designated for the installation of add-on application software packages, typically those that do not conform to standard FHS directory layout. Third-party applications and large software suites may reside here.

```
# Example of listing optional software packages
$ ls /opt
oracle  eclipse
```

- **/proc** (Process Information): A virtual filesystem that provides an interface to kernel data structures. It's dynamically generated and used to access process and system information, such as system uptime (/proc/uptime) and CPU info (/proc/cpuinfo).

```
# Viewing process information
$ cat /proc/cpuinfo
processor   : 0
vendor_id   : GenuineIntel
cpu family  : 6
...
```

- **/root** (Root Home Directory): The home directory of the root user, separate from the rest of the users in /home. This distinction ensures that root's files are available even if other filesystems are not mounted.

```
# Checking root user home directory
$ ls /root
.bashrc  .profile
```

- **/run** (Runtime Data): Used for storing transient files that describe the running system since the last boot. These include process identifiers and runtime data.

```
# Viewing runtime data
$ ls /run
utmp  systemd
```

- **/sbin** (System Binaries): Contains essential system binaries and executables intended for system administration tasks. Examples include ip, systemctl, fdisk.

```
# Example of listing system binaries
$ ls /sbin
ip systemctl fdisk
```

- **/srv** (Service Data): Holds data for services provided by the system. This directory is useful for servers that need to reference hosted data directories, such as web servers calling files from /srv/www.

```
# Viewing service data directory
$ ls /srv
www ftp
```

- **/tmp** (Temporary Files): Temporary files created by system and user processes are stored here. This directory is often cleared upon system reboot, ensuring that temporary data does not persist.

```
# Listing temporary files
$ ls /tmp
tempfile sessionid
```

- **/usr** (User Binaries and Read-Only Data): Contains the majority of user utilities and applications, organized into subdirectories like /usr/bin for user binaries, /usr/lib for libraries, and /usr/share for shared data such as documentation.

```
# Listing user binaries
$ ls /usr/bin
python gcc perl
```

- **/var** (Variable Data): This directory includes files that are expected to grow over time, such as log files (/var/log), mail queues (/var/spool), and other variable-length files that persist between reboots.

```
# Viewing variable data directories
$ ls /var
log spool tmp
```

Understanding these standard directories and their purposes is fundamental for navigating the Linux filesystem effectively. Each directory holds unique significance and provides a structural organization that supports the complexity and functionality of Linux systems.

2.4 File Types and Extensions

In Linux, the filesystem is a highly organized structure where different file types coexist, each serving a specific purpose. Even though Linux is less dependent on file extensions compared to operating systems like Windows, they still play a role in identifying or categorizing files. This section will elucidate the various file types and their extensions, along with the commands used to interact with them.

Linux supports several file types categorized into regular files, directories, device files, links, sockets, and named pipes. Recognizing these file types is essential for proper system administration and usage.

Regular Files Regular files contain data such as text, binaries, or executables. They can be further classified based on their content or usage:

- **Text Files:** These are files containing readable characters. Common text editors like nano, vim, and gedit can be used to create and edit these files. Examples include .txt, .log, .conf.
- **Binary Files:** These files contain binary data and are not directly readable by humans. These are usually executables compiled from source code, such as .out, .bin, .exe (in a cross-platform context).
- **Image Files:** Images are stored in formats such as .jpg, .png, .gif.
- **Audio and Video Files:** These multimedia files are stored with extensions like .mp3, .wav for audio, and .mp4, .avi for video.

To identify a periodic file, the file command is used:

```
$ file example.txt
example.txt: ASCII text
```

This command analyzes the file and returns its type based on content rather than extension.

Directories Directories, or folders, are special files that contain other files and directories. They serve as organizational units within the filesystem hierarchy. The command ls lists directory contents, while mkdir and rmdir can create and remove directories, respectively.

```
$ mkdir my_directory
$ ls -l
drwxr-xr-x 2 user user 4096 Apr 5 12:34 my_directory
```

Device Files Device files interface with hardware devices, providing means to communicate with system hardware. They reside in the /dev directory and are categorized into character (e.g., /dev/ttyS0) and block devices (e.g., /dev/sda1).

Creating a device file involves the mknod command:

```
$ sudo mknod myblock b 7 61
$ sudo mknod mychar c 7 61
```

Symbolic and Hard Links Links are pointers to files, serving as references rather than storing data. A hard link points directly to the inode of a file, while a symbolic link (symlink) points to the file's path. The creation of links involves the ln command:

```
$ ln original.txt hardlink.txt
$ ln -s original.txt symlink.txt
```

Sockets Sockets facilitate inter-process communication (IPC), allowing data exchange between processes running on the same or different machines. Socket files are commonly used by network services and can be identified in the file system with ls:

```
$ ls -l /var/run/docker.sock
srw-rw---- 1 root docker 0 Apr 5 12:34 /var/run/docker.sock
```

Named Pipes Named pipes (FIFOs) enable unidirectional data flow between processes. These special files are created using the mkfifo command:

```
$ mkfifo my_pipe
$ ls -l my_pipe
prw-r--r-- 1 user user 0 Apr 5 12:34 my_pipe
```

Extensions While Linux does not strictly require file extensions, they are useful for human operators to quickly identify file types. For instance, script files may have extensions signifying their interpreter:

- **Shell Scripts:** Often have .sh extension.
- **Python Scripts:** Typically use .py extension.
- **Perl Scripts:** Identified with .pl extension.

This facilitates easier manipulation and execution of scripts by using the appropriate interpreter:

```
$ bash script.sh
$ python script.py
$ perl script.pl
```

Linux's versatility lies in its flexible yet robust handling of different file types. Understanding these fundamental aspects allows users to manage the filesystem effectively, enhance productivity, and ensure efficient system operation.

2.5 Mounting and Unmounting Filesystems

The process of mounting a filesystem attaches the filesystem to a directory (mount point), making it accessible to the system. Conversely, unmounting a filesystem detaches it, ensuring that data integrity is preserved before removal. Understanding these processes is fundamental for managing storage media, such as hard drives, SSDs, USB drives, and network shares, in a Linux environment.

To mount a filesystem, use the mount command. The basic syntax is:

```
mount [options] device directory
```

Here, *device* refers to the block device or partition (e.g., /dev/sda1), and *directory* is the mount point where the filesystem is attached (e.g., /mnt).

Consider the example of mounting a USB drive formatted with the ext4 filesystem:

```
mkdir /mnt/usbdrive
mount /dev/sdb1 /mnt/usbdrive
```

The first command creates a directory to serve as the mount point. The second command mounts the USB drive's partition /dev/sdb1 to /mnt/usbdrive. After mounting, you can access the USB drive's contents through the /mnt/usbdrive directory.

To verify that the filesystem is mounted, examine the output of either the mount command or /proc/mounts:

```
mount | grep sdb1
```

or

```
cat /proc/mounts | grep sdb1
```

Another common utility used for mounting filesystems is the /etc/fstab file, which provides a way to automatically mount filesystems at boot. Each entry in fstab follows the format:

```
device mount_point filesystem_type options dump pass
```

For example:

```
UUID=12345678-9abc-def0-1234-56789abcdef0 /mnt/usbdrive ext4 defaults 0 2
```

In the fstab entry above, the partition identified by its UUID (Universally Unique Identifier) is set to be mounted on /mnt/usbdrive with the ext4 filesystem type.

Unmounting a filesystem is performed with the umount command:

```
umount directory
```

Using the previous USB drive example, unmounting is done via:

```
umount /mnt/usbdrive
```

Ensure no files are open and no process uses the filesystem to avoid errors. Use lsof or fuser to check:

```
lsof | grep /mnt/usbdrive
```

or

```
fuser -v /mnt/usbdrive
```

For mounting network filesystems, such as NFS or SMB/CIFS, use similar commands with respective network filesystem types. For instance, to mount an NFS share:

```
mount -t nfs 192.168.0.100:/shared_folder /mnt/network_share
```

To unmount the NFS share:

```
umount /mnt/network_share
```

Mounting with specific options can enhance performance and security. Common options include rw (read/write), ro (read-only), noexec (no execution of binaries), and nosuid (ignore set-user-identifier or set-group-identifier bits). For example:

```
mount -o rw,noexec,nosuid /dev/sdb1 /mnt/usbdrive
```

Modern Linux distributions often use systemd for mounting. To create a systemd mount unit:

```
[Unit]
Description=Mount USB Drive

[Mount]
What=/dev/sdb1
Where=/mnt/usbdrive
Type=ext4
Options=rw

[Install]
WantedBy=multi-user.target
```

Save this as /etc/systemd/system/mnt-usbdrive.mount, then enable and start the mount:

```
systemctl enable mnt-usbdrive.mount
systemctl start mnt-usbdrive.mount
```

Through these mounting and unmounting techniques, managing filesystems in Linux becomes efficient, ensuring reliable access and data integrity. Understanding and correctly implementing these processes is critical for system administration tasks, particularly concerning storage management and system stability.

2.6 Creating and Managing Partitions

In Linux, managing storage requires creating and managing partitions on storage devices. A partition can be thought of as a distinct section of a hard disk or other block device. Each partition can be formatted with a specific filesystem, allowing the operating system to read and write data to it. Proper partition management ensures effective utilization of disk space and contributes to system efficiency and organization.

To create and manage partitions in Linux, a variety of tools can be employed, such as fdisk, parted, and gparted. In this section, we will delve into using fdisk and parted, two of the most commonly utilized partitioning tools.

Firstly, fdisk is a command-line utility for manipulating disk partition tables. It supports MBR (Master Boot Record) and GPT (GUID Partition Table) formats.

```
sudo fdisk /dev/sdX
```

Replace /dev/sdX with the actual device identifier (e.g., /dev/sda).

The following prompt appears:

```
Command (m for help):
```

Pressing ‘m‘ displays available commands:

```
Command action
   a   toggle a bootable flag
   d   delete a partition
   l   list known partition types
   m   print this menu
   n   add a new partition
   p   print the partition table
   q   quit without saving changes
   t   change a partition's system id
   v   verify the partition table
   w   write table to disk and exit
```

To create a new partition, press ‘n‘:

```
Command (m for help): n
```

You are then prompted to specify whether the partition should be primary or extended (with MBR):

```
Partition type:
   p   primary (0 primary, 0 extended, 4 free)
   e   extended
Select (default p):
```

After choosing ‘p‘ for a primary partition, specify the partition number (1-4 with MBR), first sector, and last sector. Defaults are often acceptable.

Once the partition is created, pressing ‘w‘ writes changes to disk and exits:

```
Command (m for help): w
```

The changes take effect, and the new partition appears in the partition table.

The parted utility, accommodating both MBR and GPT, offers an interactive mode with enhanced capabilities, including resizing of partitions.

Launch parted on a disk:

```
sudo parted /dev/sdX
```

Replace /dev/sdX accordingly.

The prompt appears:

```
(parted)
```

Create a new partition table (e.g., GPT):

```
(parted) mklabel gpt
```

To create a new partition, use the mkpart command:

```
(parted) mkpart primary ext4 1MiB 100%
```

This command creates a primary partition spanning from 1MiB to the end of the disk, formatted as ext4. Adjust the values as necessary for specific requirements.

View the partition table to verify changes:

```
(parted) print
```

This displays:

```
Model: ATA VBOX HARDDISK (scsi)
Disk /dev/sdX: 42.9GB
Sector size (logical/physical): 512B/512B
Partition Table: gpt
Disk Flags:

Number  Start    End     Size    File system  Name     Flags
 1      1.00MiB  42.9GB  42.9GB  ext4         primary
```

To apply and exit:

```
(parted) quit
```

After creating partitions, filesystems must be formatted. The mkfs command formats partitions with a specified filesystem type.

For example, to format a partition with ext4:

```
sudo mkfs.ext4 /dev/sdX1
```

Replace /dev/sdX1 with the partition identifier.

Verification of the filesystem creation:

```
sudo blkid /dev/sdX1
```

This displays attributes of the partition, confirming the filesystem:

```
/dev/sdX1: UUID="abcd-1234" TYPE="ext4"
```

Through the systematic use of fdisk, parted, and mkfs, effective partition creation and management are ensured, providing the foundation for robust storage solutions within Linux environments.

2.7 Using Filesystem Utilities

In Linux, filesystem utilities play a crucial role in maintaining the integrity, performance, and overall health of the filesystem. These utilities encompass a broad range of commands that allow users and administrators to inspect, check, repair, and tune filesystems. This section elucidates several essential filesystem utilities, their applications, and usage.

The primary utilities discussed include fsck, mkfs, tune2fs, resize2fs, and e2fsck. Understanding these tools is essential for effective filesystem management.

Filesystem Check Utility - fsck

The fsck (file system consistency check) utility is used to check and optionally repair one or more Linux filesystems. It can correct inconsistencies in the filesystem data structures, ensuring filesystems remain operational.

Usage:

```
fsck [options] <filesystem>
```

Example:

```
fsck /dev/sda1
```

This command checks the filesystem on /dev/sda1. It should be noted that fsck needs to be run on unmounted filesystems or when the system is in a single-user mode to avoid potential data corruption.

```
fsck 1.45.5 (07-Jan-2020)
PASS 1: Checking inodes, blocks, and sizes
PASS 2: Checking directory structure
PASS 3: Checking directory connectivity
PASS 4: Checking reference counts
PASS 5: Checking group summary information
... (output truncated for brevity) ...
```

Filesystem Creation Utility - mkfs

The mkfs (make filesystem) utility is used to create a filesystem on a specified storage device. It formats the storage medium according to the filesystem type specified.

Usage:

```
mkfs -t <filesystem_type> <device>
```

Example:

```
mkfs -t ext4 /dev/sdb1
```

This command creates an ext4 filesystem on the partition /dev/sdb1.

```
mke2fs 1.45.5 (07-Jan-2020)
Discarding device blocks: done
Creating filesystem with 1048576 4k blocks and 262144 inodes
Filesystem UUID: 8a1a8db8-45c0-4b1f-a474-642022dc6fda
Superblock backups stored on blocks:
32768, 98304, 163840, 229376, 294912, 819200, 884736

Allocating group tables: done
Writing inode tables: done
Creating journal (16384 blocks): done
Writing superblocks and filesystem accounting information: done
```

Filesystem Tuning Utility - tune2fs

The tune2fs utility allows for the adjustment of various parameters of an ext2/ext3/ext4 filesystem, such as the maximum mount count and the interval between filesystem checks.

Usage:

```
tune2fs [options] <device>
```

Example:

```
tune2fs -c 50 /dev/sda1
```

This command sets the maximum mount count to 50 for /dev/sda1.

```
tune2fs 1.45.5 (07-Jan-2020)
Setting maximal mount count to 50
```

Filesystem Resize Utility - resize2fs

The resize2fs utility is used to resize ext2/ext3/ext4 filesystems. This is useful for modifying the size of filesystems without losing data.

Usage:

```
resize2fs <device> [size]
```

Example:

```
resize2fs /dev/sda3 10G
```

This command resizes the filesystem on /dev/sda3 to 10 GB.

```
resize2fs 1.45.5 (07-Jan-2020)
Resizing the filesystem on /dev/sda3 to 2621440 (4k) blocks.
The filesystem on /dev/sda3 is now 2621440 (4k) blocks long.
```

Filesystem Check and Repair Utility - e2fsck

The e2fsck utility, part of the e2fsprogs package, checks ext2/ext3/ext4 filesystems for errors and can also repair them.

Usage:

```
e2fsck [options] <device>
```

Example:

```
e2fsck -f /dev/sda1
```

This command forces a check on the /dev/sda1 filesystem, even if it seems clean.

```
e2fsck 1.45.5 (07-Jan-2020)
Pass 1: Checking inodes, blocks, and sizes
Pass 2: Checking directory structure
Pass 3: Checking directory connectivity
Pass 4: Checking reference counts
Pass 5: Checking group summary information
/dev/sda1: 11/128016 files (0.0% non-contiguous), 22700/512064 blocks
```

Overall, these utilities form the bedrock of filesystem management in Linux. They allow administrators to create, inspect, resize, and repair filesystems effectively, ensuring robust data integrity and optimal system performance. Each utility's correct usage can avert potential issues and maintain a well-functioning, reliable system.

2.8 Understanding Inodes

In the context of Linux filesystems, an *inode* (index node) is a fundamental data structure that stores information about a file or a directory. Each file and directory is associated with an inode, which holds metadata pertaining to that file or directory. Functions such as storing the file's type, permissions, ownership, and timestamps, among others, are efficiently managed through inodes.

An inode contains the following information:

- **File Type:** Indicates whether the inode represents a regular file, directory, symbolic link, etc.
- **Permissions:** Details the access rights granted to the owner, group, and others.

- **Owner Information:** Contains the User ID (UID) and Group ID (GID) of the file owner.
- **Timestamps:** Includes access time (atime), modification time (mtime), and change time (ctime).
- **Link Count:** The number of links (i.e., directory entries) pointing to this inode.
- **File Size:** Indicates the size of the file in bytes.
- **Data Block Pointers:** Pointers to the disk blocks that store the file's data.

Inodes do not store the file's name or its absolute path. Instead, the directory structures provide the mapping between filenames and inode numbers. This separation allows for efficient file handling and optimizes many filesystem operations.

To examine the structure of an inode, consider executing the stat command on a given file. This command provides a comprehensive overview of the inode and its attributes.

```
$ stat example.txt
```

The output will look something like:

```
  File: example.txt
  Size: 4096          Blocks: 8          IO Block: 4096   regular file
Device: 803h/2051d   Inode: 12884901891   Links: 1
Access: (0644/-rw-r--r--)  Uid: (1000/username)   Gid: (1000/groupname)
Access: 2023-10-14 10:01:32.000000000 +0000
Modify: 2023-10-14 10:02:11.000000000 +0000
Change: 2023-10-14 10:02:11.000000000 +0000
 Birth: -
```

Here, we observe the inode number, file size, access permissions, UID, GID, and timestamps. The inode number (12884901891 in this example) uniquely identifies the file within the filesystem.

File Size and Inode Allocation

Linux inodes are allocated based on a fixed ratio relative to the filesystem size, configured during the filesystem's creation. The '-i' flag in the 'mkfs' command allows you to specify the bytes-per-inode ratio. For example:

```
$ mkfs.ext4 -i 16384 /dev/sda1
```

This command creates an ext4 filesystem on /dev/sda1 with one inode per 16,384 bytes of space.

Inode Navigation with Links

Hard links and symbolic links are fundamental concepts linked to inodes. A hard link directly references an inode, and thus, multiple filenames can point to the same inode. When creating a hard link, the link count in the inode increases by one. For instance:

```
$ ln original_file hard_link
```

Both original_file and hard_link will point to the same inode. If original_file is deleted, the inode is not deallocated until hard_link is also removed.

Symbolic links, on the other hand, point to a filename rather than an inode. They are more flexible but rely on the integrity of the referenced filename. Creating a symbolic link is achieved via:

```
$ ln -s original_file symbolic_link
```

Practical Verification

It is valuable to inspect the behavior of inodes through practical experiments:

1. **Create a new file** and use stat to check its inode number:

```
$ touch testfile
$ stat testfile
```

2. **Create a hard link** to testfile and observe how the link count is updated:

```
$ ln testfile hardlink_testfile
$ stat testfile
$ stat hardlink_testfile
```

3. Notice both testfile and hardlink_testfile share the same inode number and the link count has incremented.

4. **Create a symbolic link** and observe the differences:

```
$ ln -s testfile symlink_testfile
$ stat symlink_testfile
```

The symlink_testfile will show a different inode number and points to testfile's filename.

Understanding the attributes and functions of inodes is essential in mastering the manipulation and management of filesystems in Linux. It enables efficient troubleshooting, space management, and ensures coherence and integrity across data structures.

2.9 File System Permissions and Ownership

File system permissions and ownership are foundational components of security and access control in Linux. They determine who can read, write, or execute a file or directory. Understanding and managing these permissions are critical for system administrators to maintain a secure and functional environment.

Every file and directory in Linux is associated with three types of permission classes, each governing access for different types of users:

- **Owner (User)**: The user who owns the file or directory.
- **Group**: A set of users who share certain access privileges.
- **Others**: All other users on the system who are not the owner or part of the group.

Permissions are represented in three distinct modes:

- **Read (r)**: Grants the capability to read the contents of the file or directory.
- **Write (w)**: Grants the capability to modify or remove the contents of the file or directory.
- **Execute (x)**: Grants the capability to execute the file if it is a script or program. For directories, it allows access to the directory contents.

Permissions are typically represented in a string of characters, such as drwxr-xr-x, where each set of three characters represents the permissions for the owner, group, and others, respectively. The initial character indicates the type (e.g., 'd' for directories).

To view the permissions of files in a directory, the ls -l command is used:

```
$ ls -l
total 20
drwxr-xr-x 2 root root 4096 Apr 10 12:30 bin
drwxr-xr-x 3 root root 4096 Apr 10 12:30 boot
-rw-r--r-- 1 user user 1384 Jun 5 10:54 file.txt
```

The output lists the permissions, number of links, owner, group, size, modification date, and file or directory name. For file.txt, the permissions are 'rw-r–r–', which means:

- **Owner:** has read and write permissions ('rw-').
- **Group:** has read-only permission ('r–').
- **Others:** have read-only permission ('r–').

Changing permissions is accomplished using the chmod command, which can use symbolic or numeric modes. For symbolic mode (modifying specific permissions):

```
$ chmod u+rwx,g+rw,o-r file.txt
```

This command adds read, write, and execute permissions to the owner (u), adds read and write permissions to the group (g), and removes read permission for others (o).

Numeric mode uses a three-digit octal number where each digit represents the permissions for owner, group, and others, respectively. The digits are calculated by summing the permission values:

- Read (r) = 4
- Write (w) = 2
- Execute (x) = 1

For example, setting full permissions for the owner, read and write for the group, and read-only for others is represented as 764:

```
$ chmod 764 file.txt
```

This command sets the permissions to rwxrw-r–.

Changing ownership is managed via the chown command. It updates the owner and group of a file or directory. For example, to change the owner to 'admin':

```
$ sudo chown admin file.txt
```

To change both the owner and the group:

```
$ sudo chown admin:staff file.txt
```

In addition to basic permissions, Linux supports advanced permission settings like SUID (Set User ID), SGID (Set Group ID), and the sticky bit:

- **SUID (Set User ID)**: When applied to an executable file, it allows the file to be run with the privileges of the file owner. Set using chmod u+s filename.
- **SGID (Set Group ID)**: When applied to a file, similar to SUID but applies to the group. On a directory, new files inherit the group ID. Set using chmod g+s directory.
- **Sticky Bit**: When set on a directory, files within can only be deleted by the file owner, the directory owner, or root. Commonly used in directories like /tmp. Set using chmod +t directory.

For instance, to set the SUID on a script:

```
$ sudo chmod u+s script.sh
```

To set the SGID on a directory:

```
$ sudo chmod g+s /path/to/directory
```

Understanding and correctly implementing file system permissions and ownership is essential for maintaining a secure Linux environment, ensuring that files are accessible only to intended users and processes. Clear delineation of permissions prevents unauthorized access and modification, thereby safeguarding system integrity and data security.

2.10 Symbolic and Hard Links

Linux filesystems support two primary types of links: symbolic links and hard links. Both are used to create references to files or directories, but they operate differently and have distinct use cases. Understanding these differences is crucial for effective filesystem management and ensuring efficient access to files.

A **symbolic link** (also known as a soft link) is a special type of file that points to another file or directory. Symbolic links are akin to shortcuts in other operating systems. The symbolic link is a file that contains a path referencing the target file or directory. If the target file is moved or deleted, the symbolic link becomes a dangling link, whose path leads nowhere. It is crucial to note that symbolic links work across different filesystems.

We can create a symbolic link using the ln -s command. The general syntax for creating a symbolic link is:

```
ln -s <target_file> <link_name>
```

Here is an example to illustrate its usage:

```
ln -s /home/user/original.txt /home/user/link_to_original.txt
```

This command creates a symbolic link named link_to_original.txt pointing to original.txt. When performing file operations such as reading or writing, the filesystem resolves the symbolic link to the target file. Below is a representation of a symbolic link.

```
$ ls -l /home/user/link_to_original.txt
lrwxrwxrwx 1 user user 20 Jan 1 12:34 /home/user/link_to_original.txt -> /home/user/original.txt
```

The '$\rightarrow$' symbol indicates that link_to_original.txt is a symbolic link pointing to original.txt.

A **hard link**, on the other hand, directly associates a directory entry with a file on the filesystem. Unlike symbolic links, which contain a path to the target, hard links are additional directory entries for the actual file data. This means that hard links point directly to the inode of the target file. Consequently, hard links are indistinguishable from the target file itself. Both the original file and any hard links to it share the same inode.

To create a hard link, use the ln command without the -s option. The syntax is as follows:

```
ln <target_file> <link_name>
```

An example command to create a hard link:

```
ln /home/user/original.txt /home/user/hardlink_to_original.txt
```

This command creates a hard link named hardlink_to_original.txt pointing to the same inode as original.txt. Listing the files with ls -l shows that they share the same inode:

```
$ ls -li /home/user/original.txt /home/user/hardlink_to_original.txt
123456 -rw-r--r-- 2 user user 0 Jan 1 12:34 /home/user/original.txt
123456 -rw-r--r-- 2 user user 0 Jan 1 12:34 /home/user/hardlink_to_original.txt
```

The inode number (in this case, 123456) is the same for both entries, indicating they reference the same file on the disk. Deleting any one of the hard links does not remove the file data itself, as long as at least one link remains.

There are several distinctions and implications of these differences:

- **Cross-filesystem limitations:** Hard links cannot span across different filesystems, whereas symbolic links can.
- **Directory linking:** Hard links to directories are generally not allowed to prevent filesystem loops and maintain a coherent directory structure.
- **Deletion behavior:** Deleting the original file does not affect a hard link. The data persists until all linked directory entries are deleted. Conversely, deleting the target of a symbolic link leaves the link dangling.
- **Disk space:** Hard links do not consume additional disk space for file data, whereas a symbolic link is a small file itself, adding minimal overhead.
- **Link validation:** Hard links maintain a persistent direct link to the inode of the actual file data, ensuring data access even if the file is moved or renamed within the same filesystem. Symbolic links require explicit updates if the target file path changes.

Understanding these characteristics allows practitioners to leverage the appropriate type of link based on their needs, enhancing the flexibility and efficiency of file management in the Linux environment.

The distinction between symbolic and hard links is critical for robust system administration and file organization, enabling multifaceted access and reference mechanisms within and across filesystems.

2.11 Introduction to File System Tuning

File system tuning refers to the process of optimizing the performance and reliability of a filesystem by adjusting various parameters and employing different techniques. Efficiently tuned filesystems can significantly enhance system throughput, reduce latency, and ensure better resource utilization. The objectives of file system tuning include improving read and write speeds, minimizing disk space usage, and ensuring the longevity of storage devices.

Linux provides a plethora of tools and options for file system tuning. These tools can be broadly categorized into those applicable during filesystem creation, options available during filesystem mounting, and runtime tuning utilities. Understanding and using these tools effectively requires a deep knowledge of the underlying mechanisms of the filesystem and storage devices.

When creating a filesystem, mkfs (make filesystem) is the primary tool used. With mkfs, administrators can specify various parameters that affect the performance and efficiency of the filesystem. For example, the block size, the number of inodes, and the type of journaling can be configured during the creation phase.

```
sudo mkfs.ext4 -b 4096 -i 8192 -J size=1024 /dev/sda1
```

In the above example, the mkfs command is used to create an ext4 filesystem with a block size of 4096 bytes, an inode ratio of 8192 bytes per inode, and a journal size of 1024 KB on the /dev/sda1 device.

Mount options can also have a significant impact on filesystem performance. The mount command allows specifying various options that affect caching, access time recording, and I/O behavior. The noatime mount option, for example, disables the recording of file access times, which can reduce write operations and improve performance.

```
sudo mount -o noatime,defaults /dev/sda1 /mnt/data
```

Runtime tuning involves adjusting filesystem parameters while the filesystem is mounted and in use. The tune2fs utility for ext2/ext3/ext4 filesystems is particularly useful. With tune2fs, administrators can adjust reserved block percentages, enable or disable journaling features, and optimize filesystem performance according to specific workload patterns.

```
sudo tune2fs -m 1 -O dir_index /dev/sda1
```

In this example, the tune2fs command sets the reserved block count to 1% and enables the directory index feature on the ext4 filesystem on /dev/sda1.

The kernel's I/O scheduler, which determines the order in which disk operations are performed, also plays a crucial role in filesystem performance. Linux provides several I/O schedulers, such as cfq, deadline, and noop, each suited for different workloads. The choice of scheduler can be changed at runtime using the sysfs interface.

```
echo deadline | sudo tee /sys/block/sda/queue/scheduler
```

In this command, the I/O scheduler for the /dev/sda device is set to 'deadline', which is suitable for environments where predictable latency is important.

Filesystems such as Btrfs provide advanced tuning options like subvolume creation and snapshots. Btrfs allows defragmentation and compression settings to be adjusted dynamically. The btrfs filesystem can be tuned using the btrfs command-line utility.

```
sudo btrfs filesystem defragment -r -v /mnt/data
sudo btrfs property set /mnt/data compression lzo
```

The first command defragments the Btrfs filesystem at /mnt/data recursively with verbose output, and the second command sets the compression method to LZO to save disk space and potentially improve performance.

Monitoring tools like iostat, vmstat, and sar provide valuable insights into filesystem and device performance. These tools help identify bottlenecks and understand the impact of tuning efforts.

```
iostat -x 5 3
```

The above command provides extended I/O statistics every 5 seconds for 3 intervals, enabling administrators to monitor performance metrics such as utilization and average wait times.

By integrating effective file system tuning strategies, administrators can achieve a balanced system that meets the specific performance and reliability requirements of their use case.

2.12 Backup and Restore Operations

Backup and restore operations are critical for ensuring data integrity and system reliability in Linux environments. These processes allow administrators to safeguard data against loss due to hardware failures, software errors, accidental deletions, or malicious activities. Below, we delve into the strategies and tools available for effective backup and restoration.

1. Backup Strategies

Developing an effective backup strategy involves determining the appropriate backup type, schedule, and storage location. Common types of backups include:

- **Full Backup**: Captures the entire filesystem or specified data. While comprehensive, it is time-consuming and requires significant storage space.
- **Incremental Backup**: Backs up only the data that has changed since the last backup (whether full or incremental). It is faster and uses less storage but can complicate the restoration process.
- **Differential Backup**: Backs up data that has changed since the last full backup. It strikes a balance between full and incremental backups in terms of speed, storage, and ease of restoration.

2. Backup Tools

Linux offers a diverse array of tools for performing backups, each with its unique features and capabilities:

- **tar** (tape archive): A widely-used command-line utility to create archive files. It can combine multiple files into a single archive for easier backup.
- **rsync**: Efficiently synchronizes files and directories between locations with options for differential backups.
- **dd**: Directly copies and converts raw data from one location to another, useful for creating disk images.
- **Bacula**: A comprehensive suite for enterprise-level backup, providing automated and scheduled backups.
- **Amanda** (Advanced Maryland Automatic Network Disk Archiver): Manages the backup process for multiple clients over a network.

Using the tar Command

The tar utility is often used for creating backups in Linux. Below is an example of its use:

```
tar -cvzf /backup/home.tar.gz /home
```

This command creates a compressed archive home.tar.gz of the /home directory. The flags used are:

- -c: Create a new archive.
- -v: Verbose output, showing the progress.

- -z: Compress the archive using gzip.
- -f: Specify the filename.

Using the rsync Command

rsync is favored for its efficiency and flexibility. The following example demonstrates a basic backup command:

```
rsync -av --delete /home /backup/home
```

Here, rsync synchronizes the contents of the /home directory with the /backup/home directory. The options are:

- -a: Archive mode, which preserves permissions, timestamps, and other attributes.
- -v: Verbose output.
- –delete: Deletes files in the destination directory that are not present in the source directory.

Using the dd Command

The dd command is often utilized for creating full disk backups or cloning. For example:

```
dd if=/dev/sda of=/backup/sda.img bs=64K conv=noerror,sync
```

This command creates an image of the /dev/sda disk. Parameters include:

- if: Input file (source disk).
- of: Output file (destination image).
- bs: Block size; here set to 64K for efficiency.
- conv=noerror,sync: Continue on read errors and pad blocks with zeros.

Automating Backups with Cron

Automating backup tasks can significantly enhance reliability. This can be achieved using cron jobs:

```
0 2 * * * /usr/bin/rsync -av --delete /home /backup/home
```

This crontab entry schedules rsync to run every day at 2 AM, ensuring regular backups without manual intervention.

3. Restoration Process

Ensuring a backup is only half the job; the ability to restore data is equally important. The restoration process should be periodically tested to verify its efficacy.

Restoring with tar

To restore data from a tar archive:

```
tar -xvzf /backup/home.tar.gz -C /
```

This command extracts the home.tar.gz archive to the root directory. Parameters used include:

- -x: Extract the archive.
- -v: Verbose output.
- -z: Decompress the gzipped file.
- -f: Specify the filename.
- -C: Change to the specified directory before extracting.

Restoring with rsync

Restoring data with rsync is straightforward:

```
rsync -av /backup/home/ /home
```

This command mirrors the backup back to the original location.

Restoring with dd

To restore a disk image created by dd:

```
dd if=/backup/sda.img of=/dev/sda bs=64K
```

This command writes the disk image back to the /dev/sda disk, effectively restoring its previous state.

By employing these tools and strategies, Linux administrators can ensure robust backup and restoration processes, safeguarding critical data and maintaining system integrity.

Chapter 3

Basic Linux Commands

This chapter introduces essential Linux commands for navigating and managing the system. It covers basic operations in the command line interface, such as file and directory navigation, viewing and editing files, and manipulating files and directories. Additionally, it explains text handling, process management, input and output redirection, and combining commands. The chapter also includes guidelines for using help resources and documentation, ensuring a solid foundation for further command-line proficiency.

3.1 Introduction to the Command Line Interface (CLI)

The Command Line Interface (CLI) is a powerful tool that allows users to interact directly with the operating system through text-based commands. Unlike Graphical User Interfaces (GUIs), which rely on visual elements like buttons and menus, a CLI requires the user to type specific commands to perform tasks. This section delves into the essentials of the CLI, laying the groundwork for mastering Linux commands and optimizing system management.

At its core, the CLI is an interface that processes text input from the user and returns text-based output. It provides a streamlined and efficient way to perform a wide array of tasks, such as navigating the file system, managing processes, and handling files. Familiarity with the CLI is essential for becoming proficient with Linux, as it facilitates deeper control and scripting capabilities that are often not possible or efficient through GUI.

A terminal emulator is a software application that emulates a classic terminal within a GUI. It allows users to enter commands and view the output. Common terminal emulators include GNOME Terminal, Konsole, and xterm. These terminal emulators can be started from the application menu in your Linux desktop environment, or, in some distributions, through a keyboard shortcut like Ctrl+Alt+T.

Basic Command Structure

A fundamental understanding of the command structure is necessary to use the CLI effectively. In Linux, commands are typically issued in the following format:

```
command [options] [arguments]
```

- command is the name of the program or utility you want to run. - [options] are optional modifiers that alter the behavior of the command. - [arguments] are the targets of the command, such as file or directory names.

Consider the ls command, which lists the contents of a directory. It can be used with various options to display different details, and with arguments specifying the target directory. For example:

```
ls -l /home/user/Documents
```

In this example: - ls is the command. - -l is an option that tells the command to list the contents in long format, providing more details about each item. - /home/user/Documents is an argument specifying the directory to be listed.

Command Execution and Output

Commands in the CLI are executed by typing the command and pressing the Enter key. The system processes the command and provides output directly in the terminal. The output can include information about files, system status, or can even be messages confirming that a particular task has been completed.

Consider the following example where the pwd command is used to print the current working directory:

```
pwd
```

The output will be the absolute path of the current directory, such as:

/home/user

This straightforward interaction demonstrates the efficiency and clarity of using the CLI for immediate and precise tasks.

Common Key Combinations

Interacting with the CLI efficiently also involves familiarity with certain key combinations that enhance command entry and management:

- Tab: Auto-completes file and directory names. If multiple options are available, pressing Tab twice displays the available options. - Ctrl+C: Terminates the current command or process. - Ctrl+Z: Suspends the current foreground process. This can later be resumed with the fg command. - Ctrl+D: Ends the terminal session or logs out the current user.

These key combinations save time and help to manage the workflow effectively.

Accessing Command History

Linux shells typically store a history of executed commands. This history can be navigated using the up and down arrow keys. Pressing the up arrow key displays previously executed commands in reverse chronological order, allowing quick reuse or modification without retyping. Additionally, the history command lists all past commands with a numerical index:

```
history
```

To execute a command from the history by its index number, use the exclamation mark followed by the index. For example, to re-run command #45:

```
!45
```

Command Aliases

Aliases allow for the creation of shortcuts for longer commands, enhancing productivity by reducing typing. The alias command is used to define an alias:

```
alias ll='ls -l'
```

With this alias, typing ll will execute ls -l. Aliases are typically defined in shell configuration files such as .bashrc or .bash_profile to persist across sessions.

Conclusion and Further Learning

The CLI is a fundamental aspect of Linux that empowers users with control and flexibility. Understanding basic command structures, execution methods, key combinations, accessing command history, and using aliases equips users with essential skills to navigate and manage the system effectively. Subsequent sections will build upon these foundations, introducing more complex commands and functionalities to further enhance Linux proficiency.

3.2 Navigating the File System with CD, LS, and PWD Commands

Navigating the file system is a fundamental skill for any Linux user. Understanding how to move between directories, list their contents, and confirm your current location within the directory hierarchy is crucial. We will delve into three essential commands: cd, ls, and pwd.

The cd (change directory) command allows you to switch from your current directory to another directory. Its syntax is straightforward:

```
cd [directory]
```

If you want to change to your home directory, you can simply use:

```
cd
```

or

```
cd ~
```

To navigate to a specific directory, you need to provide the path to that directory. Paths can be absolute or relative. An absolute path defines a location from the root directory, while a relative path is based on the current directory. For example:

```
cd /usr/local/bin
```

Here, /usr/local/bin is an absolute path. In contrast, consider:

```
cd ../etc
```

This command uses a relative path, indicating to move up one directory before entering the etc directory.

To return to the previous directory you were in, you can use:

```
cd -
```

Next, the ls command lists the contents of a directory. Its basic usage is as follows:

```
ls
```

However, ls has several options that can modify its behavior. For example, to list all files, including hidden ones (which start with a dot), you use:

```
ls -a
```

For a detailed listing with file permissions, ownership, size, and modification date, the -l option is used:

```
ls -l
```

To combine both options:

```
ls -la
```

Additionally, you can use the -h option to make file sizes human-readable:

```
ls -lh
```

If you prefer to list directories and their contents recursively, the -R option is useful:

```
ls -R
```

Furthermore, the ls command supports sorting the output based on various criteria. For example, to sort by modification time, use:

```
ls -lt
```

Finally, the pwd (print working directory) command displays your current directory. Its usage is simple:

```
pwd
```

This command is particularly useful when you need to ascertain your current location within the directory hierarchy. For instance, executing pwd from the /usr/local/bin directory would yield:

```
/usr/local/bin
```

Together, these commands equip you with the ability to navigate through the file system efficiently. Understanding and utilizing cd, ls, and pwd are core competencies for managing files and directories in a Linux environment.

3.3 Viewing and Editing Files with CAT, LESS, and NANO

Understanding how to view and edit files in Linux is fundamental to effective system administration and everyday command-line use. This section delves into the functionalities and command-line usage of cat, less, and nano, which are standard utilities for interacting with file contents. Their usage spans simple content display to comprehensive file editing, thus enhancing a user's proficiency in managing text files on a Linux system.

The cat command, short for "concatenate," is frequently employed to display the contents of a file. It can also be used to concatenate multiple files and direct them to standard output (the screen) or another file. The basic syntax of the cat command is as follows:

```
cat [OPTION]... [FILE]...
```

A straightforward use case involves displaying the contents of a single file:

```
cat filename.txt
```

This command reads the file named filename.txt and displays its content on the screen. To concatenate and display multiple files, the command can be used with multiple file arguments:

```
cat file1.txt file2.txt
```

In addition to viewing and concatenating files, cat can be used with output redirection to create new files or append content to existing files. For example, to concatenate file1.txt and file2.txt into a new file output.txt, the following command can be executed:

```
cat file1.txt file2.txt > output.txt
```

If the goal is to append the contents of file2.txt at the end of file1.txt, the » operator is used:

```
cat file2.txt >> file1.txt
```

These basic operations with cat provide efficient methods for quick file review and content manipulation. However, for larger files or when browsing file content incrementally, less is a more suitable utility.

The less command is a pager program optimized for viewing large text files. Unlike cat, less allows the user to navigate through the file content interactively. It automatically handles long files by providing navigation commands to scroll through the content, making it more practical for extensive file reviews. The syntax for less is:

```
less [options] [file]
```

A typical example includes viewing a file with:

```
less filename.txt
```

Upon execution, less opens the specified file and awaits user input for navigation. The essential commands within less include:

- Space - Scroll down one page
- b - Scroll up one page
- Enter - Scroll down one line
- y - Scroll up one line
- q - Quit less
- /pattern - Search for pattern downwards
- ?pattern - Search for pattern upwards

These controls enhance the user's capability to inspect file content meticulously. Moreover, less allows backward navigation, a feature not present in cat.

When it comes to file editing directly within the terminal, nano is among the most accessible text editors, offering a simple interface and essential editing functionalities. The command syntax is:

```
nano [options] [file]
```

To edit or create a file named filename.txt, the command would be:

```
nano filename.txt
```

This command opens filename.txt in the nano editor, providing a familiar text-based interface for text manipulation. The command bar at the bottom of the nano interface lists the most necessary commands, such as:

- Ctrl+O - Write (save) the file
- Ctrl+X - Exit the editor
- Ctrl+K - Cut text
- Ctrl+U - Uncut (paste) text
- Ctrl+W - Search within the file
- Ctrl+G - Display help menu

The simplicity and prevalence of nano make it ideal for beginners or users requiring straightforward file editing without the complexity of more robust text editors like vi or emacs.

Thus, by utilizing cat, less, and nano, users gain a versatile toolkit for viewing and editing text files effectively within the Linux command-line environment.

3.4 File Manipulation: CP, MV, RM, and TOUCH

Mastering the basic file manipulation commands in Linux is pivotal for effective system management. This section delves into four essential commands: cp, mv, rm, and touch. Each of these commands plays a crucial role in everyday tasks such as copying, moving, renaming, deleting, and creating files.

The **cp** command is utilized for copying files and directories. Its basic syntax is:

```
cp [options] source destination
```

The above command copies the source file or directory to the specified destination. For example, to copy a file named example.txt from the current directory to a directory named backup, use:

```
cp example.txt backup/
```

To copy a directory and its contents recursively, the -r option is used. For instance:

```
cp -r project/ backup/
```

The cp command also supports additional options such as -v for verbose mode, which displays a message for each file copied, and -i for interactive mode, prompting before overwriting files:

```
cp -vi example.txt backup/
```

Next, the **mv** command is used to move or rename files and directories. Its syntax is similar to cp:

```
mv [options] source destination
```

To move a file from one location to another, execute:

```
mv example.txt backup/
```

If destination is a directory, example.txt will simply be moved there. To rename a file:

```
mv example.txt sample.txt
```

The mv command can also be used with the -i option to prompt before overwriting a file, or -v to output the details of the move operation:

```
mv -vi example.txt sample.txt
```

For file deletion, the **rm** command is employed. Its basic form is:

```
rm [options] file
```

To delete a file named example.txt, execute:

```
rm example.txt
```

For deleting a directory and its contents, the -r (recursive) option is necessary:

```
rm -r backup/
```

Options like -i (prompting before each removal) and -v (verbose) are also available for rm:

```
rm -vi example.txt
```

It is important to use the rm command cautiously, as it permanently removes files and directories. There is no recycle bin to recover deleted files.

The **touch** command is used to create an empty file, or to change the access and modification timestamps of an existing file. Its basic syntax is:

```
touch [options] file
```

To create an empty file named newfile.txt, use:

```
touch newfile.txt
```

If newfile.txt already exists, the touch command will update its timestamps to the current time. The -a option changes only the access time, the -m option changes only the modification time, and the -t option allows specifying a specific timestamp:

```
touch -a example.txt
touch -m example.txt
touch -t 202301010101.01 example.txt
```

Here, the timestamp format for -t is [[CC]YY]MMDDhhmm[.ss], where optional parts are in brackets.

Practical knowledge of these commands is essential for efficient file management in Linux. Through these examples and explanations, one can gain proficiency in crucial file manipulation operations.

3.5 Directory Management: MKDIR, RMDIR, and RM -R

Managing directories is a fundamental skill in Linux. This section delves into three essential commands for directory management: mkdir, rmdir, and rm -r. These commands help in creating, removing, and forcefully deleting directories.

The mkdir command, short for "make directory," is used to create one or more empty directories. The basic syntax for mkdir is straightforward:

```
mkdir [options] directory_name
```

For example, to create a directory named project in the current directory, use:

```
$ mkdir project
```

To create a nested directory structure, such as a directory project with a subdirectory src, the -p option is useful. This option allows the creation of parent directories as needed:

```
mkdir -p project/src
```

rmdir, or "remove directory," is used to delete empty directories. Its basic syntax is as follows:

```
rmdir [options] directory_name
```

For example, to remove an empty directory named oldproject, use:

```
$ rmdir oldproject
```

It is important to note that rmdir will not remove directories that contain files or other directories. Attempting to remove a non-empty directory with rmdir will result in an error:

```
$ rmdir project
rmdir: failed to remove 'project': Directory not empty
```

For cases where non-empty directories need to be deleted, the rm command with the -r option should be used. The rm command is used to remove files, but the -r (recursive) option extends its capability to directories, allowing it to remove directories and their contents recursively:

```
rm -r [options] directory_name
```

To remove a directory and all of its contents, such as project, use:

```
$ rm -r project
```

It is recommended to proceed with caution when using the rm -r command, as it will delete all files and subdirectories within the specified directory permanently. An additional safety measure involves using the -i option, which prompts for confirmation before each removal:

```
rm -ri project
```

For automated scripts or scenarios where prompting is not feasible, the -f (force) option can be combined with rm -r to suppress prompts and error messages:

```
rm -rf project
```

The combined command rm -rf is powerful and should be used with caution to avoid unintentional data loss. Always double-check the directory path before executing this command.

In practice, using these commands involves understanding their scope and the context in which they are deployed, ensuring efficient and safe directory management in Linux systems.

3.6 Finding Files and Directories: FIND and LOCATE

The task of locating files and directories in a filesystem is fundamental for efficient system management. Two powerful utilities, find and locate, are frequently employed for this purpose in Linux environments. This section provides a comprehensive overview of these tools, elucidates their usage scenarios, and demonstrates their implementation through practical examples.

The find command is a versatile and exhaustive tool that searches the directory tree recursively. It offers numerous options and parameters, enabling users to precisely specify criteria such as file type, name, size, modification date, and permissions. On the other hand, locate leverages a pre-built database, offering rapid search capabilities, albeit with a potential trade-off in immediacy due to the periodic nature of database updates.

To utilize the find command effectively, one must understand its syntax and the various parameters it supports. The general syntax of find is:

```
find [path] [expression]
```

- [path]: Starting point in the directory hierarchy where the search begins. If omitted, find defaults to the current directory.
- [expression]: Criteria that files or directories must meet to be considered a match.

To illustrate, consider the following examples:

1. Finding files by name:

```
find /home name ”example.txt”
```

This command searches for files named example.txt beginning from the /home directory.

2. Finding directories by name:

```
find /var -type d -name "logs"
```

Here, the search is restricted to directories (-type d) named logs within the /var directory.

3. Finding files by size:

```
find /tmp -size +50M
```

This locates files larger than 50 megabytes in the /tmp directory.

4. Finding files by modification time:

```
find /usr -mtime -7
```

Files modified within the last 7 days in the /usr directory are identified by this command.

Actions can also be specified for find to execute upon locating a match. For example:

```
find / -type f -name "*.log" -exec rm {} \;
```

This command locates files with a .log extension and deletes them. The -exec option initiates a specified command (rm in this case) on each found item, where {} acts as a placeholder for the current file path. The command sequence ends with a semicolon escaped by a backslash ( ).

Contrastingly, locate operates by querying a database that contains a snapshot of the filesystem. The database is typically updated periodically by the updatedb command, often managed by a cron job. The simplicity and speed of locate make it ideal for quick searches, albeit with the caveat that recent changes to the filesystem may not be immediately reflected until the next database update.

To use locate, the syntax is straightforward:

```
locate [filename]
```

For instance:

```
locate example.txt
```

An optional but useful feature of locate is the -i flag, which makes the search case-insensitive:

```
locate -i example
```

Given the inherent differences between find and locate, each has scenarios where it is preferred. find excels in real-time searches with precise criteria and immediate reflection of the current filesystem state, whereas locate offers expedited searches for frequent or non-time-sensitive queries.

For instance, the command

```
find /home -type f -perm 644
```

searches for files in /home with permissions set to 644, indicating read and write permissions for the owner, and read-only for the group and others. Using locate for a similar task requires prior familiarity with the specific paths or filenames and does not afford the same granularity in permission-based searches.

When using these tools, one must balance the immediacy and precision of find with the efficiency of locate, selecting the tool best suited to the specific requirements at hand.

3.7 Understanding and Using Wildcards

Wildcards in Linux serve as powerful tools for pattern matching, allowing users to perform operations on multiple files or directories efficiently. They are particularly useful when dealing with groups of files that share similarities in their names or extensions. Wildcards simplify tasks such as searching, listing, moving, or deleting files, thereby enhancing productivity in command-line operations.

Common Wildcards

Three primary wildcards are used in Linux: the asterisk (*), the question mark (?), and square brackets ([]). Each wildcard has unique characteristics and usage:

- **Asterisk (*)**: Matches zero or more characters. It can represent any string of characters, including an empty string.
- **Question Mark (?)**: Matches exactly one character. It can represent any single character.
- **Square Brackets ([])**: Matches any one character within the brackets. It can be used to specify a range or a set of specific characters.

Wildcard: Asterisk (*)

The asterisk (*) wildcard matches any string of characters, including an empty string. This means it can represent a part of a filename or an entire filename.

```
# List all files in the current directory
ls *

# List all '.txt' files in the current directory
ls *.txt

# List all files that start with 'file' and have any extension
ls file*
```

If the current directory contains files named example1.txt, example2.txt, and test.doc, the command ls *.txt will output:

```
example1.txt
example2.txt
```

Wildcard: Question Mark (?)

The question mark (?) wildcard matches exactly one character. It is useful when you want to specify filenames with variable characters at certain positions.

```
# List all files with names consisting of five characters
ls ?????

# List all files that start with 'file' and have a single character extension
ls file.?
```

Assuming the directory contains files named file1.txt, file2.doc, and file3.xls, the command ls file.? will output:

```
file2.doc
file3.xls
```

Wildcard: Square Brackets ([])

The square brackets ([]) wildcard matches any one character within the brackets. It can be used to specify a set or range of characters.

```
# List files that start with 'file' followed by any digit between 1 and 5
ls file[1-5].txt

# List files that start with 'data' followed by either 'a' or 'b'
ls data[a-b].txt
```

If the current directory contains file1.txt, file3.txt, and file6.txt, executing the command ls file[1-5].txt will result in:

```
file1.txt
file3.txt
```

Combining Wildcards

To maximize efficiency, wildcards can be combined to create more complex patterns.

```
# List files that start with 'file', followed by zero or more characters, and end with '.txt'
ls file*.txt

# List files that start with 'data', followed by any single character, and end with '.log'
ls data?.log

# List files that start with 'report', followed by any one of '1', '3', or '5', and end with
    '.csv'
ls report[135].csv
```

Suppose the directory contains file1.txt, file2.log, data2.log, report1.csv, and report5.csv. Running the following command will produce:

```
ls data?.log
data2.log

ls report[135].csv
report1.csv
report5.csv
```

Practical Applications of Wildcards

Wildcards prove to be versatile in a variety of practical scenarios:

- **Moving Multiple Files:** Move all text files to a backup directory.

```
mv *.txt backup/
```

- **Deleting Multiple Files:** Remove all log files that start with "error".

```
rm error*.log
```

- **Copying Subsets of Files:** Copy all '.png' files that have names starting with "img".

```
cp img*.png /path/to/destination/
```

- **Listing Specific Files:** List all files that contain digits in their names.

```
ls *[0-9]*
```

Mastering wildcards is essential for efficient file management in the Linux command line. By enabling the execution of operations on multiple files and directories simultaneously, wildcards significantly reduce the complexity and time required for routine tasks.

3.8 Managing Processes with PS, TOP, KILL, and NICE

Process management is a vital aspect of Linux administration, enabling users to monitor and control the processes running on the system. This section delves into the primary commands used for these tasks: ps, top, kill, and nice. Understanding and utilizing these commands effectively ensures that you can manage system resources optimally and maintain system stability.

ps is a versatile command for reporting a snapshot of current processes. When used without options, ps displays processes associated with the current terminal session. Here is a simple use case:

```
ps
```

The output from the above command typically includes four columns: PID, TTY, TIME, and CMD.

```
  PID TTY          TIME CMD
 1234 pts/0    00:00:00 bash
 4567 pts/0    00:00:00 ps
```

- **PID**: Process ID, a unique identifier for each running process. - **TTY**: Terminal type associated with the process. - **TIME**: CPU time consumed by the process. - **CMD**: Command that initiated the process.

The ps command supports various options to filter and format output. For example, using ps -e lists all system processes:

```
ps -e
```

For a more detailed overview, ps aux provides extensive information about all processes. The options here are: - a: Display processes from all users. - u: Show process owner and additional details. - x: Include processes not associated with a terminal.

```
ps aux
```

The output includes columns like USER,

```
USER       PID %CPU %MEM    VSZ   RSS TTY      STAT START   TIME CMD
root         1  0.0  0.1  19312  1592 ?        Ss   08:56   0:01 /sbin/init
user       568  0.0  0.3  36784  1664 ?        S    08:56   0:02 /usr/sbin/cron
```

top is an interactive command that provides a real-time overview of system processes. Invoking top displays a dynamic view that continually updates, showing processes, memory usage, and CPU utilization:

```
top
```

The screen is divided into several sections:

- **Summary area**: Displays system uptime, number of users, load average, tasks (total, running, sleeping, stopped, zombie), CPU usage, memory (physical and swap) details. - **Task list area**: Lists processes sorted by CPU usage by default, with columns for PID, USER, PR (Priority), NI (Nice Value), VIRT (Virtual Memory), RES (Resident Memory), SHR (Shared Memory), S (State), and command name.

Users can interact with top through keyboard commands to sort, filter, and manage processes. For example:

- k: Prompts for a PID to terminate a process. - r: Prompts for a PID to renice (change priority) a process. - h: Displays help.

To exit top, press q.

Terminating processes is indispensable for managing unresponsive or unnecessary tasks. The kill command sends signals to processes. The most common signal is SIGTERM (terminate gracefully), but if a process fails to respond, SIGKILL (forceful termination) can be used:

```
kill PID
kill -9 PID
```

In the examples above, replace PID with the process ID. Using kill -9 PID sends the SIGKILL signal, which instantly stops the process without allowing cleanup.

The killall command terminates all processes matching a specific name:

```
killall processname
```

nice and renice commands adjust the priority of a process, affecting its CPU scheduling. The nice command launches a new process with a specified priority, while renice changes the priority of an existing process. The priority range is from -20 (highest priority) to 19 (lowest priority). Without a specified priority, nice applies a default of 10:

```
nice -n 10 command
renice 15 -p PID
```

In these examples, command is the executable to launch, and PID is the process ID of an existing process.

By mastering the use of ps, top, kill, and nice, users gain robust control over system processes, ensuring efficient and stable operation.

3.9 Handling Text with GREP, SED, and AWK

Handling text efficiently in the Linux command line interface involves utilizing powerful tools such as grep, sed, and awk. Each of these tools offers unique capabilities for searching, transforming, and processing text. Mastering them provides significant flexibility and control over text data.

grep, short for "global regular expression print", is used to search for specific patterns within files. It supports various options for matching patterns such as fixed strings, regular expressions, and word boundaries. The basic syntax for grep is:

```
grep [OPTIONS] PATTERN [FILE...]
```

For example, to search for the word "Linux" in a file named sample.txt, use:

```
grep "Linux" sample.txt
```

This command prints each line in sample.txt containing the word "Linux". Common options include -i for case-insensitive search, -r or -R for recursive search through directories, -v to invert the match, showing lines that do not match the pattern, and -c to count the number of matching lines.

sed, which stands for "stream editor", is used for parsing and transforming text. It employs a simple, compact programming language to specify text transformations. Its general syntax is:

```
sed [OPTIONS] 'SCRIPT' [INPUTFILE...]
```

A common sed operation is replacing text. For instance, to replace "Linux" with "Unix" in sample.txt, use:

```
sed 's/Linux/Unix/g' sample.txt
```

In this example, s/old/new/g signifies a substitution command where old is replaced by new globally on each line. The g at the end ensures every occurrence in a line is replaced, rather than just the first one. Other useful sed options include -n to suppress automatic printing of pattern space, and -e to add multiple scripts to be executed sequentially.

awk is a powerful programming language designed for text processing and typically used for data extraction and reporting. Named after its creators Aho, Weinberger, and Kernighan, awk reads input data line by line, splits each line into fields, and allows the execution of specified actions on matched lines. The basic syntax is:

```
awk 'PATTERN { ACTION }' [INPUTFILE...]
```

For example, to print the second field of each line in sample.txt, which is typically a column in tabular data, use:

```
awk '{print $2}' sample.txt
```

Here, the curly braces { } contain the awk action print $2, which prints the second field. awk allows for more complex operations, including mathematical computations, using built-in variables (NR for the current record number, NF for the number of fields in the current record), and conditional constructs (if statements, loops).

Consider an example where awk prints lines where the third field is greater than 100:

```
awk '$3 > 100' sample.txt
```

In this command, $\$3 > 100$ serves as the pattern, and the default action is to print lines that match the pattern.

The combined use of grep, sed, and awk enables intricate text processing workflows. For instance, suppose you need to find all lines containing "error" in a log file, replace occurrences of "404" with "Page Not Found" in those lines, and then extract the timestamp field (assumed to be the second field in the log entries):

```
grep "error" logfile.txt | sed 's/404/Page Not Found/g' | awk '{print $2}'
```

First, grep filters lines with "error", sed performs the replacement, and awk extracts the desired field. This demonstrates the powerful, modular nature of these text-processing tools. Real-world scenarios often require chaining multiple commands to achieve precise results, highlighting the importance of understanding each tool's unique capabilities and how they interoperate.

3.10 Redirecting Input and Output: >, », and |

Understanding how to redirect input and output streams is fundamental in mastering Linux command line operations. This section delves into the use of redirection operators '>', '»', and the pipe '|' to control the flow of data between commands and files.

The command line interface (CLI) in Linux operates with three primary data streams:

- **Standard Input (stdin)**: Typically, the keyboard, which provides input to commands.
- **Standard Output (stdout)**: The terminal, which displays command results.
- **Standard Error (stderr)**: Also the terminal, where error messages are shown.

Redirection changes where these streams originate or terminate. We will begin by discussing the '>' operator.

Output Redirection with '>'

The '>' operator redirects the standard output of a command to a file, overwriting the file if it exists. This is particularly useful for saving command outputs.

```
$ echo "Hello, Linux World!" > greetings.txt
```

In this example, the string "Hello, Linux World!" is directed to the file greetings.txt. If greetings.txt already exists, it is overwritten. To examine the contents of greetings.txt, the cat command can be used:

```
$ cat greetings.txt
Hello, Linux World!
```

Appending Output with '»'

The '»' operator appends the standard output to the specified file, preserving the existing contents.

```
$ echo "Learning Linux is fun!" >> greetings.txt
```

Here, the string "Learning Linux is fun!" is added to the end of the greetings.txt file. Using cat again shows the combined content:

```
$ cat greetings.txt
Hello, Linux World!
Learning Linux is fun!
```

Error Redirection

To redirect stderr, use 2>. The number 2 represents the stderr stream.

```
$ ls non_existent_file 2> error.log
```

Since non_existent_file does not exist, an error message is generated and stored in error.log.

Combining Standard Output and Error

To redirect both stdout and stderr to the same file, use &>.

```
$ ls non_existent_file exist_file &> combined.log
```

This ensures that both standard output and standard error messages are written to combined.log.

Piping with '|'

The pipe operator '|' enables the output of one command to serve as the input to another, facilitating the creation of powerful command combinations.

```
$ ls -l | grep "txt"
```

Here, the ls -l command lists directory contents in long format, and the output is piped to grep, which searches for entries containing "txt".

grep can also receive its input from a file using the cat command in conjunction with a pipe:

```
$ cat greetings.txt | grep "Linux"
```

This filters the contents of greetings.txt, displaying only lines with the word "Linux".

Combining multiple pipes allows for more complex operations. For instance:

```
$ cat /var/log/syslog | grep "error" | wc -l
```

In this sequence, cat reads the /var/log/syslog file; grep filters lines containing "error"; wc -l counts those lines.

Redirection in Command Examples

Consider a use case where we need to compile a C program, monitoring both the output and errors.

```
$ gcc program.c > output.log 2> error.log
```

Here, the standard output is saved in output.log and errors in error.log.

For scenarios requiring combined output and error logging:

```
$ gcc program.c &> all.log
```

This directs both streams into all.log for comprehensive logging.

Through these mechanisms, the manipulation of input and output in the CLI becomes streamlined, empowering users to efficiently manage data and troubleshoot processes. Integrating output and error redirection with piping creates extensive capabilities for handling and transforming information.

3.11 Using the MAN and HELP Commands

When navigating the myriad of commands and utilities in Linux, it is essential to have access to documentation and help resources that provide detailed information about command usage, options, and examples. The man and help commands are indispensable tools for this purpose, offering in-depth manuals and assistance directly from the command line.

The man command, short for "manual," retrieves the user manual for a given command or utility. These manuals, called "man pages," encapsulate a wealth of information including a description of the command, its syntax, available options, and often examples of usage. The basic syntax of the man command is as follows:

```
man <command>
```

For instance, to view the manual page for the ls command, which lists directory contents, you would execute:

```
man ls
```

Within the man page, you'll find structured sections such as:

- **Name**: Brief command description.

- **Synopsis**: Command syntax, showing various command arguments and options.
- **Description**: Detailed explanation of the command.
- **Options**: List and description of command options.
- **Examples**: Usage examples, useful for practical understanding.
- **See Also**: Related commands or documentation references.

Navigating the man page is similar to using the less pager command. Standard navigation commands include:

- Press q to quit the manual and return to the shell prompt.
- Use the Up and Down arrow keys to scroll line-by-line.
- Press Space to scroll down one page.
- Type / followed by a keyword to search for that keyword in the manual.

Another significant resource comes in the form of the help command. Unlike man, which serves a broader range of programs and utilities, help is restricted to shell built-in commands. Shell built-ins are commands integrated into the shell itself, rather than separate executable files. The syntax for using help is:

```
help <builtin>
```

For example, to view help information about the cd (change directory) built-in command, you would type:

```
help cd
```

The output provided by help is typically more concise but covers the essential usage and options for the shell built-in commands. Here is what the output might look like:

```
cd: cd [-L|-P] [dir]
    Change the shell working directory.

    Change the current directory to DIR. The default DIR is the value of the
    HOME shell variable.
    ...
```

For commands that are not built-ins but standard executables, using –help often provides a quick overview of the command syntax and options without delving into the more extensive content of a man page. The usage is as follows:

```
<command> --help
```

Taking the grep command as an instance, execute:

```
grep --help
```

This would yield an output similar to:

```
Usage: grep [OPTION]... PATTERN [FILE]...
Search for PATTERN in each FILE or standard input.
Example: grep -i 'hello world' menu.h main.c

Pattern selection and interpretation:
  -E, --extended-regexp     PATTERN is an extended regular expression (ERE)
  -F, --fixed-strings      PATTERN is a set of newline-separated strings
  -G, --basic-regexp       PATTERN is a basic regular expression (default)
  -P, --perl-regexp        PATTERN is a Perl regular expression
  ...
```

The –help output offers practicality for quickly referencing a command without the need to navigate through the entire manual. Both man and help commands, supplemented by –help, equip users with the necessary tools to confidently explore and utilize Linux commands efficiently.

Mastery of these tools is pivotal for successfully navigating the command line environment, ensuring that users can access relevant information promptly and accurately.

3.12 Combining Commands: &&, ||, and ;

Combining commands in Linux can optimize workflows and improve the efficiency of executing multiple commands. Using the logical operators &&, ||, and the command separator ; enables more control over command execution sequences based on the success or failure of preceding commands. This section details the functionality and appropriate usage of these operators.

&& (Logical AND):

The && operator allows for the sequential execution of commands where the subsequent command is executed only if the preceding command completes successfully (typically indicated by an exit status of 0). This operator is useful when a command depends on the successful completion of a previous command.

```
command1 && command2
```

For example, to create a directory and then change into that directory, you can use:

```
mkdir new_directory && cd new_directory
```

If mkdir new_directory is successful, cd new_directory will be executed. If the directory creation fails, the change directory command will not run. Additionally, this ensures that errors in the first command do not propagate unnecessary execution of dependent commands.

|| **(Logical OR):**

The || operator performs command execution in such a way that the next command is executed only if the preceding command fails (indicated by a non-zero exit status). This operator typically comes into play for fallback or error-handling mechanisms.

```
command1 || command2
```

For example, if a file download fails, you might want to attempt an alternative download source:

```
wget http://example.com/file.tar.gz || wget http://backup.example.com/file.tar.gz
```

If wget http://example.com/file.tar.gz fails, wget http://backup.example.com/file.tar.gz will be attempted. This ensures that an error in the primary download attempt triggers the secondary attempt without requiring manual intervention.

; **(Command Separator):**

The ; command separator allows multiple commands to be executed sequentially, regardless of the success or failure of the preceding commands. Unlike && and ||, ; does not control the flow based on exit statuses but simply separates commands to be executed in order.

```
command1; command2; command3
```

For example, to update the package list, upgrade installed packages, and then clean up redundant packages, you can use:

```
sudo apt-get update; sudo apt-get upgrade -y; sudo apt-get autoremove -y
```

Each command is executed in sequence, with no dependency on the success or failure of the others. This method ensures that all commands are attempted in the given order.

Combining Operators:

Combining these operators within a single line can create complex command sequences for robust script execution. Careful structuring based on logical dependencies and error-handling needs can streamline operations.

For example, consider a scenario where a user needs to download data, extract it, and process it with error checking at each step:

```
wget http://example.com/data.tar.gz && tar -xzf data.tar.gz && ./process_data.sh ||
    echo "There was an error with processing data"
```

Here, wget http://example.com/data.tar.gz is executed first. If the download succeeds, tar -xzf data.tar.gz runs to extract the archive. If both these commands succeed, ./process_data.sh is executed to process the data. If any command in the sequence fails, an error message is printed.

Command chaining provides significant flexibility and efficiency in executing multiple commands. Understanding and utilizing &&, ||, and ; effectively enable users to construct powerful command sequences, improve script reliability, and ensure precise control over command execution.

Chapter 4

User and Group Management

This chapter focuses on managing users and groups in Linux. It explains the structure and purpose of key files like /etc/passwd, /etc/shadow, and /etc/group. The chapter provides detailed instructions on creating, modifying, and deleting users and groups, and discusses assigning and modifying group memberships. Additionally, it covers setting user passwords, managing user profiles and environments, implementing administrative access with sudo, and access control and login management, providing a comprehensive understanding of user and group administration.

4.1 Introduction to User and Group Management

Managing users and groups is one of the fundamental responsibilities of a Linux system administrator. Proper user and group management ensures that a system's resources are used efficiently, securely, and conveniently. This section introduces the key concepts and tools necessary for effective management of users and groups in a Linux environment.

A Linux system supports multiple users and user accounts, which require various levels of access rights to files, directories, and applications. User accounts are designed to segregate user processes and data from other users' data. Each user account is unique and managed through a username and a corresponding user ID (UID). Group accounts, on the other hand, are used to simplify user permissions and facilitate collaboration by grouping users with similar access needs. A group is identified by a group name and a corresponding group ID (GID).

Linux employs several critical files that store user and group information, the most prominent being /etc/passwd, /etc/shadow, and /etc/group. Understanding the structure and function of these files is essential for user and group management.

The /etc/passwd file contains essential information about all user accounts on the system. Each line in this file represents a single user account and includes fields such as the username, UID, GID, home directory, and the default shell. The /etc/shadow file stores secure user password information and related account properties. Entries in this file are readable only by the root user to maintain password confidentiality and system security. It includes fields for the encrypted password, password expiration information, and account lockout settings. The /etc/group file lists all the groups on the system, where each line represents a group and includes fields such as the group name, GID, and member users.

Below is an example of what these files might look like:

```
# /etc/passwd
root:x:0:0:root:/root:/bin/bash
john:x:1001:1001:John Doe:/home/john:/bin/bash

# /etc/shadow
root:$6$randomsalt$encryptedpassword:18337:0:99999:7:::
john:$6$randomsalt$encryptedpassword:18337:0:99999:7:::

# /etc/group
root:x:0:
john:x:1001:
users:x:100:
```

System administrators use various command-line tools to manage user and group accounts. Key commands include useradd, usermod, userdel for user management, and groupadd, groupmod, groupdel for group management. The passwd command is utilized for setting and updating user passwords, while the gpasswd command is used for managing group memberships.

Creating a new user account involves specifying the username and may include options such as setting the home directory, shell, and user

ID. For example, the command to create a user named alice with a specific home directory would look like this:

```
sudo useradd -m -d /home/alice alice
```

To assign a password to the new user, the following command is employed:

```
sudo passwd alice
```

Similarly, creating a new group requires providing a group name, and optionally a GID. The command to create a group named developers is:

```
sudo groupadd developers
```

Assigning a user to a group can be conducted with the usermod or gpasswd commands. For example, to add alice to the developers group, the command used is:

```
sudo usermod -aG developers alice
```

Group memberships are critical for managing file permissions, which are controlled via the ownership and group assignments on files and directories. For instance, setting the group ownership of a directory can be completed with the following command:

```
sudo chown :developers /srv/project
```

Effective user and group management also encompasses proper password policies, defining user environments, and securing administrative access. The /etc/skel directory contains files and directories to be automatically copied to a new user's home directory, thus establishing a standardized initial setup for users. Configuring sudoers appropriately allows users to perform tasks requiring elevated privileges without necessitating full-time root access, adding a layer of security.

Understanding and implementing these concepts ensures robust user and group management, promoting system integrity and security.

4.2 The /etc/passwd File

The /etc/passwd file is a fundamental component of Unix and Linux systems, serving as the central registry for user account information. It is a plain text file that maintains essential details for each user account on the system. Each line in the /etc/passwd file corresponds to a single user account and adheres to a standardized format. The structure of a single entry in the /etc/passwd file is composed of seven fields, each separated by a colon (":"):

```
username:x:uid:gid:full_name:home_directory:shell
```

Here is a detailed breakdown of each field:

- **username**: This field contains the user's login name. It is typically a string of up to 32 characters that uniquely identifies the user within the system. The username must be unique and adhere to specific rules, such as starting with a letter and optionally followed by letters, digits, underscores, or hyphens.

- **x** (Password Placeholder): Historically, the second field held the user's encrypted password. However, for enhanced security, modern Unix and Linux systems store actual password hashes in the /etc/shadow file, which is discussed in the subsequent section of this chapter. The /etc/passwd file now stores an "x" in this field to indicate the presence of the password hash in the /etc/shadow file.

- **uid** (User ID): This numeric value uniquely identifies the user within the system. It is used by the kernel and various utilities to differentiate users. The root user always has a UID of 0, while regular users typically have UIDs starting from 1000 or 500, depending on the distribution.

- **gid** (Group ID): This field contains the primary group ID associated with the user. The GID maps to an entry in the /etc/group file, which specifies the user's primary group. Group memberships are fundamental for controlling access permissions to files and resources.

- **full_name** (GECOS field): The GECOS field is a comma-separated list of user information intended for human use. Typically, it includes the user's full name, and optionally, it can contain fields for office number, work phone, and home phone. However, using only the user's full name is common practice.

- **home_directory**: This field specifies the absolute path to the user's home directory. The home directory is the user's primary workspace, where personal files, configurations, and environment settings are stored. On most systems, this is located at /home/username.

- **shell**: This field indicates the path to the user's login shell, which is the program that runs when the user logs in. Common shell paths include /bin/bash for the Bourne-Again Shell and /bin/sh for the Bourne Shell. This can be customized to any valid shell available on the system.

A sample entry in the /etc/passwd file might look like this:

```
john:x:1001:1001:John Doe:/home/john:/bin/bash
```

In this example, 'john' is the username, 'x' indicates that the password is stored securely in the /etc/shadow file, '1001' is the UID, '1001' is the primary GID, full name is 'John Doe', the home directory is '/home/john', and '/bin/bash' is the user's login shell.

To access and view the contents of the /etc/passwd file, with necessary permissions, the cat command can be used:

```
cat /etc/passwd
```

The above command will output the entire content of the file:

```
root:x:0:0:root:/root:/bin/bash
daemon:x:1:1:daemon:/usr/sbin:/usr/sbin/nologin
bin:x:2:2:bin:/bin:/usr/sbin/nologin
john:x:1001:1001:John Doe:/home/john:/bin/bash
```

The /etc/passwd file must remain readable by all users, as several programs rely on the ability to read user account details. However, to ensure security, it should not be writable by regular users, and write permissions should be restricted to the root or superuser.

Moreover, secure management of the /etc/passwd file is crucial. Unauthorized changes can impair system functionality, compromise user accounts, and pose significant security risks. Tools such as vipw can be employed to safely edit the /etc/passwd file:

```
sudo vipw /etc/passwd
```

The vipw command locks the file during editing, preventing concurrent modifications that may corrupt the file. It employs the default text editor (such as vi) to safely make necessary alterations.

Understanding the structure and role of the /etc/passwd file is fundamental to effective user and group management in Linux systems. It lays the foundation for more advanced topics like user authentication, user profile management, and system security. Proper configuration and maintenance of this file ensure orderly user account operations and robust system integrity.

4.3 The /etc/shadow File

The /etc/shadow file stores essential security information related to user authentication. It includes hashed passwords and other security-related attributes for user accounts. This file is essential for maintaining system security and is readable only by the root user or processes running with elevated privileges.

The structure of the /etc/shadow file consists of multiple lines, each corresponding to a single user account. Each line contains several fields separated by colons. Below is a typical structure of an entry in the /etc/shadow file:

```
/etc/shadow:
username:password:lastchange:minimum:maximum:warn:inactive:expire:reserved
```

The fields in each line are interpreted as follows:

- **username**: The user's login name. This field must match an entry in the /etc/passwd file.
- **password**: The hashed password. If this field contains an asterisk (*) or an exclamation mark (!), it indicates that the account is disabled.
- **lastchange**: The number of days since January 1, 1970, when the password was last changed. Using the chage command, this value can be modified.
- **minimum**: The minimum number of days required between password changes. A value of zero indicates no minimum requirement.
- **maximum**: The maximum number of days a password is valid before a user must change it.
- **warn**: The number of days before the password expiry date during which the user is warned to change the password.
- **inactive**: The number of days of inactivity after a password expires before the account is locked.

- **expire**: The number of days since January 1, 1970, when the user account will be disabled. A value of blank implies that the account will never expire.
- **reserved**: This field is reserved for future use.

Here is an example of an entry in the /etc/shadow file:

```
johndoe:$6$salt$hashedpassword$abcd12345:18547:7:90:7:14:19000:
```

For clarity, let us examine the example with respect to each attribute:

- **username**: johndoe
- **password**: 6salt$hashedpassword$abcd12345
- **lastchange**: 18547 (days since January 1, 1970)
- **minimum**: 7 (days)
- **maximum**: 90 (days)
- **warn**: 7 (days before expiry)
- **inactive**: 14 (days after expiry)
- **expire**: 19000 (days since January 1, 1970)
- **reserved**: empty

The hash algorithm used for the password is identified by the prefix in the hashed password field. Common prefixes include:

- 1 - MD5
- $2a$ or $2y$ - Blowfish
- 5 - SHA-256
- 6 - SHA-512

These hashed passwords are generated by applying a one-way hash function to the user's actual password, combined with a cryptographic salt, to produce a fixed-length string.

To adjust password and account expiration dates, the chage command can be employed. Here are some practical examples:

```
# View password aging information for a user
chage -l johndoe

# Set user password to expire in 30 days
sudo chage -M 30 johndoe

# Force user to change password on their next login
sudo chage -d 0 johndoe
```

The output of the chage -l johndoe command:

```
Last password change                                   : Jan 30, 2023
Password expires                                       : Apr 30, 2023
Password inactive                                      : never
Account expires                                        : never
Minimum number of days between password change         : 7
Maximum number of days between password change         : 90
Number of days of warning before password expires      : 7
```

By efficiently managing the /etc/shadow file and its configurations, system administrators ensure secure and well-maintained user authentication processes.

4.4 The /etc/group File

The */etc/group* file in Linux is an integral component of the system's user and group management. It delineates all the groups present on the system and links them to their respective members. This file enables easier administrative tasks by allowing efficient categorization and permission assignment for users based on their group membership. Understanding the structure and manipulation of the */etc/group* file is crucial for maintaining a secure and well-organized multi-user environment.

Syntax and Structure: The */etc/group* file adopts a simple format, where each line corresponds to a single group. The fields in each line are separated by colons (":"). The file consists of four fundamental fields:

- **group_name**: The name assigned to the group, which is a user-friendly identifier.
- **password**: This field is generally not used or is set to 'x'. In modern systems, group passwords are rarely utilized.
- **group_ID (GID)**: A unique numerical identifier for the group.
- **member_list**: A comma-separated list of users who belong to the group.

A typical entry in the */etc/group* file appears as follows:

```
group_name:password:group_ID:member1,member2,member3
```

For instance:

```
developers:x:1001:alice,bob,carol
```

Field Descriptions:

Group Name: This is the human-readable name given to the group. It can comprise both letters and numbers but traditionally adheres to lowercase alphanumeric characters. This name is used in configuration files and commands for group-based permission assignments.

Password: Most contemporary systems use a placeholder 'x' or '*' in this field. Historically, this field could contain an encrypted password for the group, but this practice is obsolete and largely unsupported.

Group ID (GID): The Group ID is a unique integer assigned to each group. It functions analogously to user IDs (UIDs) but pertains specifically to groups. Each GID must be unique to ensure correct group identification.

Member List: This comprises login names of users who are members of the group, separated by commas. If multiple users are added to a single group, this list reflects the membership. This field can be left blank if the group has no users.

Managing the /etc/group File:

Modifying the */etc/group* file directly should be done cautiously, as incorrect modifications can lead to security vulnerabilities or system misconfigurations. Below, we explore some command-line utilities for managing this file safely:

```
sudo groupadd developers
```

This command creates a new group named developers. The system automatically assigns a unique GID.

```
sudo groupdel developers
```

This command deletes the group developers from the */etc/group* file. It removes the group but not the users listed under this group.

```
sudo usermod -a -G developers alice
```

This command appends (-a) alice to the existing group developers without affecting her membership in other groups.

```
sudo gpasswd -d alice developers
```

This command removes the user alice from the developers group.

Verification of Group Memberships:

To verify the group memberships of a particular user, the following command proves useful:

```
groups alice
```

Executing this will display the groups to which alice belongs:

```
alice : alice developers sudo
```

To view all groups available on the system, the */etc/group* file can be examined directly:

```
cat /etc/group
```

Implementing these techniques ensures the administrator efficiently handles group-related tasks while maintaining system integrity. Familiarity with the */etc/group* file's structure and associated commands has practical implications for orchestrating user permissions and fostering secure collaborative environments.

4.5 Creating and Deleting Users with useradd and userdel

Creating and managing user accounts is a critical task for Linux system administrators. The useradd and userdel commands are two fundamental utilities used to add and remove users from the system respectively. Proficiency with these commands ensures that administrators can efficiently manage user access and maintain system security.

The useradd Command

The useradd command is used to create a new user. This command, when executed, makes entries in several key files, including /etc/passwd, /etc/shadow, and /etc/group, ensuring the new user is fully integrated into the system's user management framework.

The basic syntax for useradd is:

```
useradd [options] username
```

A detailed breakdown of important options is as follows:

- -c, –comment: Adds a comment, typically the user's full name.
- -d, –home: Defines the user's home directory. If not specified, the default /home/username is used.
- -e, –expiredate: Sets the expiry date for the user account.
- -G, –groups: Specifies a list of supplementary groups.
- -s, –shell: Sets the login shell.
- -u, –uid: Sets the user ID.
- -p, –password: Sets the encrypted password for the new account.

To create a user named john with a specific home directory and shell, the command would be:

```
useradd -d /customhome/john -s /bin/bash john
```

This command does the following:

- Adds an entry in /etc/passwd for user john.
- Creates the home directory /customhome/john.
- Sets the login shell to /bin/bash.

The administrator can then set a password for john using the passwd command:

```
passwd john
```

Content of /etc/passwd After Adding User

The contents of /etc/passwd after creating the user john might look like:

john:x:1001:1001::/customhome/john:/bin/bash

The userdel Command

The userdel command is used to remove a user from the system. This command can also remove the user's home directory and mail spool if specified. The basic syntax is:

```
userdel [options] username
```

Important options include:

- -r: Removes the user's home directory and mail spool along with the user account.

To delete the user john and remove his home directory, the command would be:

```
userdel -r john
```

This command performs the following actions:

- Removes john's entry from /etc/passwd.
- Deletes the home directory /customhome/john.
- Removes any mail files associated with john.

Verification

After deletion, the /etc/passwd file no longer contains an entry for john:

```
/etc/passwd entry for 'john' is deleted
```

Accurate use of useradd and userdel commands coupled with proper option usage ensures effective user account management, preserving both system integrity and security.

4.6 Modifying Users with usermod

The usermod command in Linux is a powerful utility used for modifying existing user accounts. This command allows administrators to change various user attributes, update user information, and manage user attributes effectively. The comprehensive functionality of usermod facilitates maintaining an organized and secure user environment.

The basic syntax of the usermod command is:

```
usermod [options] USERNAME
```

The USERNAME parameter specifies the account to be modified. Various options are available to alter the user's characteristics.

-c: usermod -c "COMMENT" USERNAME

This option updates the comment field in the /etc/passwd file, typically used for the user's full name or other descriptive details.

```
usermod -c "John Doe" johnd
```

After executing this command, the comment field of the user johnd becomes "John Doe".

-d: usermod -d HOME_DIR USERNAME

To change the user's home directory to a new location, use this option. For simultaneous creation of the new directory and transfer of contents from the old one, combine with the -m option.

```
usermod -d /new/home/directory -m johnd
```

This command sets /new/home/directory as johnd's home directory and migrates the existing contents.

-e: usermod -e EXPIRE_DATE USERNAME

Setting an account expiration date is crucial for temporary accounts. The expiration date needs to be in the format YYYY-MM-DD.

```
usermod -e 2023-12-31 johnd
```

Here, johnd's account is scheduled to expire on December 31, 2023.

-g: usermod -g GID USERNAME

Primary group changes are accomplished using this option. The GID represents the Group ID of the new primary group.

```
usermod -g developers johnd
```

Executing the above assigns developers as the primary group for johnd.

-G: usermod -G GROUP1,GROUP2,... USERNAME

Supplementary group memberships are managed through this option. It sets the user's groups to the provided list, replacing any previous memberships.

```
usermod -G wheel,sudo johnd
```

With this, johnd is added to the wheel and sudo groups. To preserve existing memberships while adding new ones, use -aG.

```
usermod -aG audio johnd
```

Here, johnd is added to the audio group, retaining his existing group memberships.

-l: usermod -l NEW_USERNAME OLD_USERNAME

For renaming a user account, utilize this option.

```
usermod -l john.doe johnd
```

After this, the user account johnd is renamed to john.doe.

-L and -U: usermod -L USERNAME and usermod -U USERNAME

Account locking and unlocking are essential for access control. The -L option locks and -U unlocks the specified user's account.

```
usermod -L johnd
usermod -U johnd
```

The first line disables johnd's login, while the second re-enables it.

-s: usermod -s SHELL USERNAME

Modifying the default login shell is done through this option.

```
usermod -s /bin/zsh johnd
```

This command sets /bin/zsh as the login shell for johnd.

-u: usermod -u UID USERNAME

User ID modification is managed with this option.

```
usermod -u 2001 johnd
```

Here, johnd's UID changes to 2001. Ensure the new UID is unique.

Executing these commands requires root or sudo privileges. The following example demonstrates combining multiple usermod options in one command:

```
usermod -c "John Doe" -d /new/home -m -g developers -G wheel,audio -s /bin/zsh
    johnd
```

This command updates the comment, home directory (and moves its contents), primary and supplementary groups, and the login shell for johnd.

Attention to details such as UID, GID uniqueness, and the accurate syntax is critical when using the usermod command, ensuring seamless modifications without disrupting user access or system stability.

4.7 Creating and Deleting Groups with groupadd and groupdel

The management of groups is a fundamental aspect of user administration in Linux. Groups provide a convenient way to assign permissions to multiple users simultaneously. This section will cover the tools and commands used to create and delete groups, specifically focusing on the utilities groupadd and groupdel.

Creating Groups with groupadd

The groupadd command is utilized to create new groups on the system. Its basic syntax is straightforward:

```
groupadd [options] group_name
```

Where group_name is the name of the group to be created. By default, the new group is assigned the next available group ID (GID). However, this can be customized using the -g option.

Options for groupadd

Several options can be used with groupadd. The most frequently used ones include:

- -g gid : Assigns a specific GID to the new group.
- -r : Creates a system group (with a GID less than 1000).
- -K KEY=VALUE : Overrides settings in /etc/login.defs.

Creating a Simple Group

To create a group named developers, the following command can be used:

```
groupadd developers
```

This will create a group with the name developers and assign it the next available GID.

Creating a Group with a Specific GID

To create a group named testers with a specific GID, such as 1500, the -g option is used:

```
groupadd -g 1500 testers
```

This command ensures that the testers group is created with the GID 1500.

Creating a System Group

System groups are typically used for system processes and usually have GIDs less than 1000. The -r option creates a system group:

```
groupadd -r sysadmins
```

This command creates a system group named sysadmins with an appropriate GID for system groups.

Deleting Groups with groupdel

The groupdel command is used to delete groups from the system. Its basic syntax is:

```
groupdel group_name
```

Where group_name is the name of the group to be deleted. This command removes the group entry from the /etc/group file but does not affect any files owned by the group. Only groups that are not associated with any users can be deleted directly.

Deleting a Simple Group

To delete a group named obsolete_group, the following command can be issued:

```
groupdel obsolete_group
```

After executing this command, the obsolete_group will be removed from the system.

Potential Issues and Error Handling

groupadd and groupdel commands should be executed with caution. Some common errors include attempting to create a group with a name or GID that already exists, or trying to delete a group that is still associated with users or system processes.

For instance, attempting to create a group with a duplicate GID will produce an error:

```
groupadd -g 1000 groupname
# groupadd: GID '1000' already exists
```

Similarly, attempting to delete a group that is associated with existing users will result in an error message suggesting the group cannot be deleted.

It is often useful to check the existence and details of groups using the getent group command before attempting to create or delete groups:

```
getent group group_name
```

This will display the group details if it exists.

Creating and deleting groups efficiently is critical for maintaining a well-organized and secure environment in Linux systems. Proper understanding and usage of the groupadd and groupdel commands enhance the administrator's ability to manage groups effectively.

4.8 Assigning and Modifying Group Membership with gpasswd and usermod

The process of managing group memberships in Linux is crucial for establishing permissions and access control on a multi-user system. Two essential commands for modifying group memberships are gpasswd and usermod. We will explore both commands in depth, providing examples to illustrate their usage.

gpasswd is specifically designed for group membership administration. It allows an administrator to add or remove users from groups and set group passwords if necessary. In contrast, usermod is a more general command for modifying user accounts, including their group memberships.

Adding Users to Groups with gpasswd

gpasswd offers a straightforward method for adding a user to an existing group. The syntax is:

```
gpasswd -a username groupname
```

For example, to add a user named alice to the developers group, the command is:

```
gpasswd -a alice developers
```

Executing the above command would yield an output confirming the action:

```
Adding user alice to group developers
```

Removing Users from Groups with gpasswd

Similarly, removing a user from a group can be achieved with:

```
gpasswd -d username groupname
```

To remove alice from the developers group, the command is:

```
gpasswd -d alice developers
```

The system confirms the user removal as follows:

Removing user alice from group developers

Setting Group Administrators with gpasswd

gpasswd also supports the assignment of group administrators, allowing specified users within the group to modify the group membership. To add a group administrator:

```
gpasswd -A user1,user2 groupname
```

To make alice an administrator of the developers group:

```
gpasswd -A alice developers
```

Clearing Group Administrators

If you need to remove existing group administrators and leave the group without any specific administrators, the following command is used:

```
gpasswd -A "" groupname
```

Adding Users to Groups with usermod

Whereas gpasswd focuses on the modification of group memberships, usermod allows for a broader range of modifications to user accounts. To add a user to supplementary groups, use the -aG options:

```
usermod -aG groupname username
```

To add alice to the developers group without removing her from other groups, the command is:

```
usermod -aG developers alice
```

The -a option (append) ensures that the user is added to the group without affecting their existing group memberships.

Changing Primary Group with usermod

Each user has a primary group, reflected in the /etc/passwd file. To change the primary group for a user:

```
usermod -g new_primary_group username
```

For example, to change alice's primary group to developers, the command is:

```
usermod -g developers alice
```

Replacing All Secondary Group Memberships

If the goal is to replace all of a user's secondary groups rather than appending new ones, omit the -a option:

```
usermod -G group1,group2,group3 username
```

To set alice to be a member exclusively of developers and testers groups, use:

```
usermod -G developers,testers alice
```

Limitations and Considerations

While gpasswd and usermod commands offer similar functionalities, gpasswd is often preferred for managing multi-user group memberships due to its specificity and additional administrative capabilities. Changes made using these commands take immediate effect but may require the user to re-login to apply the new group memberships to their active session. Always ensure user processes utilizing group permissions are appropriately restarted to reflect changes fully.

4.9 Understanding and Setting User Passwords with passwd

The passwd command is integral to managing user security in a Linux environment. It allows the system administrator, as well as users, to set or change passwords, an essential aspect of protecting user accounts. This section elucidates the usage of this command, including both command-line options and the underlying mechanisms it triggers.

The basic syntax of the passwd command is:

```
passwd [OPTIONS] [USERNAME]
```

By default, if executed without specifying a USERNAME, the command changes the password of the user currently logged in. When executed by the root user, specifying a USERNAME allows changing the password for any user.

To understand the passwd command comprehensively, consider the following commonly used options:

- -d: Deletes the password for the specified user account, leaving the account without a password. This is typically used with caution, as it can leave user accounts vulnerable unless accompanied by other forms of authentication.
- -e or –expire: Forces the user to change their password upon their next login. This is especially useful for administrative actions where security policies require periodic password changes.
- -l or –lock: Locks the specified user account, effectively disabling the account while keeping all user files and settings intact.
- -u or –unlock: Unlocks the specified user account, reversing the effect of the -l option.
- -i INACTIVE: Sets the account to be disabled after the specified number of days from the password's expiration if the password is not changed.
- -n MIN_DAYS: Sets the minimum number of days required between password changes.
- -x MAX_DAYS: Sets the maximum number of days the password remains valid.
- -w WARN_DAYS: Sets the number of days of warning before a password change is required.

Executing the passwd command without any options will follow a standard process, prompting the user for the current password (if applicable), the new password, and a confirmation of the new password:

```
$ passwd
Changing password for username.
(current) UNIX password:
Enter new UNIX password:
Retype new UNIX password:
passwd: password updated successfully
```

When the passwd command is initiated, it performs several critical operations integral to password management in Linux:

1. **Password Authentication**: Validates the current user's password against the encrypted password in the /etc/shadow file.

2. **Password Strength Validation**: Checks the strength of the new password according to the policies defined in /etc/pam.d/passwd, ensuring it meets the complexity requirements.

3. **Password Encryption**: Encrypts the new password and updates the entry in the /etc/shadow file.

4. **Metadata Update**: Updates the password change timestamps and any related user account fields.

The /etc/shadow file plays a pivotal role in the password management process. Each line in this file corresponds to a user and contains the following fields:

```
username:password:lastchg:min:max:warn:inactive:expire:
```

- username: The name of the user. - password: The user's encrypted password. - lastchg: The last password change date, in the number of days since Jan 1, 1970 (Unix epoch). - min: The minimum number of days between password changes. - max: The maximum number of days before a password change is required. - warn: The number of days before password expiration during which the user will receive a warning. - inactive: The number of days after password expiration before the account is disabled. - expire: The absolute date when the account will be disabled, in the number of days since Jan 1, 1970 (Unix epoch).

For example, to force a user named alice to change her password at the next login, the system administrator would use:

```
sudo passwd --expire alice
```

To lock the account of bob:

```
sudo passwd --lock bob
```

Unlocking the same account would require:

```
sudo passwd --unlock bob
```

To delete the password for charlie, making his account password-less:

```
sudo passwd --delete charlie
```

Enforcing password aging policies ensures users regularly update their passwords and adhere to organizational security standards. Setting these policies can prevent misuse and unauthorized access. An example command to set the password policy for user david is:

```
sudo passwd -n 5 -x 90 -w 7 david
```

Here, -n 5 means the password must be at least 5 days old before it can be changed again, -x 90 means the password expires after 90 days, and -w 7 means the user gets a warning 7 days before password expiration.

Understanding the intricacies of setting and managing passwords with the passwd command and its impact on security policies is essential for effective system administration in any Linux environment.

4.10 Managing User Profiles and Environments

In Linux, user profiles and environments play a critical role in personalizing and customizing the user's interaction with the system. These aspects define the system behavior, the user's interface, the commands available through the user's shell, and various other preferences that enhance user productivity. This section delves into the configuration files and parameters that control user environments, emphasizing practical management techniques to ensure optimal user experience and system efficiency.

Configuration files, such as ~/.bashrc, ~/.bash_profile, and ~/.profile, are essential in defining user environments. Understanding the differences between these files is fundamental for effective user environment management.

~/.bashrc is executed for interactive non-login shells. This file typically contains commands and settings to configure the prompt, set shell aliases, and define environment variables. Here is an example of a typical ~/.bashrc file:

```
# ~/.bashrc: executed by bash(1) for non-login shells.
# Note: the following command lines are examples and can be customized as needed.

# Enable color support for ls and add handy aliases
if [ -x /usr/bin/dircolors ]; then
    eval "$(dircolors -b)"
    alias ls='ls --color=auto'
```

```
    alias grep='grep --color=auto'
    alias fgrep='fgrep --color=auto'
    alias egrep='egrep --color=auto'
fi

# Alias definitions.
alias ll='ls -alF'
alias la='ls -A'
alias l='ls -CF'

# Add user-specific environment variables
export HISTCONTROL=ignoredups:erasedups
export HISTFILESIZE=2000
export HISTSIZE=1000

# Source global definitions if present
if [ -f /etc/bashrc ]; then
    . /etc/bashrc
fi
```

~/.bash_profile and ~/.profile are executed for login shells. These files often contain commands that set up environment variables, initiate custom scripts, and start essential services. The choice between ~/.bash_profile and ~/.profile can depend on the user shell's configuration and the specific needs of the environment.

Below is a simple example of a ~/.bash_profile file:

```
# ~/.bash_profile: executed by bash(1) for login shells.
# Note: the following command lines are examples and can be customized as needed.

# If running interactively, source ~/.bashrc
if [ -n "$PS1" ]; then
    if [ -f ~/.bashrc ]; then
        . ~/.bashrc
    fi
fi

# Set PATH for user-specific binaries
export PATH=$HOME/bin:$PATH

# Customize user prompt (PS1)
export PS1="\u@\h \w\$ "
```

The initialization process for these files involves, first, a system-wide configuration through files like /etc/profile and /etc/bash.bashrc, followed by user-specific configuration files. Therefore, changes made at the user level can override the global settings, providing scope for extensive customization.

To illustrate, we can view how changes in these files impact a user's environment. Consider a scenario where an alias for a frequently used command is added or modified. By adding the following alias to ~/.bashrc:

```
alias gs='git status'
```

the command gs can be used as a shortcut for git status. After editing ~/.bashrc, the user must re-source the file with:

```
source ~/.bashrc
```

Another critical aspect of managing user profiles involves environment variables. These variables can control various shell behaviors and software configurations. For instance,

```
export EDITOR=nano
```

sets the default text editor to nano. This environment variable can be added in ~/.bash_profile or ~/.profile to ensure it is available globally across login sessions.

Beyond individual-user configurations, it's sometimes important to enforce or recommend certain settings globally. System administrators can place common configuration snippets in /etc/profile.d/. Scripts within this directory are executed for all users, ensuring consistent environment settings across the system.

To create a new script in /etc/profile.d/, the following minimal script ensures all users have a default editor set to nano:

```
# /etc/profile.d/default_editor.sh
export EDITOR=nano
```

Managing user profiles and environments effectively prevents common pitfalls associated with environment misconfigurations, such as incorrect PATH settings or conflicting variable definitions. This precision not only enhances user satisfaction but also ensures system stability and security.

4.11 Implementing Sudo for Administrative Access

Sudo, or "superuser do," is a program designed to allow a permitted user to execute a command as the superuser or another user, as specified in the /etc/sudoers file. Utilizing sudo enhances security as it allows for controlled, temporary administrative access without exposing the root user login.

The sudo configuration is managed through the /etc/sudoers file. This file controls how sudo behaves and dictates which users or groups can execute which commands. Direct edits to this file are discouraged; instead, the visudo command ensures safe editing practices.

To edit the sudoers file:

```
sudo visudo
```

Within the sudoers file, entries follow a specific format:

```
user host=(user:group) commands
```

An example entry:

```
john ALL=(ALL:ALL) ALL
```

This grants the user "john" the ability to execute any command as any user on any host.

For group-based permissions:

```
%admin ALL=(ALL) ALL
```

Here, all users in the "admin" group are given full sudo access. The leading percent sign (

To grant a user restricted access, explicitly specify commands:

```
jane ALL=(root) /usr/bin/apt-get, /usr/bin/dpkg
```

In this case, user "jane" is permitted to execute apt-get and dpkg commands as root.

Configuring Alias for Commands, Users, and Groups

Aliases simplify configuration in the sudoers file:

```
Cmnd_Alias STORAGE = /bin/mount, /bin/umount
User_Alias OPERATORS = alice, bob
```

Here, STORAGE is an alias for the mount and umount commands, while OPERATORS refers to users "alice" and "bob". These aliases can be used:

```
OPERATORS ALL=(root) STORAGE
```

Defaults and Fine-tuning Behavior

Customize sudo behavior with the Defaults option:

```
Defaults timestamp_timeout=10
```

This example sets the sudo password prompt timeout to 10 minutes. For tailored configurations, combine defaults with command or user-specific rules:

```
Defaults:alice !requiretty
```

This exempts "alice" from needing a terminal to use sudo.

Managing Sudo in Practice

Adding a User to the Sudo Group:

Most distributions create a "sudo" or "wheel" group. To grant a user sudo access, add them to this group:

```
sudo usermod -aG sudo newuser
```

Verifying User Privileges:

Check a user's sudo capabilities:

```
sudo -l
```

This command lists permitted (and forbidden) commands for the user, based on sudoers entries.

Testing and Logging

Test sudo configurations to verify correctness:

```
sudo -u user command
```

Analyze sudo logs for security audits. By default, sudo logs to /var/log/auth.log, detailing each command execution attempt:

```
Mar 10 15:43:20 hostname sudo: pam_unix(sudo:session): session opened for user root by john(uid=1001)
```

This ensures that administrative actions are traceable to individual users.

For optimal security, only grant necessary privileges, regularly review configurations, and educate users on responsible sudo usage.

4.12 Access Control and Login Management

Access control and login management are critical components of Linux system administration, ensuring that only authorized users can access the system and its resources. This section delves into various tools and configurations that administrators can use to enhance security, control login behavior, and monitor user activities.

Access control can be broadly categorized into discretionary access control (DAC), managed through file permissions, and mandatory access control (MAC), implemented through security modules like SELinux and AppArmor.

File Permissions: File permissions in Linux are specified using a numerical or symbolic format, representing access rights for the file's owner, group, and others. File permissions can be viewed and modified using commands like ls, chmod, chown, and chgrp.

```
# View file permissions
ls -l filename

# Change file permissions using symbolic notation
chmod u+rwx,go=r filename

# Change file permissions using numerical notation
chmod 755 filename

# Change file owner
chown newowner filename

# Change file group
chgrp newgroup filename
```

In the output of the ls -l command, the first column displays the file type and permissions. For example:

```
-rwxr-xr--
```

The above string indicates that the owner has read, write, and execute permissions (rwx), the group has read and execute permissions (r-x), and others have only read permissions (r–).

Access Control Lists (ACLs): ACLs provide a finer-grained security policy for files and directories, allowing specific permissions for individual users and groups.

```
# Enable ACL on a filesystem
```

```
mount -o remount,acl /mountpoint

# View ACL for a file
getfacl filename

# Set ACL for a file
setfacl -m u:username:rwx filename

# Remove ACL for a file
setfacl -x u:username filename
```

Pluggable Authentication Modules (PAM): PAM is a suite of shared libraries that enable the dynamic authentication of users. PAM configuration files are located in /etc/pam.d/, and each service has its own file detailing the modules it uses for authentication, account management, session management, and password management.

An example of a PAM configuration for the login service may look like this:

```
/etc/pam.d/login:
auth       required    pam_securetty.so
auth       requisite   pam_nologin.so
auth       include     system-auth
account    required    pam_access.so
password   include     system-auth
session    include     system-auth
session    optional    pam_lastlog.so
session    optional    pam_motd.so
```

Each line in the PAM configuration file consists of a module interface, control flag, module name, and optional arguments. The control flags determine the operations of the modules: required, requisite, sufficient, and optional.

Security-Enhanced Linux (SELinux): SELinux enforces mandatory access control policies that limit the resources that processes can access. It integrates with file contexts, policy rules, and user attributes to offer a higher degree of security.

Basic SELinux commands include:

```
# Check the current SELinux mode
getenforce

# Set SELinux mode to enforcing
setenforce 1

# Set SELinux mode to permissive
setenforce 0

# View SELinux context of files
ls -Z filename

# Change SELinux context of a file
chcon -t httpd_sys_content_t filename
```

AppArmor: AppArmor is another MAC system that confines programs to a limited set of resources by using profiles. AppArmor profiles can be in enforcing mode or complaint mode, allowing administrators to audit capabilities without blocking access initially.

Basic AppArmor commands include:

```
# Enable a profile
aa-enforce /etc/apparmor.d/profile_name

# Put a profile in complain mode
aa-complain /etc/apparmor.d/profile_name

# Check AppArmor status
aa-status
```

Login Management: Managing logins involves configuring settings in various system files to restrict or allow certain behaviors. Important files include /etc/nologin, /etc/securetty, and /etc/ssh/sshd_config.

```
# Create /etc/nologin to prevent non-root users from logging in
echo "System maintenance in progress" > /etc/nologin

# Only allow root login from specified ttys
echo "tty1" > /etc/securetty
echo "tty2" >> /etc/securetty

# Configure SSH settings in /etc/ssh/sshd_config
# Disable root login
PermitRootLogin no

# Specify allowed users
AllowUsers username1 username2
```

By utilizing these tools and configurations, administrators can effectively manage access control and login policies to ensure a secure Linux environment.

Chapter 5

File Permissions and Security

This chapter explains file permissions and security in Linux. It covers the basics of read, write, and execute permissions, and details how to view and change these permissions using commands like ‘ls‘, ‘stat‘, and ‘chmod‘. The chapter discusses file ownership and the use of ‘chown‘ and ‘chgrp‘, as well as setting default permissions with ‘umask‘. It introduces special permissions such as SUID, SGID, and the sticky bit, and explores access control lists (ACLs) and security frameworks like SELinux and AppArmor. The chapter concludes with techniques for file integrity monitoring to maintain system security.

5.1 Introduction to File Permissions

File permissions in Linux are a fundamental aspect of the operating system's security and access control mechanisms. These permissions dictate who can read, write, or execute a file. Understanding and managing file permissions effectively is crucial for maintaining system security and ensuring the appropriate access levels to files and directories.

In Linux, file permissions are represented in a structured manner, associated with every file and directory. When you execute the ‘ls -l‘ command, you'll see a detailed list of files and directories along with their permissions. The permissions for each file are displayed as a string of ten characters. Here is an example of the output from this command:

```
-rw-r--r--
```

This string can be broken down into distinct sections that provide specific information about the file permissions and other attributes:

1. The first character indicates the file type. A hyphen (-) represents a regular file, a 'd' represents a directory, and other characters such as 'l' can represent symbolic links or special files. 2. The remaining nine characters are divided into three sets, each comprising three characters. These sets represent the permissions for the file's owner, the group, and others, respectively.

Each set of three characters follows the pattern 'rwx', where: - 'r' stands for read permission. - 'w' stands for write permission. - 'x' stands for execute permission. - A hyphen (-) indicates the absence of a permission.

For example:

- 'rw-' means read and write permissions are granted, but execute permission is not.
- 'r–' means only read permission is granted.
- 'r-x' means read and execute permissions are granted, but write permission is not.

To illustrate, let's consider the following output for a specific file:

```
-rwxr-xr--
```

This indicates: - The first character '-' signifies that the item is a regular file. - The next three characters 'rwx' indicate that the owner of the file has read, write, and execute permissions. - The following three characters 'r-x' indicate that the group assigned to the file has read and execute permissions, but not write permissions. - The final three characters 'r–' indicate that others (anyone who is not the owner or part of the group) have only read permissions.

Now, if we look at a directory:

```
drwxr-xr-x
```

Here: - The first character 'd' indicates that the item is a directory. - The next three characters 'rwx' show that the owner has read, write, and execute permissions. - The following three characters 'r-x' indicate that the group has read and execute permissions. - The final three characters 'r-x' reveal that others have read and execute permissions as well.

Directories require execute permission for users to enter the directory and read its contents, while files primarily use execute permissions to denote whether they can be executed as programs or scripts.

Understanding these components is essential for managing access control to files and directories effectively. Linux uses these permission strings to enforce security and control access rights, making it imperative for users and administrators to understand and utilize these permissions correctly.

Let's move forward by exploring how to view and change these permissions using various commands like 'ls', 'stat', and 'chmod'. We'll also delve into the categorization of users into owners, groups, and others, and how these categories interact with the permission sets to dictate access control across the system.

5.2 Understanding Read, Write, and Execute Permissions

In Linux, file permissions are fundamental to the security and proper functioning of the system. Understanding these permissions is essential for both system administrators and users. Each file and directory has an associated set of permissions that dictate who can read, write, or execute it. These permissions ensure that only authorized users have access to certain data or functionalities.

Permissions are typically represented in three distinct sets: owner (user), group, and others (world). These sets of permissions are broken down further into three types of permissions: read (r), write (w), and execute (x). Each type has specific implications depending on whether it is assigned to a file or a directory:

- **Read (r)**: For files, this permission allows the contents of the file to be viewed. For directories, read permission enables the listing of the directory's contents.
- **Write (w)**: For files, write permission allows modifications to the file's contents. For directories, it permits the creation, deletion, or

renaming of files within the directory.

- **Execute (x)**: For files, execute permission allows the file to be run as a program or script. For directories, it enables the traversal of the directory, i.e., the ability to enter the directory and access files and subdirectories.

Each of these permissions can be set individually for the owner, the group, and others. Consider an example of a typical permission string:

-rwxr-xr–

The structure of this string is as follows:

- The first character indicates the file type: a dash (-) signifies a regular file, d indicates a directory, l a symbolic link, etc.
- The next three characters (rwx) represent the permissions for the file owner. In this case, the owner can read, write, and execute the file.
- The subsequent three characters (r-x) indicate the permissions for the group. Here, group members can read and execute the file, but cannot modify it.
- The final three characters (r–) specify the permissions for others (world). Others can only read the file.

Permissions play a crucial role in multi-user environments, where control over who can access or modify information is essential for maintaining security and organization. We can use the ls command with the -l option to view detailed permission settings of files and directories. Consider the following example:

```
$ ls -l example.txt
-rw-r--r-- 1 user group 1045 Aug 10 14:35 example.txt
```

Here, the output provides comprehensive details about example.txt:

```
-rw-r--r-- 1 user group 1045 Aug 10 14:35 example.txt
```

Breaking down the elements from left to right:

- -rw-r–r–: The permission string.

- 1: The number of hard links to the file.
- user: The user (owner) of the file.
- group: The group associated with the file.
- 1045: The file size in bytes.
- Aug 10 14:35: The last modified date and time.
- example.txt: The file name.

To modify these permissions, we use the chmod command. Permissions can be represented both symbolically with letters (r, w, x) and numerically using octal values. The symbolic mode involves explicitly setting the permissions using u (user), g (group), o (others), and a (all). For instance:

```
$ chmod u+r example.txt
```

This command adds read permission for the user (owner) on example.txt. Symbolic mode allows fine-grained, human-readable permission modifications. Alternatively, the numeric mode uses a three-digit octal number, where each digit corresponds to the permissions for user, group, and others, respectively. Each permission type is represented by a specific value:

- r (read) = 4
- w (write) = 2
- x (execute) = 1

The numeric value for a set of permissions is the sum of these values. For example, 7 (read, write, execute) is calculated as 4 + 2 + 1. Therefore, to set read and write permissions for the user, read for the group, and no permissions for others, one would use:

```
$ chmod 640 example.txt
```

This translates to:

```
$ ls -l example.txt
-rw-r----- 1 user group 1045 Aug 10 14:35 example.txt
```

Understanding and properly setting read, write, and execute permissions is vital in Linux for system security and functionality. This holistic grasp of file permissions enables users and administrators to manage access control effectively, ensuring that only authorized users perform specific actions on files and directories.

5.3 Using the ls and stat Commands to View Permissions

One of the most fundamental aspects of managing file permissions in a Linux environment is the ability to view and interpret existing permissions. Two primary commands facilitate this task: ls and stat. Each command offers a unique set of features to display detailed information about files and directories, including their permissions.

The ls command is widely used to list files and directories in the file system. Adding specific options to the basic ls command can provide a more detailed view of file permissions.

```
ls -l
```

The -l option produces a long-format listing, displaying detailed information about each file. The output is organized into several columns, and the first column shows the file's permissions in a string of ten characters. Here is a breakdown of a standard ls -l output:

```
-rwxr-xr--
```

- The first character indicates the file type:

- - for a regular file
- d for a directory
- l for a symbolic link

- The next nine characters are grouped into three sets of three, representing the permissions for the file owner, the group, and others, respectively:

- r stands for read permission.
- w stands for write permission.
- x stands for execute permission.

- - indicates the absence of the corresponding permission.

To illustrate, consider the following output from the ls -l command:

```
-rwxr-xr-- 1 user group 12345 Jan 1 12:34 example.txt
```

- -rwxr-xr–: This indicates a regular file with read, write, and execute permissions for the owner, read and execute permissions for the group, and read-only permissions for others.
- 1: This is the number of hard links to the file.
- user: This shows the owner of the file.
- group: This shows the group associated with the file.
- 12345: This displays the size of the file in bytes.
- Jan 1 12:34: This gives the last modification date and time.
- example.txt: This is the name of the file.

Another useful option is -a, which lists all files and directories, including hidden ones (those starting with a period). Combining ls -a with the long format -l provides a comprehensive view of all files and their permissions in the directory.

```
ls -la
```

While ls provides a quick view of permissions and other file attributes, the stat command delivers more detailed and comprehensive information about a file. The stat command presents a structured output of various file properties, including permissions in both textual and octal (numeric) format.

To use the stat command, run:

```
stat example.txt
```

The output of the stat command may look like this:

```
  File: example.txt
  Size: 12345           Blocks: 24          IO Block: 4096   regular file
Device: 801h/2049d      Inode: 1234567      Links: 1
Access: (0754/-rwxr-xr--)  Uid: ( 1000/    user)   Gid: ( 1000/   group)
Access: 2021-01-01 12:34:56.000000000 +0000
Modify: 2021-01-01 12:34:56.000000000 +0000
Change: 2021-01-01 12:34:56.000000000 +0000
 Birth: -
```

Key components of this stat output include:

- **File**: The name of the file. - **Size**: The file size in bytes. - **Blocks**: The number of 512-byte blocks allocated to the file. - **IO Block**: The size of the filesystem's block size in bytes. - **Type**: Indicates the file type (e.g., regular file, directory). - **Device**: Device number in hexadecimal and decimal. - **Inode**: Unique inode number assigned to the file. - **Links**: Number of hard links to the file. - **Access**: Permission string and corresponding numeric mode (octal). - **Uid/Gid**: User ID and Group ID along with their respective names. - **Access/Modify/Change**: Timestamps for the last access, modification, and status change. - **Birth**: Creation time (if available on the filesystem).

An essential part of the stat output is the **Access** field, which displays the file permissions in a comprehensive format:

```
Access: (0754/-rwxr-xr--)
```

Here, 0754 is the octal representation of the file permissions, and -rwxr-xr– is the textual representation.

Combining both ls and stat commands can provide a thorough understanding of the file permissions and attributes, crucial for effective file security management in a Linux system.

5.4 Changing Permissions with chmod

The command chmod, short for "change mode," is a fundamental utility for modifying file and directory permissions in Linux. Understanding how to effectively use chmod is essential for ensuring the correct access control of system resources. This section provides a comprehensive guide on using chmod, explaining both its symbolic and numeric modes.

Permissions in Linux are divided into three classes: user (owner), group, and others. Each class has three types of permissions: read (r), write (w), and execute (x). The chmod command facilitates changing these permissions in either symbolic form, where permissions are represented by letters, or numeric form, where permissions are represented by numbers.

First, consider the symbolic form. The syntax for changing permissions using the symbolic mode with chmod is as follows:

```
chmod [who][operator][permission] filename
```

Here, who represents the class of permissions to be modified and can be any combination of:

- u for user (owner)
- g for group
- o for others
- a for all (user, group, and others)

The operator specifies the action to perform on the permissions:

- + to add permissions
- - to remove permissions
- = to set permissions exactly

The permission specifies the type of permission:

- r for read
- w for write
- x for execute

For example, to add execute permissions for the user on a file named example.txt, you would use the command:

```
chmod u+x example.txt
```

To remove write permissions for the group and others, the command would be:

```
chmod go-w example.txt
```

To set the permissions of the file so that only the user has read and write permissions, while the group and others have no permissions, use:

```
chmod u=rw,go= example.txt
```

In contrast, the numeric mode represents permissions as a three-digit octal number, where each digit corresponds to a class (user, group, and others). The permission bits are represented as follows:

Permission	Value	Binary Representation	Meaning
Read (r)	4	100	Permits reading
Write (w)	2	010	Permits writing
Execute (x)	1	001	Permits execution

To form the numeric representation, add the values of the permissions you want to set. For instance, to give read (4), write (2), and execute (1) permissions to the user, you sum the values: 4 + 2 + 1 = 7. If the group should have read (4) and execute (1), the value is 4 + 1 = 5. If others should only have read (4), the value is 4.

Combining these values, the numeric representation for setting read, write, and execute permissions for the user, read and execute permissions for the group, and read permissions for others is 755. The command in numeric mode would be:

```
chmod 755 example.txt
```

This method is often quicker and preferred for experienced users familiar with octal representations.

Consider another example. To grant only read and write permissions to the user, and no permissions to the group and others, the numeric value is 600:

```
chmod 600 example.txt
```

Executing the chmod command without proper understanding can lead to unintended permission settings, potentially compromising system security or functionality. Therefore, cautious application of these principles ensures that files and directories have the appropriate level of access.

Running chmod on directories requires special consideration, particularly with the execute permission. For directories, the execute permission allows a user to enter (also called cd into) the directory. For example, to make a directory project accessible to its owner (with full permissions), while making it readable and executable (but not writable) to the group and others, use:

```
chmod 755 project
```

By understanding and utilizing both symbolic and numeric modes of the chmod command, users can precisely control the access rights of their files and directories, ensuring both flexibility and security within the Linux environment.

5.5 Using Symbolic and Numeric Modes in chmod

The Linux chmod command is an essential tool for modifying file permissions. It allows users to change the access rights for files and directories. Permissions can be set in two primary ways: symbolic modes and numeric modes. Each mode offers a distinct approach to specifying permissions, providing flexibility and control to the user.

Symbolic mode employs a combination of characters to adjust permissions. This method utilizes letters to represent the users (owner, group, and others) and permissions (read, write, execute). For example, in symbolic notation, we use 'u' for user (owner), 'g' for group, 'o' for others, and 'a' for all users. The permissions themselves are denoted as 'r' for read, 'w' for write, and 'x' for execute. To modify permissions, symbolic mode employs operators such as '+' (to add a permission), '-' (to remove a permission), and '=' (to set a permission explicitly).

For example, consider a file example.txt. To add execute permission for the owner, the following command can be used:

```
chmod u+x example.txt
```

To remove the write permission for the group, the following command is utilized:

```
chmod g-w example.txt
```

Setting all permissions for others (read, write, execute) can be achieved using:

```
chmod o=rwx example.txt
```

Conversely, numeric mode uses octal (base-8) numbers to define permissions. Each permission is represented by a single digit from 0 to 7. The permission digits are derived as follows: read equals 4, write equals 2, and execute equals 1. These values are summed to determine the permission settings. For example, a value of 7 (4+2+1) grants all permissions (read, write, execute), while a value of 6 (4+2) grants read and write permissions.

In numeric mode, three digits are used to represent the permissions for the owner, group, and others respectively. For example, to set permissions for the owner (7 - read, write, execute), the group (5 - read and execute), and others (0 - no permissions), the following command is used:

```
chmod 750 example.txt
```

Consider an example where we need to modify the permissions of `script.sh` such that the owner's permissions are read, write, and execute (7), the group's permissions are read and execute (5), and others have no permissions (0). The following `chmod` command achieves this:

```
chmod 750 script.sh
```

The permissions can be verified through the `ls -l` command:

```
ls -l script.sh
```

```
-rwxr-x--- 1 user group 1234 Apr 11 12:34 script.sh
```

The above output confirms the permissions have been set correctly: the owner has read, write, and execute permissions; the group has read and execute permissions; and others have no permissions.

Leveraging both symbolic and numeric modes of `chmod` is crucial for efficiently managing file and directory permissions. Users can choose whichever method aligns best with their needs and preferences. Symbolic modes may be more intuitive when making incremental changes, while numeric modes can provide a succinct and direct way to set permissions comprehensively. Understanding both methods empowers users to enforce precise access controls, thereby enhancing the security and functionality of their Linux systems.

5.6 Understanding File Ownership

File ownership in Linux is a fundamental concept that plays a critical role in the system's security model. Each file in a Linux file system is associated with an owner and a group, which defines who has permissions to access or modify the file.

Every file in Linux has three ownership attributes:

- **User (Owner)**: The individual user who owns the file.
- **Group**: The group to which the file belongs.
- **Other**: All other users who are not the owner or part of the group associated with the file.

These attributes allow Linux to maintain granular control over who can read, write, or execute a particular file.

User (Owner): The user who owns the file is responsible for the file's contents and how it can be accessed. The owner's permissions can be very permissive or restrictive.

Group: Group ownership enables collaboration among users. When a file is assigned to a group, all users who are members of that group can have the same level of access as defined by the group's permissions. This is particularly useful in multi-user environments where teamwork and shared access to files are necessary.

Other: Users who are neither the file owner nor members of the file's group fall under the 'other' category. Permissions for 'other' users are generally the most restrictive to prevent unauthorized access.

To view the ownership and permissions of files and directories, the 'ls' command is frequently used with the '-l' flag to display detailed information. Consider the following example file listing:

```
$ ls -l sample.txt
-rw-r--r-- 1 john developers 1024 Feb 2 12:34 sample.txt
```

Here is the breakdown of the 'ls -l' output:

- '-rw-r–r–': The permissions of the file ('r', 'w', and 'x' for read, write, and execute, respectively).
- '1': The number of hard links to the file.
- 'john': The owner (user) of the file.
- 'developers': The group associated with the file.
- '1024': The file size in bytes.
- 'Feb 2 12:34': The last modification date and time.
- 'sample.txt': The name of the file.

In the sample output, the file 'sample.txt' is owned by the user 'john' and belongs to the group 'developers'.

To change the ownership of a file or directory, the 'chown' (change owner) command is utilized. This command allows both user and group ownership changes, either together or individually.

For example, to change the owner of a file to a user named 'alice', the following command is used:

```
$ sudo chown alice sample.txt
```

To change both the user and the group, separate the user and group with a colon:

```
$ sudo chown alice:managers sample.txt
```

In this example, 'alice' becomes the owner of 'sample.txt', and the file now belongs to the 'managers' group.

The group ownership can be changed independently of the user ownership using the 'chgrp' command. For instance, to change only the group of the file 'sample.txt' to 'admin' while keeping the current owner intact, execute:

```
$ sudo chgrp admin sample.txt
```

All these commands typically require superuser privileges, so they are often preceded by 'sudo' to execute them with elevated permissions.

The necessity to keep precise control over file ownership becomes evident in multi-user systems. Proper file ownership helps to prevent unauthorized access and modification, ensuring that only designated users can perform specific actions on files.

Ownership and permissions can also apply recursively to directories and their contents. To change ownership for a directory and all its contents, include the '-R' (recursive) option with 'chown':

```
$ sudo chown -R alice:managers /path/to/directory
```

This command will set 'alice' as the owner and 'managers' as the group for the directory specified and all its subfiles and subdirectories.

By mastering file ownership, system administrators can enforce security policies more effectively, thereby maintaining system integrity and facilitating collaborative efforts among users without compromising security.

5.7 Changing Ownership with chown and chgrp

In Linux, the ownership of files and directories significantly impacts the security and integrity of the system. The owner of a file or directory can control who is allowed to access it and what they can do with it. The ownership encompasses two primary attributes: the user owner (often simply referred to as the owner) and the group owner. Modifying these attributes can be efficiently accomplished using the chown and chgrp commands.

The chown command is utilized to change the user and group ownership of files and directories. The general syntax for chown is as follows:

```
chown [OPTION]... [OWNER][:[GROUP]] FILE...
```

Here, OWNER denotes the new owner's username or UID (user ID), GROUP signifies the new group's name or GID (group ID), and FILE represents the target file or directory. Note that the colon (:) is utilized to separate the owner and group when both are specified.

For instance, consider a scenario where we need to change the owner of a file named examplefile to username. The command would be:

```
chown username examplefile
```

To change both the owner and the group of the file to username and usergroup respectively, the command would be:

```
chown username:usergroup examplefile
```

If only the group ownership must be changed, the chgrp command is more suitable. The syntax for chgrp is simpler and centered solely on group modification:

```
chgrp [OPTION]... GROUP FILE...
```

For example, to alter the group ownership of examplefile to usergroup, one would execute:

```
chgrp usergroup examplefile
```

Both chown and chgrp commands provide additional options to facilitate recursive changes and ensure user confirmation. To apply changes recursively, affecting all files and subdirectories within a specified directory, utilize the -R or –recursive option. For example, to recursively change the owner and group of the projectdir directory and its contents, one can use:

```
chown -R username:usergroup projectdir
```

Similarly, the -R option with chgrp allows for recursive group ownership changes:

```
chgrp -R usergroup projectdir
```

In scenarios requiring confirmation before executing a change on each file, the -c or –changes option can be used. This option causes chown and chgrp to output a diagnostic for every file whose ownership is actually modified.

Consider the following example with chown:

```
chown -c username userfile
changed ownership of 'userfile' from oldusername to username
```

Similarly, for chgrp:

```
chgrp -c usergroup userfile
changed group of 'userfile' from oldgroup to usergroup
```

The chown command also allows for more advanced options, such as preserving the original file's last access and modification times using the -p or –preserve-timestamps option. This feature is beneficial in environments where file timestamps are crucial for monitoring and auditing purposes. Here is an example:

```
chown -p username:usergroup examplefile
```

For scenarios where it is critical to ensure that ownership changes occur regardless of symbolic links, the –no-dereference option can be used. This instructs chown to affect the symbolic link itself, rather than the file it points to:

```
chown --no-dereference username:usergroup symlink
```

These commands are powerful tools for managing file and directory ownership in Linux systems. While their use is straightforward, understanding the options and syntax ensures precise control over file permissions and security.

Furthermore, robust management of file ownership is imperative in multi-user systems, where improper settings could lead to unauthorized access or data breaches. Combining chown and chgrp with traditional file permission management, ACLs, and security frameworks like SELinux or AppArmor, forms a comprehensive approach to maintaining a secure and efficient Linux environment.

5.8 Setting Default Permissions with umask

When a new file or directory is created in a Linux system, it does not automatically possess desired permissions; these are initially guided by the user file-creation mask, commonly referred to as umask. The umask command is fundamental in setting default permissions, thereby ensuring a baseline security standard for newly created files and directories.

The umask value is a permission mask that restricts the default permissions for new files and directories. It essentially subtracts permissions from the system's default permission set. Understanding the umask and how to configure it effectively is crucial for maintaining system security and operational consistency.

Default System Permissions

By default, the system sets the following permissions:

- For files, the default permissions are 666 (read and write for owner, group, and others).
- For directories, the default permissions are 777 (read, write, and execute for owner, group, and others).

The umask value modifies these defaults. For instance, a umask value of 022 results in the default permissions for files being 644 (read and write for the owner, read-only for group and others) and for directories being 755 (read, write, and execute for the owner, read and execute for group and others).

Calculating umask Values

The calculation of a umask value involves the bitwise subtraction of the umask from the default permissions. The typical default permissions (before umask is applied) are:

- 666 for files
- 777 for directories

The umask command syntax is:

```
umask [octal]
```

Here's a step-by-step example:

1. Let's consider a umask value of 027. 2. The default permissions for a file would be 666 - 027 resulting in 640. 3. For directories, the default permissions would be 777 - 027 resulting in 750.

This can be broken down into:

- Owner permissions: $7 - 0 = 7$ (Read, write, and execute)
- Group permissions: $7 - 2 = 5$ (Read and execute)
- Others permissions: $7 - 7 = 0$ (No permissions)

Setting umask in Shell Profiles

The umask value is typically set in the shell configuration files such as .bashrc, .bash_profile, .profile, or system-wide configuration files like /etc/profile and /etc/bash.bashrc. Setting umask in these files ensures that the desired file-creation mask is applied each time a shell session is initiated.

To set umask globally for all users:

```
echo "umask 027" >> /etc/profile
```

To set umask for a single user:

```
echo "umask 027" >> ~/.bashrc
```

After editing the profile script, it's necessary to reload it to apply changes immediately:

```
source ~/.bashrc
```

Verifying and Testing umask

To verify the current umask setting, execute the umask command without arguments:

```
umask
```

This will return the current umask value. To test the effect of the umask, create a new file or directory and observe the assigned permissions.

```
touch testfile
mkdir testdirectory
ls -ld testfile testdirectory
```

```
-rw-r----- 1 user user 0 date time testfile
drwxr-x--- 2 user user 4096 date time testdirectory
```

These results should reflect the permissions modified by the set umask value.

Setting appropriate umask values is imperative in maintaining a balance between accessibility and security, ensuring that newly created files and directories adhere to the desired permission policies from the outset.

5.9 Special Permissions: SUID, SGID, and Sticky Bit

In Unix-like operating systems, special permissions were developed to provide advanced security controls and functionalities necessary for specific tasks. The Set User ID (SUID), Set Group ID (SGID), and Sticky Bit permissions play pivotal roles in managing access and behavior of executable files and directories. Understanding and utilizing these permissions effectively is crucial for maintaining a secure and efficient Linux system.

The Set User ID (SUID) permission allows users to execute a file with the file owner's privileges. This is particularly useful for executables that require elevated privileges. For instance, the 'passwd' command, which enables users to change their passwords, needs root privileges to modify the system's password database. When SUID is set on an executable file, it ensures that any user executing the file temporarily gains the file owner's permissions, thus allowing the requisite actions without granting permanent elevated privileges.

To set the SUID permission, the symbolic mode involves adding an 's' to the owner's execute permission. If execute permission does not already exist for the owner, it will be symbolically represented by an 'S'.

```
# Adding SUID permission
chmod u+s /path/to/file

# Removing SUID permission
chmod u-s /path/to/file

# Check if SUID permission is set
ls -l /path/to/file
```

The numeric mode uses the value '4' in the most significant position of the three-digit permission setting.

```
# Adding SUID permission (example: 4755)
chmod 4755 /path/to/file

# Check if SUID permission is set
ls -l /path/to/file
```

The output shows an 's' in the owner's execute slot if SUID is set:

```
-rwsr-xr-x 1 root root 12345 Apr 12 12:34 /path/to/file
```

The Set Group ID (SGID) permission, similarly, allows users to execute files with the file group's privileges and affects the behavior of directories. For executable files, SGID ensures the executable runs with the permissions of the group owner. For directories, SGID ensures that new files and subdirectories inherit the group of the directory rather than the creating user's group. This is particularly useful in collaborative environments.

To set the SGID permission, the symbolic mode involves adding an 's' to the group's execute permission. If execute permission does not exist for the group, it is symbolically represented as an 'S'.

```
# Adding SGID permission to a file
chmod g+s /path/to/file

# Removing SGID permission from a file
chmod g-s /path/to/file

# Check if SGID permission is set
ls -l /path/to/file

# Adding SGID permission to a directory
chmod g+s /path/to/directory

# Removing SGID permission from a directory
chmod g-s /path/to/directory

# Check if SGID permission is set on a directory
ls -ld /path/to/directory
```

The numeric mode uses the value '2' in the most significant position:

```
# Adding SGID permission (example: 2755)
```

```
chmod 2755 /path/to/file

# Check if SGID permission is set on a file or directory
ls -l /path/to/file
ls -ld /path/to/directory
```

An executable file with SGID permission set is shown by an 's' in the group's execute slot:

```
-rwxr-sr-x 1 user group 12345 Apr 12 12:34 /path/to/file
```

For directories, the SGID permission appears similarly:

```
drwxrwsr-x 2 user group 4096 Apr 12 12:34 /path/to/directory
```

The Sticky Bit is used mainly on directories to restrict file deletion. When the Sticky Bit is set on a directory, only the file's owner, the directory's owner, or the root user can delete or rename files within that directory. This is commonly used in world-writable directories like '/tmp' to prevent users from deleting each other's files.

To set the Sticky Bit, the symbolic mode uses a 't' for the others' execute permissions. If execute permission does not exist for others, it appears as 'T':

```
# Adding Sticky Bit to a directory
chmod +t /path/to/directory

# Removing Sticky Bit from a directory
chmod -t /path/to/directory

# Check if Sticky Bit is set on a directory
ls -ld /path/to/directory
```

The numeric mode uses the value '1' in the most significant position:

```
# Adding Sticky Bit (example: 1777)
chmod 1777 /path/to/directory

# Check if Sticky Bit is set on a directory
ls -ld /path/to/directory
```

When the Sticky Bit is set, the directory listing displays it as a 't' in the others' execute spot:

```
drwxrwxrwt 2 user group 4096 Apr 12 12:34 /path/to/directory
```

Special permissions like SUID, SGID, and the Sticky Bit provide enhanced control over access and behavior of files and directories. Proper understanding and usage of these permissions can greatly enhance the security and collaborative functionality of a Unix-like operating system.

5.10 Access Control Lists (ACLs)

Access Control Lists (ACLs) provide a more fine-grained permission mechanism in Linux, extending beyond the traditional Unix file permission system that uses owner, group, and others. ACLs allow specific permissions to be set for different users and groups on a per-file or per-directory basis, thus offering greater flexibility in defining access controls.

The default Linux file permission system can sometimes be restrictive. For instance, if multiple users require different levels of access to a specific file, ACLs can be employed to define these levels without needing to modify the file's primary group or ownership attributes.

Viewing ACLs

To view the ACL settings of a file or directory, the getfacl command is utilized. Here is an example of how to use getfacl to display the ACL of a file named example.txt:

```
getfacl example.txt
```

The output of the getfacl command might look as follows:

```
# file: example.txt
# owner: user1
# group: group1
user::rw-
user:user2:r--
group::r--
mask::r--
other::---
```

In this example:

- user::rw- specifies that the owner (user1) has read and write permissions.
- user:user2:r– indicates that a specific user (user2) has read-only permission.
- group::r– shows that the group has read-only permission.
- mask::r– represents the effective rights mask, which limits the maximum permissions that can be granted through ACLs.
- other::— means all other users have no permissions.

Modifying ACLs

The setfacl command enables modification of ACLs for files and directories. To set an ACL that provides read and write permission to user2 on example.txt, the command would be:

```
setfacl -m u:user2:rw example.txt
```

This command updates the ACL, granting user2 read and write permissions. The -m option specifies that an ACL entry is to be modified.

To remove a specific ACL entry, the -x option is used. For instance, to remove the ACL entry for user2:

```
setfacl -x u:user2 example.txt
```

Default ACLs

When a directory has a default ACL set, new files and subdirectories created within that directory inherit these ACLs. To set a default ACL for a directory named example_dir such that new files have read and write permissions for user2, use the following:

```
setfacl -d -m u:user2:rw example_dir
```

In this instance, the -d option specifies the default ACL. Viewing the default ACLs for the directory can be done with:

```
getfacl example_dir
```

Copying ACLs

To copy ACLs from one file to another, the getfacl and setfacl combination can be used with pipes. For example, to copy ACLs from source.txt to destination.txt:

```
getfacl source.txt | setfacl --set-file=- destination.txt
```

Here, –set-file=- instructs setfacl to read the ACL entries from standard input, which is provided by getfacl.

ACL Mask

The ACL mask entry is crucial as it dictates the maximum permissions that can be granted via ACLs for any user or group except the file owner. To modify the ACL mask of example.txt to read and write permissions:

```
setfacl -m m::rw example.txt
```

Viewing the effective permissions after setting the mask can be done via getfacl example.txt.

Recursive ACL Changes

Applying ACLs recursively to directories and their contents is achieved with the -R option:

```
setfacl -R -m u:user2:rw example_dir
```

This command sets the read and write permissions for user2 on example_dir and all files and subdirectories contained within it.

By comprehending and employing ACLs, system administrators and users can exercise granular control over file and directory permissions, beyond the constraints of the traditional permission model.

5.11 SELinux and AppArmor Basics

Security-Enhanced Linux (SELinux) and AppArmor are two prevalent Linux security modules (LSMs) that provide a mechanism for enforcing access control security policies. These policies define how processes can access files, directories, and other resources on a Linux system. Understanding the basics of SELinux and AppArmor is crucial for enhancing the security posture of a Linux environment.

SELinux operates based on mandatory access control (MAC) policies. It was integrated into the Linux kernel starting from version 2.6. SELinux policies are centrally managed and enforce rule-based restrictions on all processes. At the core of SELinux is the concept of type enforcement and multi-level security.

Type Enforcement: Each file, directory, and process on the system is assigned a type. SELinux policies define what types of objects can be accessed by a given type of process. For example, a web server process running with the type httpd_t might be allowed to read files labeled with type httpd_sys_content_t but denied access to files labeled shadow_t. Type enforcement helps in isolating different processes and restricting their access to only the necessary files.

Multi-Level Security (MLS): MLS is an additional layer of security in SELinux that assigns sensitivity levels to files and processes, allowing for the creation of hierarchies of trust or sensitivity. This can be used in environments where varying degrees of data confidentiality are essential.

SELinux operates in three modes:

1. **Enforcing:** SELinux policies are enforced, and any violations result in access denials.
2. **Permissive:** SELinux policies are not enforced, but violations are logged. This mode is useful for debugging and policy development.
3. **Disabled:** SELinux is turned off entirely.

To manipulate SELinux modes, the setenforce command is used. For instance, to switch to permissive mode, the following command can be executed:

```
setenforce 0
```

Conversely, to return to enforcing mode, the following command would be used:

```
setenforce 1
```

To check the current SELinux status or mode, use:

```
getenforce
```

AppArmor, on the other hand, is another type of LSM that uses the Linux Security Module (LSM) framework to provide path-based access control. AppArmor allows the definition of policies based on the file system paths processes are allowed to access. Unlike SELinux, which relies on labeling and broader MAC policies, AppArmor policies are simpler and mostly file-path-centric.

AppArmor operates through profiles that explicitly outline the allowable operations for each application. These profiles are typically located in the /etc/apparmor.d/ directory. AppArmor operates in two primary modes:

1. **Complaining:** Also known as permissive mode, where violations are allowed but logged.
2. **Enforcing:** Where violations are denied and logged.

To view the AppArmor status and loaded profiles, use the command:

```
sudo apparmor_status
```

To enable AppArmor enforcement for a specific profile, the following command can be executed:

```
sudo aa-enforce /etc/apparmor.d/{profile_name}
```

Similarly, to set a profile to complain mode, use:

```
sudo aa-complain /etc/apparmor.d/{profile_name}
```

When generating or modifying profiles, the aa-genprof tool assists in creating new profiles for applications by observing their behavior:

```
sudo aa-genprof {application}
```

Both SELinux and AppArmor provide a granular level of control over process and file access, significantly enhancing the security of Linux environments. Understanding the underlying principles and basic commands for managing these security modules is essential for system administrators and security professionals aiming to protect critical systems and data effectively.

By deterring unauthorized access and limiting the potential impact of compromised processes, SELinux and AppArmor form a robust defense mechanism within the Linux security architecture.

5.12 File Integrity Monitoring

File integrity monitoring (FIM) is a critical aspect of maintaining system security in Linux environments. It involves validating the integrity of operating system and application software files by verifying that their contents have not been tampered with. Any unauthorized changes could indicate a security breach, and identifying these changes promptly is essential for mitigating potential damage. This section will delve into the tools and techniques used in Linux for FIM, providing both conceptual understanding and practical examples.

One of the most widely-used tools for FIM in Linux is 'tripwire'. This tool creates a baseline snapshot of the attributes of files and directories, which it then uses for comparison in subsequent integrity checks. Any deviations from this baseline are flagged for further investigation.

To install 'tripwire' on a Debian-based system, execute the following commands:

```
sudo apt-get update
sudo apt-get install tripwire
```

Once installed, ‘tripwire‘ needs to be configured. An integral part of this configuration is initializing the file policy database, which establishes the baseline of the file system's state. This can be done using the following commands:

```
sudo tripwire --init
```

This command initializes the database according to the policy file, typically located at /etc/tripwire/twpol.txt.

After initialization, the database can be used to compare the current file system state against the established baseline. To perform a manual integrity check, use:

```
sudo tripwire --check
```

The output will be displayed in a detailed report, which summarizes any detected changes. The report might look like this:

```
\#\#\# Section: File System
-----------------------------------------------------------------------
Rule Name: User executable (/bin)
Severity Level: 66
-----/bin/ls-----
    Property: Expected              Observed
    -----------                     -----------
    User ID: 0                      1000
-----------------------------------------------------------------------
```

This output indicates that the user ID of /bin/ls has changed, which could be a significant security concern requiring immediate attention.

Apart from ‘tripwire‘, another effective tool for file integrity monitoring is the ‘aide‘ (Advanced Intrusion Detection Environment). ‘aide‘ works similarly by creating a database of file attributes, which it uses to detect unauthorized modifications. Install ‘aide‘ using:

```
sudo apt-get update
sudo apt-get install aide
```

Once installed, initialize the ‘aide‘ database with:

```
sudo aideinit
```

The aideinit command will generate a new database at /var/lib/aide/aide.db.new. To rename the database to the expected location, use:

```
sudo mv /var/lib/aide/aide.db.new /var/lib/aide/aide.db
```

Run periodic checks by executing:

```
sudo aide --check
```

The aide –check command compares the current state of the file system with the stored database. Any discrepancies will be output for analysis:

```
AIDE found differences between database and filesystem!!
\#\#\# FILE: /bin/bash
d =..... user:root    group:root  perm: 755
.....
```

In addition to 'tripwire' and 'aide', modern Linux distributions provide kernel-level integrity-checking mechanisms like 'Inotify' and 'Auditd'. The 'Inotify' API allows programs to monitor file system events, such as modifications to files. For instance, the following script leverages 'Inotify' to monitor a directory in real time:

```
#!/bin/bash
inotifywait -m /path/to/directory -e modify -e create -e delete |
   while read path action file; do
      echo "The file '$file' at '$path' has been $action"
   done
```

Execute this script to receive notifications whenever a file in the monitored directory is modified, created, or deleted.

'Auditd' provides more comprehensive monitoring by logging information about access to system files. Install 'Auditd' using:

```
sudo apt-get install auditd
```

To add a watch on a specific file, the following command can be used:

```
sudo auditctl -w /etc/passwd -p wa -k passwd_watch
```

This command instructs 'Auditd' to watch the /etc/passwd file for write (w) and attribute (a) changes and logs them under the key passwd_watch. Use the ausearch tool to review the logged events:

```
sudo ausearch -k passwd_watch
```

The ausearch command retrieves the audit records associated with the specified key, showing details of any changes made to the monitored file.

Implementing these tools and techniques enables administrators to effectively monitor and preserve the integrity of the file system, which is a cornerstone of robust Linux system security.

Chapter 6

Shell Scripting Basics

This chapter covers the fundamentals of shell scripting in Linux, starting with writing and executing basic scripts. It explains the significance of the shebang and script execution, followed by essential concepts of variables and constants, basic input and output, and using conditional statements and loop structures. The chapter introduces functions in shell scripts, debugging and error handling techniques, command line arguments, and working with arrays. It concludes with scripting best practices to ensure clarity, maintainability, and efficiency in script development.

6.1 Introduction to Shell Scripting

Shell scripting is a critical skill for any Linux user, providing a means to automate a wide array of tasks that would otherwise involve time-consuming manual steps. By leveraging shell scripts, users can enhance efficiency, ensure reproducibility, and reduce potential for human error.

Linux, in particular, offers various shells — bash, sh, csh, to name a few — each of which can interpret commands and execute scripts. The most commonly used shell for scripting on Linux is the Bourne Again Shell (bash). A shell script is essentially a text file containing a sequence of commands for a Unix-based operating system to execute. These files can automate repetitive tasks, manage system operations, and even create complex workflows integrating various software tools.

The simplest form of a shell script is a text file with one or more Unix commands, each executed in sequence. For example, consider a script to list files in a directory, find text within files, or any number of diverse tasks. To create such scripts, understanding the Linux command-line utilities, syntax, and conventions is essential.

To begin writing a shell script, it is necessary to create a new text file with an appropriate extension, typically .sh, although this is not strictly required. Once the file is created, the first line should specify the interpreter to be used for executing the script. This line, known as the shebang (#!/bin/bash), is crucial in defining the script's execution environment.

A basic example:

```
#!/bin/bash
# This is a simple shell script

echo "Hello, World!"
```

In this example, the shebang #!/bin/bash indicates that the script should be interpreted by bash. The following line, beginning with a hash (#), is a comment, ignored during execution but invaluable for documentation. The echo command is used to print text to the terminal.

Executing a script requires modifying its file permissions to make it executable. This can be done using the chmod command:

```
chmod +x scriptname.sh
```

Once the script is executable, it can be run from the terminal:

```
./scriptname.sh
```

Understanding shell scripting extends beyond simply writing and executing commands. A proficient shell script often includes variables to store data, control constructs to make decisions, loops to repeat actions, and functions to modularize code. By crafting scripts with these elements, one can automate sophisticated and reliable solutions for numerous tasks.

Shell scripting also emphasizes the importance of robustness and error handling. Well-written scripts anticipate potential issues and include mechanisms to handle errors gracefully. This is accomplished through condition checks and appropriate use of exit statuses, which are values returned by commands or functions indicating their success or failure.

Another important aspect is the proper structuring of scripts to enhance readability and maintainability. Clear commenting, adhering to naming conventions, and organizational practices, such as modular design, are best practices to be followed.

Below is a more advanced example illustrating variables and a simple conditional statement:

```
#!/bin/bash
# Script to check for a command-line argument

if [ -z "$1" ]; then
  echo "No argument provided."
else
  echo "Argument provided: $1"
fi
```

In this script, $1 refers to the first command-line argument. The if statement checks if the argument is empty (i.e., if no argument was provided). The [-z "$1"] syntax checks for an empty string, and the script prints a message based on the condition.

To run this script:

```
./argument_check.sh Hello
```

```
Argument provided: Hello
```

With no arguments:

```
./argument_check.sh
```

```
No argument provided.
```

This introduces fundamentals like checking conditions, getting input from command-line arguments, and using variables. By progressively building on these principles, more complex and powerful scripts can be created to automate sophisticated workflows, enhance productivity, and solve intricate problems efficiently.

6.2 Writing and Executing Your First Script

Writing and executing your first script in a Linux environment is a fundamental step in mastering shell scripting. To begin, you will need a text editor to create the script. Popular choices include nano, vim, and gedit.

Create a file named first_script.sh using your preferred text editor. To do this using nano, for example, you would open the terminal and type:

```
nano first_script.sh
```

In the newly created file, the first line should be the shebang (more details are covered in the section *Shebang and Script Execution*), which indicates the script's interpreter. For a standard Bash script, this will look like:

```
#!/bin/bash
```

Next, add a simple command to the script. For instance, to print the text "Hello, World!" to the terminal, add the following line:

```
echo "Hello, World!"
```

Your first_script.sh should now contain:

```
#!/bin/bash
echo "Hello, World!"
```

Save the file and exit the text editor. In nano, you can do this by pressing CTRL+X, then Y to confirm changes, and Enter to finalize.

Before executing the script, you need to ensure it has executable permissions. You can modify the file's permissions using the chmod command:

```
chmod +x first_script.sh
```

Now, execute the script by typing the following command in the terminal:

```
./first_script.sh
```

The expected output should be:

```
Hello, World!
```

This basic script demonstrates the fundamental components: the shebang line and a single command.

Adding More Complexity

To enhance your script, you can incorporate variables, user input, and control structures. Consider the following extended script that asks for the user's name and then greets them.

```
#!/bin/bash
echo "Please enter your name:"
read user_name
echo "Hello, $user_name!"
```

When executed, this script will prompt the user to input their name and then greet them using the entered value. The read command waits for user input and stores it in the user_name variable, which is subsequently used in the echo command to display a personalized message.

```
Please enter your name:
John
Hello, John!
```

Handling Script Execution Errors

It is crucial to handle potential errors in a script, ensuring robust and reliable operation. Consider a scenario where a command fails. Adding an exit status after critical commands helps in managing script execution flow:

```
#!/bin/bash
echo "Attempting to create a directory named 'test_directory'."
mkdir test_directory
if [ $? -eq 0 ]; then
  echo "Directory created successfully."
else
  echo "Failed to create directory."
  exit 1
fi

cd test_directory || exit
echo "Currently in $(pwd)"
```

The $? variable captures the exit status of the last executed command, where 0 indicates success, and any nonzero value indicates failure. In this script, failure to create the directory results in an error message and script termination with exit 1. The next command changes the current directory to the new directory and confirms the path using the pwd command.

```
Attempting to create a directory named 'test_directory'.
Directory created successfully.
Currently in /home/user/test_directory
```

Combining Commands and Using Comments

It is often necessary to combine multiple commands in a script. You can use logical operators such as && and || to combine commands conditionally.

```
#!/bin/bash
# Check if the specified file exists
file="example.txt"
[ -e "$file" ] && echo "$file exists." || echo "$file does not exist."
```

Moreover, adding comments using the # character improves the script's readability and maintainability. Comments provide context and explanation without affecting the script's execution.

Practicing Best Practices in Script Writing

Adhering to best practices ensures scripts are clear and maintainable. Use meaningful variable names, clear commenting, and consistent indentation. Regularly check for errors and handle them gracefully, ensuring the script remains robust under various conditions.

Combine these practices to write a simple utility script that combines several commands into a reusable tool.

By mastering these basic principles of writing and executing scripts, you lay a strong foundation for more sophisticated script development covered in subsequent sections, enhancing efficiency and automation in your Linux environment.

6.3 Shebang and Script Execution

The start of any shell script is distinctively marked by the "shebang" (#!), which is the character combination that informs the operating system of the script's interpreter. Positioned at the very top of the file, the shebang guides the OS on how to execute the script. Let's explore this concept in detail.

A shebang line in a script looks like the following:

```
#!/bin/bash
```

Here, #!/bin/bash instructs the system to use the Bash shell to interpret the script, indicating that the Bash shell should execute the following script commands. The path /bin/bash specifies the location of the Bash interpreter. This location can vary based on the system, but /bin/bash is common in most Linux distributions. In the case of a script intended for Python, the shebang might look like:

```
#!/usr/bin/env python3
```

Where #!/usr/bin/env invokes the env command to find python3 in the user's PATH, allowing for more flexibility.

Executing a shell script can be approached in several ways:

- **Direct Execution:**

  To execute a script directly, it must have execute permission. This can be set using the following command:

```
chmod +x script_name.sh
```

Once the proper permissions are set, the script can be executed with:

```
./script_name.sh
```

- **Via an Interpreter:**

  Execution can also proceed by passing the script as an argument to an interpreter, bypassing the need for the shebang:

  ```
  bash script_name.sh
  ```

  This approach does not require the script to have execute permissions.

Let's consider a simple script example to demonstrate these concepts:

```
#!/bin/bash

echo "Hello, World!"
```

To run this script:

- Save it to a file named hello_world.sh.
- Make it executable with:

  ```
  chmod +x hello_world.sh
  ```

- Execute it with:

  ```
  ./hello_world.sh
  ```

The output will be:

```
Hello, World!
```

An important aspect of script execution is understanding the environment in which scripts are run. When a script executes, it inherits the environment variables and current working directory from its parent shell. This inheritance can be harnessed for adding flexible behavior to scripts. For instance, using the PATH variable to locate commands and ensuring scripts run in specific directories through cd commands.

While understanding script execution, it is crucial to be aware of potential pitfalls. A common error arises when the specified interpreter in the shebang is either incorrect or missing; this leads to execution failures. It is advisable to double-check the interpreter's path on different systems to ensure cross-system compatibility.

Execution errors can also stem from incorrect use of relative and absolute paths. Relative paths are interpreted relative to the current working directory, while absolute paths are fully qualified from the root directory. Scripts relying on relative paths can face issues if executed from unexpected locations.

In addition, setting the environment explicitly at the start of a script can mitigate issues from uninitialized or incorrectly set environment variables. For example:

```
#!/bin/bash

export PATH=/usr/local/bin:/usr/bin:/bin
cd /home/user/scripts

echo "Script is running in $(pwd)"
```

The export command ensures the PATH variable contains specific directories for finding executable binaries, and cd changes the working directory to /home/user/scripts.

In summary, the shebang line is critical for specifying the script's interpreter and facilitating proper script execution. By understanding script execution methods, setting appropriate permissions, and managing the execution environment, one can write robust, portable scripts. This foundational knowledge is essential for further exploration of shell scripting intricacies.

6.4 Variables and Constants

Variables in shell scripting are used to store data that can be referenced and manipulated throughout the execution of the script. Shell variables do not require explicit declaration and are weakly typed, which means their data type is inferred based on usage. Constants, on the other hand, are variables whose values are not intended to be modified once set. This section delves into the syntax and best practices for defining and using variables and constants in shell scripts.

The syntax to assign a value to a variable is straightforward. No spaces should exist between the variable name, the assignment operator =, and the value. Here is an example:

```
# Assigning a value to a variable
greeting="Hello, World!"
```

To reference the value of a variable, precede the variable name with a dollar sign $. Consider the following example, which prints the greeting stored in the variable:

```
# Referencing a variable's value
echo $greeting
```

Variables can hold different types of data, such as strings, integers, and even the output of commands:

```
# Integer assignment
number=42

# Command substitution
current_date=$(date)
```

It is crucial to note that variable names in shell scripting are case-sensitive. Conventionally, shell variable names use uppercase characters to enhance readability, particularly for environment variables and constants.

Quoting Variables

Quoting variables correctly is essential to handle spaces and special characters in their values. The shell offers three types of quoting: double quotes " ", single quotes ' ', and backticks ` `. Double quotes allow variable expansion within the quoted string, single quotes treat the enclosed string as literal text, and backticks execute commands and capture their output.

```
# Double quotes: variable expansion is performed
echo "Today is $current_date"

# Single quotes: literal string, no variable expansion
echo 'Today is $current_date'

# Backticks: command substitution
echo `date`
```

Constants

In shell scripting, constants can be defined using the readonly keyword or through the declare command with the -r option. Once set, a constant's value cannot be modified.

```
# Using readonly
readonly pi=3.14159
```

```
# Using declare -r
declare -r e=2.71828

# Attempting to change the value will result in an error
# pi=3.14 # This will cause an error
```

Exporting Variables

Variables defined within a script are local to that script by default. To make a variable available to other programs or scripts executed in the current shell session, use the export command.

```
# Define a variable
path="/usr/local/bin"

# Export the variable
export path

# Now $path is available to other scripts and programs
```

Dynamic Variables and Indirection

Shell scripting supports dynamic variable usage, sometimes referred to as indirection, where one variable's value determines another variable's name. This can be achieved using the eval command or through complex parameter expansion.

```
# Direct assignment
var1="name"
name="Alice"

# Indirection using eval
eval echo \$$var1

# Indirection using parameter expansion
echo ${!var1}
```

Special Variables

The shell provides several special variables that have predefined meanings. Some of these include:

- $0: The name of the script.
- $1, $2, ..., $N: Positional parameters representing the arguments passed to the script.
- $@: All the arguments passed to the script.
- $*: Similar to $@ but treats all arguments as a single word.
- $#: The number of arguments passed to the script.

- $?: The exit status of the last executed command.
- $$: The process ID of the current shell.
- $: The process ID of the last background command.

Unsetting Variables

To remove a variable's definition and value, use the unset command:

```
# Define a variable
temp_variable="temporary data"

# Unset the variable
unset temp_variable

# The variable is no longer available
```

Careful management and understanding of variables and constants are vital for writing effective and efficient shell scripts. Through proper usage, scripts become more readable, maintainable, and less prone to errors.

6.5 Basic Input and Output

In the context of shell scripting, basic input and output operations form the cornerstone of interactive and automated script behavior. It is essential to understand how to handle data input from users or files and how to display output efficiently. This section delves into these fundamental concepts with systematic examples and detailed explanations.

In shell scripting, the primary means of outputting text to the terminal is the echo command. This command is invaluable for displaying messages, debugging information, and the results of script computations. The basic syntax for the echo command is as follows:

```
echo [options] [string...]
```

For instance, you can use the echo command to display a simple message:

```
echo "Hello, World!"
```

When executed, this script will produce the following output:

```
Hello, World!
```

The double quotes are used to encapsulate the string and ensure that it is treated as a single argument, even if it contains spaces.

To gather input from the user, shell scripts often utilize the read command. This command reads a line of input from standard input (stdin) and assigns it to a variable. The basic syntax for the read command is:

```
read [options] [variable...]
```

For example, a script might prompt the user for their name and then greet them personally:

```
#!/bin/bash
echo "Please enter your name:"
read name
echo "Hello, $name!"
```

Execution of this script would behave as follows:

```
Please enter your name:
John
Hello, John!
```

In this case, the input provided by the user (John) is stored in the variable name and then used within the echo command to personalize the greeting.

To combine strings with variable values, shell scripts employ concatenation. This process can be seamlessly integrated using the $ symbol alongside the variable name. For example:

```
#!/bin/bash
greeting="Good morning"
name="Alice"
echo "$greeting, $name!"
```

When this script is executed, it will output:

```
Good morning, Alice!
```

Special characters and formatting can also be managed within the echo command by utilizing escape sequences. For instance, to include a newline character or a tab, the -e option must be provided:

```
echo -e "Line 1\nLine 2"
echo -e "Item 1\tItem 2"
```

The output of this script will be:

```
Line 1
Line 2
Item 1	Item 2
```

Reading input from files instead of directly from the user is another vital concept. This can be achieved by redirecting file content to the read command. For example:

```
#!/bin/bash
while read line; do
    echo "$line"
done < inputfile.txt
```

In this script, inputfile.txt is read line by line, and each line is displayed on the terminal. The while loop continues until all lines in the file have been processed.

Shell scripts often require reading multiple values from a single line of input. This can be facilitated by specifying multiple variables with the read command. For instance:

```
#!/bin/bash
echo "Enter two numbers separated by space:"
read num1 num2
sum=$((num1 + num2))
echo "The sum is: $sum"
```

Execution of this script will appear as follows:

```
Enter two numbers separated by space:
3 5
The sum is: 8
```

The read command splits the input into separate variables based on whitespace by default. Each number entered by the user is assigned to num1 and num2 respectively, and their sum is computed and displayed.

Another essential feature of handling input and output in shell scripts is the ability to control the visibility of input using the -s option with the read command. This is particularly useful for password prompts:

```
#!/bin/bash
echo "Enter your password:"
read -s password
echo "Password entered"
```

When executed, the input provided by the user will not be displayed on the terminal, maintaining its confidentiality:

```
Enter your password:
Password entered
```

In script development, ensuring input validation and appropriate error handling is paramount. For instance, to check if a variable is non-empty:

```
#!/bin/bash
echo "Enter a value:"
read value
```

```
if [ -z "$value" ]; then
    echo "No value entered"
else
    echo "You entered: $value"
fi
```

This script will output either a confirmation of the user's input or a message indicating that no input was provided:

```
Enter a value:
You entered: 42
```

```
Enter a value:
No value entered
```

Understanding and mastering these basic input and output mechanisms are essential for creating sophisticated and interactive shell scripts. Through practical implementation and adhering to best practices, you will develop scripts that are robust, efficient, and user-friendly.

6.6 Using Conditional Statements: if, elif, else

Conditional statements are fundamental constructs in shell scripting that allow for decision-making and branching of code execution based on specified conditions. The three primary keywords used for conditional statements in shell scripting are if, elif (else if), and else. This section will delve into the syntax and usage of these conditional statements, enabling you to create more dynamic and responsive scripts.

The basic structure of an if statement in shell scripting is as follows:

```
if [ condition ]
then
    # Commands to execute if condition is true
fi
```

Several components form an if statement:

- **condition**: A test expression, usually enclosed in square brackets []. It is evaluated by the test command or its alias [. The condition can involve comparisons using logical operators.
- **then**: Marks the beginning of the command block to execute if the condition is true.
- **fi**: Ends the if block.

For example, to check if a file exists and is readable, you could use:

```
if [ -r /path/to/file ]
then
    echo "File is readable."
fi
```

Conditions can use a variety of test expressions, as demonstrated in Table 6.1.

Test Expression	Description
-e file	True if the file exists.
-d file	True if the file is a directory.
-f file	True if the file is a regular file.
-r file	True if the file is readable.
-w file	True if the file is writable.
-x file	True if the file is executable.
string1 = string2	True if the strings are equal.
string1 != string2	True if the strings are not equal.
-z string	True if the string is empty.
-n string	True if the string is not empty.
num1 -eq num2	True if the numbers are equal.
num1 -ne num2	True if the numbers are not equal.
num1 -lt num2	True if num1 is less than num2.
num1 -le num2	True if num1 is less than or equal to num2.
num1 -gt num2	True if num1 is greater than num2.
num1 -ge num2	True if num1 is greater than or equal to num2.

Table 6.1: Common Test Expressions for Conditional Statements

When there are multiple conditions to evaluate, elif and else can be used to extend the if statement. The structure is as follows:

```
if [ condition1 ]
then
    # Commands to execute if condition1 is true
elif [ condition2 ]
then
    # Commands to execute if condition2 is true
else
    # Commands to execute if none of the above conditions are true
fi
```

elif (else if) allows for the evaluation of additional conditions if the preceding if condition is false. If none of the provided conditions are true, the else block will be executed.

For instance, consider a script that checks for a file type:

```
file="/path/to/file"

if [ -d "$file" ]
then
    echo "$file is a directory."
elif [ -f "$file" ]
then
    echo "$file is a regular file."
else
    echo "$file is of another type."
fi
```

Logical operators can combine multiple conditions in a single test expression for more complex decision-making. The key logical operators are:

- **AND**: -a or &&
- **OR**: -o or ||
- **NOT**: !

For example, to check if a file is both readable and writable:

```
if [ -r "$file" -a -w "$file" ]
then
    echo "$file is readable and writable."
fi
```

Or using the && operator:

```
if [ -r "$file" ] && [ -w "$file" ]
then
    echo "$file is readable and writable."
fi
```

Similarly, using the OR logical operator:

```
if [ -d "$file" ] || [ -f "$file" ]
then
    echo "$file is either a directory or a regular file."
fi
```

Negating a condition with the NOT operator:

```
if [ ! -e "$file" ]
then
    echo "$file does not exist."
```

```
fi
```

Conditionals can also be nested to manage complex decision-making scenarios:

```
if [ -e "$file" ]
then
    if [ -d "$file" ]
    then
        echo "$file is a directory."
    else
        echo "$file exists but is not a directory."
    fi
else
    echo "$file does not exist."
fi
```

This section has provided an in-depth overview of using conditional statements in shell scripting. Mastering conditional constructs is crucial for writing scripts that perform tasks based on dynamic conditions, enhancing the script's capability to handle a variety of real-world scenarios efficiently.

6.7 Loop Structures: for, while, until

Loop structures are essential for performing repetitive tasks in shell scripts. They allow the script to iterate over a set of values or execute a block of code multiple times until a certain condition is met. In shell scripting, the primary loop constructs are for, while, and until loops. Each loop type serves specific purposes and can be used to enhance the control flow of a script.

The for loop iterates over a list of items and executes a block of code for each item. Its syntax is straightforward:

```
for item in list
do
   command1
   command2
   ...
done
```

Consider an example where we want to iterate over a list of filenames and display each filename:

```
#!/bin/bash
for filename in file1.txt file2.txt file3.txt
do
   echo "Processing $filename"
```

```
done
```

The output of the script will be:

```
Processing file1.txt
Processing file2.txt
Processing file3.txt
```

The for loop can also iterate over the contents of a directory:

```
#!/bin/bash
for file in /path/to/directory/*
do
  echo "Found file: $file"
done
```

This script will print the names of all files and directories in the specified directory.

The while loop executes a block of code repeatedly as long as a specified condition evaluates to true. The syntax for the while loop is:

```
while [ condition ]
do
  command1
  command2
  ...
done
```

Consider a scenario where we want to read numbers from the user until they enter a negative number:

```
#!/bin/bash
number=0
while [ $number -ge 0 ]
do
  echo "Enter a number (negative to quit): "
  read number
  echo "You entered: $number"
done
```

The script will continue to prompt for a number as long as the entered number is non-negative.

The until loop, conversely, executes a block of code until a specified condition becomes true. Its syntax is similar to the while loop but with the condition negated:

```
until [ condition ]
do
  command1
  command2
  ...
done
```

For example, we can rewrite the previous while loop example using an until loop:

```
#!/bin/bash
number=0
until [ $number -lt 0 ]
do
  echo "Enter a number (negative to quit): "
  read number
  echo "You entered: $number"
done
```

This script performs the same task as the earlier while loop but uses the until construct to handle the condition.

Loops can also be combined with break and continue statements for greater control over their execution. The break statement exits the loop immediately, while the continue statement skips the remaining commands in the current iteration and proceeds with the next iteration.

Here is an example using break in a while loop:

```
#!/bin/bash
while true
do
  echo "Enter a number (0 to quit): "
  read number
  if [ $number -eq 0 ]; then
    break
  fi
  echo "You entered: $number"
done
echo "Exiting loop."
```

If the user enters 0, the loop will terminate.

Similarly, an example utilizing continue in a for loop:

```
#!/bin/bash
for number in {1..10}
do
  if [ $((number % 2)) -eq 0 ]; then
    continue
  fi
  echo $number
done
```

This script prints only the odd numbers between 1 and 10 by skipping even numbers.

Understanding and mastering these loop structures will significantly enhance your ability to write efficient and effective shell scripts, allowing you to handle repetitive tasks with ease and precision.

6.8 Functions in Shell Scripts

Functions in shell scripts provide a powerful way to modularize code by encapsulating a sequence of commands in a named block. This promotes code reuse, maintainability, and clarity. Functions allow the script to execute a sequence of commands wherever necessary and also facilitate easier debugging and testing.

A function in a shell script is defined using the following syntax:

```
function_name () {
    commands
}
```

For example:

```
greet() {
    echo "Hello, $1!"
}
```

In this example, the function greet takes one parameter and prints a greeting message. To call this function, simply use its name followed by any arguments:

```
greet "World"
```

The output will be:

```
Hello, World!
```

Functions can be defined anywhere in the script, but it is a good practice to define them at the beginning. This helps in keeping the script organized and ensures that all functions are available before being called.

Passing Arguments to Functions

Functions can accept arguments just like scripts. These arguments are accessed using the positional parameters $1, $2, etc., within the function. For example:

```
sum() {
    local result=$(( $1 + $2 ))
    echo "The sum is: $result"
}
```

In this example, the function sum takes two arguments, calculates their sum, and prints the result. You can call this function and pass the required arguments as follows:

```
sum 5 10
```

The output will be:

```
The sum is: 15
```

Returning Values from Functions

Unlike some programming languages, shell functions do not return values in the traditional sense. Instead, they return an exit status code using the return command, where 0 typically denotes success and any non-zero value indicates an error.

To capture the output of a function, command substitution is used:

```
multiply() {
    echo $(( $1 * $2 ))
}
result=$(multiply 4 5)
echo "The result is: $result"
```

The output of this script will be:

```
The result is: 20
```

However, if you need to use the exit status:

```
check_file() {
    if [ -f "$1" ]; then
        return 0
    else
        return 1
    fi
}
check_file "/etc/passwd"
if [ $? -eq 0 ]; then
    echo "File exists."
else
    echo "File does not exist."
fi
```

The function check_file checks if a file exists and returns 0 if it does and 1 if it does not. The special variable $? captures the return value, which is then used in the subsequent if statement.

Using Local Variables

Variables within functions are global by default, which means their values can be accessed and modified outside the function. To limit the scope of a variable to the function, use the local keyword:

```
math_operations() {
    local a=5
    local b=3
    echo $(( a + b ))
}
```

Here, a and b are local to the math_operations function and cannot be accessed outside of it.

Function Libraries

For more complex scripts, it's beneficial to create libraries of functions that can be sourced and reused across multiple scripts. This can be achieved by placing function definitions in a separate file and sourcing it in your script using the source or . command:

```
# mylib.sh
my_function() {
    echo "This is a library function."
}

# main_script.sh
#!/bin/bash
source ./mylib.sh
my_function
```

This approach keeps your scripts clean and promotes reusability.

By understanding and utilizing functions in shell scripts, you can enhance the modularity, readability, and maintainability of your code. Functions allow for easier debugging and can make complex scripts simpler to understand and manage.

6.9 Debugging and Error Handling

In the development and maintenance of shell scripts, debugging and error handling are critical competencies. Efficient debugging aids in identifying and resolving issues quickly, while robust error handling ensures scripts can manage unexpected situations and fail gracefully. This section delves into both aspects in detail.

To begin with, consider the common pitfalls in shell scripting, such as syntax errors, logical errors, and runtime errors. Syntax errors occur when the script fails to adhere to the shell's syntactical rules, leading to immediate script termination. Logical errors, though syntactically correct, result in incorrect behavior or outputs and can be challenging to detect. Runtime errors arise during script execution due to unforeseen conditions, such as missing files or incorrect permissions.

Using the set Command

The set command is a powerful tool for debugging. It changes the behavior of the shell and can provide valuable insights. To enable debugging, use:

```
set -x
```

This command instructs the shell to print each command and its arguments as they are executed, thus providing step-by-step feedback.

To disable debugging, use:

```
set +x
```

Embedding these commands around suspected errors can isolate problematic code sections. For instance:

```
#!/bin/bash

echo "Starting script..."
set -x
# Debugging enabled
cp source.txt destination.txt
set +x
# Debugging disabled
echo "Script ended."
```

Using trap for Signal Handling

Signals provide a method for handling exceptional conditions. The trap command specifies commands to execute upon receiving signals. Common signals include EXIT, ERR, INT, and TERM.

Example:

```
#!/bin/bash

trap 'echo "Error occurred!"' ERR
trap 'echo "Script interrupted!"' INT
trap 'echo "Script exited!"' EXIT

echo "Running script..."
# Code that might cause errors
```

Here, if an error occurs (signal ERR), or if the script is interrupted (signal INT), custom messages are displayed.

Error Handling with Conditional Constructs

Explicit error checks can be implemented using conditional constructs like if, else, elif, and case. Consider:

```
#!/bin/bash

if cp source.txt destination.txt; then
  echo "File copied successfully."
else
  echo "File copy failed."
```

```
fi
```

This structure ensures that appropriate action is taken based on the success or failure of cp command.

Additionally, exit statuses can be captured and used as follows:

```
#!/bin/bash

cp source.txt destination.txt
status=$?

if [ $status -eq 0 ]; then
  echo "Success"
else
  echo "Failure"
fi
```

Using the exit Command

The exit command terminates a script and can return a status code to the calling process, usually indicating success (0) or failure (non-zero). For example:

```
#!/bin/bash

echo "Performing checks..."
# If any check fails, exit with status 1
if [ ! -f source.txt ]; then
  echo "source.txt not found"
  exit 1
fi

# If all checks pass
exit 0
```

Redirecting Output and Error Messages

Redirecting standard output (stdout) and standard error (stderr) can also aid in debugging. For instance:

```
#!/bin/bash

command > output.log 2> error.log
# Redirects stdout to output.log and stderr to error.log

command &> combined.log
# Redirects both stdout and stderr to combined.log
```

Here, any standard output and error messages are captured in separate or combined log files, facilitating post-execution analysis.

Debugging with the debug Keyword

In newer shells like bash-4.1 and later, debugging can be aided with the

DEBUG trap, which triggers before every command:

```
#!/bin/bash

trap 'echo "Executing: $BASH_COMMAND"' DEBUG

cp source.txt destination.txt
# Each command is preceded by a debug message
```

By integrating these techniques, shell scripts become more robust and maintainable, providing clear diagnostics and actionable error messages. This ensures smoother execution and easier troubleshooting, significantly enhancing the script's reliability and efficiency.

6.10 Using Command Line Arguments

Command line arguments are a powerful feature in shell scripting, enabling the user to pass input values to a script from the command line itself. This allows scripts to be more flexible and useful in various situations without needing to modify the script's code. Shell scripts can accept any number of arguments, and these are accessed within the script using special positional parameters.

In a shell script, command line arguments are referenced by position using the variables $1, $2, $3, and so on, where $1 represents the first argument, $2 the second argument, etc. The system also provides other special parameters such as $#, which gives the number of arguments passed to the script, and $* or $@, which provide all the arguments as a single string.

Consider the following example of a script named welcome.sh that greets the user by their name and age passed as command line arguments.

```
#!/bin/bash

# Welcome script that takes name and age as arguments
echo "Hello, $1!"
echo "You are $2 years old."
```

When executing this script, you pass the name and age as arguments:

```
$ ./welcome.sh Alice 30
Hello, Alice!
You are 30 years old.
```

In this example, $1 is Alice, and $2 is 30.

To handle an arbitrary number of arguments, you can iterate over the arguments using a loop. For instance, the following script prints all of its arguments:

```
#!/bin/bash

# Script to print all provided arguments
echo "You provided $# arguments."
for arg in "$@"
do
    echo "$arg"
done
```

Execute the script with multiple arguments:

```
$ ./printargs.sh one two three
You provided 3 arguments.
one
two
three
```

Here, $# gives the number of arguments, and $@ expands to each argument in the list. Note the use of double quotes around "$@" to preserve the integrity of each argument even if they contain spaces.

Another illustrative example demonstrates the difference between $* and $@. Both are typically used to pass all arguments to another command or loop, but they handle quoting variations differently.

```
#!/bin/bash

# Script to demonstrate difference between $* and $@
echo "Using \$*:"
for arg in $*
do
    echo "$arg"
done

echo "Using \$@:"
for arg in "$@"
do
    echo "$arg"
done
```

Consider the following script invocation:

```
$ ./args_diff.sh "arg with space" arg2
Using $*:
arg
with
space
arg2
Using $@:
arg with space
arg2
```

When using $*, the arguments are concatenated into a single string with spaces, which can split individual arguments if they contain spaces. In contrast, $@ preserves each argument as a distinct entity.

Argument handling also integrates seamlessly with conditional statements and functions. For example, verifying that the required number of arguments is provided before performing actions:

```
#!/bin/bash

# Check for exactly two arguments
if [ $# -ne 2 ]; then
    echo "Usage: $0 <arg1> <arg2>"
    exit 1
fi

echo "Argument 1: $1"
echo "Argument 2: $2"
```

This script checks if exactly two arguments are passed and provides usage instructions if not. It exits with a status code 1, indicating an error condition if the check fails.

Combining argument handling with functions can make scripts modular and reusable. The following example shows a script that takes arguments and utilizes functions to process them:

```
#!/bin/bash

# Function to display usage
usage() {
    echo "Usage: $0 <name> <age>"
}

# Main function to greet user
greet() {
    local name=$1
    local age=$2
    echo "Hello, $name. You are $age years old."
}

# Check for exactly two arguments
if [ $# -ne 2 ]; then
    usage
    exit 1
fi

# Call greet function with provided arguments
greet "$1" "$2"
```

This script ensures the correct number of arguments are provided, uses a function for usage instructions, and a function to greet the user, exemplifying structured and maintainable shell scripting practices.

6.11 Working with Arrays

In shell scripting, arrays provide a powerful mechanism for storing multiple values under a single variable name. This section delves into the definition, initialization, and manipulation of arrays within a shell script, enhancing script functionality and efficiency.

Defining and Initializing Arrays

Arrays in bash are zero-indexed. To define an array, use parentheses with space-separated elements. For example:

```
# Defining an array with explicit elements
my_array=(value1 value2 value3)

# Alternatively, an array can be defined element by element
my_array[0]=value1
my_array[1]=value2
my_array[2]=value3
```

You can also create an empty array and append elements to it later:

```
# Creating an empty array
empty_array=()

# Appending elements
empty_array+=("element1")
empty_array+=("element2")
```

Accessing Array Elements

Elements in an array are accessed using their indices. The syntax is $array[index]. For instance:

```
echo ${my_array[0]} # Outputs: value1
echo ${my_array[1]} # Outputs: value2
```

To iterate over all elements in an array:

```
for element in "${my_array[@]}"; do
    echo $element
done
```

The @ symbol allows access to all array elements. Similarly, using * instead of @ will produce the same result.

Array Length

To find the number of elements in an array, use the following syntax:

```
echo ${#my_array[@]} # Outputs the number of elements in my_array
```

Modifying Arrays

Elements within an array can be modified by directly assigning a new value to a specific index:

```
# Modifying the second element
my_array[1]="new_value"
echo ${my_array[1]} # Outputs: new_value
```

Elements can be removed from an array using the unset command:

```
unset my_array[1]
# This will remove the second element, shifting is not performed, index 1 is now unset
```

The unset command does not reindex the array, creating a gap in the indices.

Slicing Arrays

Array slicing allows retrieval of a subset of array elements:

```
# Syntax: ${array[@]:start:length}
echo ${my_array[@]:1:2} # Outputs the second and third elements
```

Multi-dimensional Arrays

Although bash does not natively support multi-dimensional arrays, associative arrays can emulate similar behavior. Associative arrays are declared using declare -A:

```
declare -A matrix
matrix[0,0]="a"
matrix[0,1]="b"
matrix[1,0]="c"
matrix[1,1]="d"

echo ${matrix[0,0]} # Outputs: a
```

Examples and Practical Applications

Arrays are particularly useful when dealing with lists retrieved from commands or data manipulation. Consider a script designed to process filenames in a directory:

```
# Listing .txt files in a directory
file_list=($(ls *.txt))

# Renaming files by appending suffix '_backup'
for file in "${file_list[@]}"; do
    mv "$file" "${file%.txt}_backup.txt"
done
```

Another example involves numerical data processing, where arrays can store and calculate values:

```
numbers=(1 2 3 4 5)
sum=0

# Calculating sum of the array elements
for num in "${numbers[@]}"; do
    let sum+=num
done
echo "Sum: $sum" # Outputs: Sum: 15
```

When combined with functions, arrays provide enhanced modularity and reusability, fostering script robustness. Here, a function utilizes an array to return multiple values:

```
# Function to calculate minimum and maximum values
find_min_max() {
    local arr=("$@")
    local min=${arr[0]}
    local max=${arr[0]}

    for val in "${arr[@]}"; do
        ((val < min)) && min=$val
        ((val > max)) && max=$val
    done

    echo $min $max
}

# Defining an array
numbers=(43 56 23 89 88 90 4 28 65 12)
# Capturing min and max
read min max < <(find_min_max "${numbers[@]}")
echo "Min: $min, Max: $max" # Outputs: Min: 4, Max: 90
```

Utilizing arrays efficiently requires understanding their implementation and manipulation techniques, which provides a strong foundation for creating dynamic and robust shell scripts.

6.12 Scripting Best Practices

Adhering to best practices in shell scripting is crucial for developing scripts that are not only functional but also efficient, readable, and maintainable. Well-written scripts minimize errors and improve collaboration across teams. Below are the key guidelines that should be followed to achieve these outcomes:

Use Meaningful Names for Variables and Functions: Always choose descriptive names for your variables and functions. This clearly documents the purpose of each variable and function, improving readability. For example:

```
# Poor naming
a=5
b=10
c=$((a + b))

# Good naming
start_value=5
end_value=10
total_value=$((start_value + end_value))
```

Comment Your Code: While concise code is often the goal, sometimes clarity can be lost in brevity. Use comments to explain the purpose of complex commands or logic blocks. This helps other developers (or your future self) understand the reasoning behind your code choices.

```
# Calculate the sum of the start and end values
total_value=$((start_value + end_value))
```

Use Indentation and Spacing: Consistent indentation and spacing make the script easier to read and debug. Adopting a standard style guide within your team can further streamline this process.

```
# Good indentation
if [ $a -lt $b ]; then
    echo "a is less than b"
else
    echo "a is not less than b"
fi
```

Validate Inputs: Always check for valid input values before using them in your script. This helps prevent unexpected behavior and crashes.

```
# Check if an argument is passed
if [ -z "$1" ]; then
    echo "No argument supplied"
    exit 1
fi
```

Use Functions to Encapsulate Logic: Functions should be used to encapsulate logic that is reused or logically distinct. This enhances modularity and readability.

```
# Define a function to calculate factorial
factorial() {
    local n=$1
    local result=1
    while [ $n -gt 0 ]; do
        result=$((result * n))
        n=$((n - 1))
    done
    echo $result
}
# Call the function
```

```
factorial_result=$(factorial 5)
```

Use Shell Built-in Commands When Possible: Built-in commands in the shell are more efficient than external commands as they avoid the overhead of running a new process.

```
# Use 'echo' (built-in command) instead of 'print'
echo "Hello, World!"
```

Check the Exit Status of Commands: Always check the exit status of commands to verify that they completed successfully. This helps in diagnosing issues promptly.

```
# Check if mkdir succeeds
mkdir new_directory
if [ $? -ne 0 ]; then
    echo "mkdir command failed"
    exit 1
fi
```

Use 'ShellCheck': ShellCheck is a static analysis tool that can detect common issues in shell scripts. Incorporate ShellCheck in your development workflow to catch bugs early.

```
$ shellcheck myscript.sh
```

Limit the Use of Root Privileges: Only use root privileges when absolutely necessary. Avoid running scripts as root if possible to mitigate security risks.

Handle Errors Gracefully: Implement error handling to manage unexpected situations effectively. Use traps to catch signals and clean up resources.

```
# Trap EXIT signal to perform clean up
trap 'echo "Cleaning up..."; rm -f temp_file' EXIT

# Rest of the script
```

Test Scripts Thoroughly: Test your scripts in a controlled environment before deploying them to production. Ensure they handle various edge cases and input scenarios effectively.

Use Version Control: Keep your scripts under version control (e.g., Git). This allows tracking changes over time, collaborating with other developers, and reverting to previous versions if necessary.

Log Actions and Results: Implement logging to record the script's actions and results. This assists in debugging and understanding the script's behavior over time.

```
# Logging example
exec > >(tee -i logfile.txt)
exec 2>&1

echo "Script started"
# Rest of the script
```

Avoid Hardcoding Values: Where possible, parameterize values instead of hardcoding them. This makes your script more flexible and easier to adjust as needs change.

```
# Use variables instead of hardcoding
data_directory="/path/to/data"
backup_directory="/path/to/backup"

# Perform backup
cp -r "$data_directory" "$backup_directory"
```

Integrating these best practices into your shell scripting workflow will result in scripts that are efficient, maintainable, secure, and easier for others to understand and use.

Chapter 7

Package Management

This chapter provides an overview of package management in Linux, detailing key concepts and terms. It covers managing DEB packages using APT and DPKG for Debian-based systems, and RPM packages using YUM and DNF for Red Hat-based systems. The chapter also includes installation from tarballs and source code, use of Snap and Flatpak packages, and managing software repositories. It discusses verifying package integrity, handling dependencies, and procedures for upgrading and removing packages. Finally, it addresses automating package management tasks to streamline system maintenance.

7.1 Introduction to Package Management

Linux systems rely heavily on package management to handle the installation, upgrade, configuration, and removal of software. A package manager is a collection of tools designed to automate the process of installing, upgrading, configuring, and removing software packages from a computer's operating system in a consistent manner. The role of a package manager is crucial for maintaining a clean, efficient, and secure system.

At the core of any package management system are packages. A package is an archive file containing a piece of software and metadata necessary for its installation. This metadata typically includes the software's name, version, description, dependencies (other packages required for the software to work), and any configuration files.

A package manager performs several key tasks:

- **Package Retrieval**: Downloading the software package from a repository.
- **Installation**: Placing files in the appropriate directories and configuring the software to work in the user's environment.
- **Dependency Resolution**: Ensuring all required software libraries and components are installed.
- **Upgrading**: Updating the software package to a newer version.
- **Uninstallation**: Removing the software package and cleaning up any unnecessary files.

In Linux, there are several popular package management systems. The choice of system is often tied to the Linux distribution in use. For example, Debian-based distributions like Ubuntu use APT (Advanced Package Tool), while Red Hat-based distributions like Fedora use YUM (Yellowdog Updater Modified) or DNF (Dandified YUM).

The following examples demonstrate basic package management operations on a Debian-based system using APT. Ensure you have root privileges or use sudo for the commands:

```
# Updating the package list
sudo apt-get update

# Installing a package
sudo apt-get install package_name

# Upgrading all packages
sudo apt-get upgrade

# Removing a package
sudo apt-get remove package_name

# Searching for a package
apt-cache search package_name
```

Output from these commands can vary based on the specific configuration of your system and the availability of packages. For example, running the apt-get update command will refresh the package list from the repositories configured on your system:

```
Hit:1 http://archive.ubuntu.com/ubuntu focal InRelease
Get:2 http://archive.ubuntu.com/ubuntu focal-updates InRelease [114 kB]
Get:3 http://archive.ubuntu.com/ubuntu focal-backports InRelease [101 kB]
Get:4 http://archive.ubuntu.com/ubuntu focal-security InRelease [114 kB]
Fetched 329 kB in 2s (178 kB/s)
Reading package lists... Done
```

It is important to keep the package list updated to ensure that you have the latest information on what packages are available and their versions. This allows for efficient package upgrades and installations.

Packages can be classified into three main types:

- **Binary Packages**: Contain precompiled programs ready to be installed and executed.
- **Source Packages**: Include the source code and instructions specified for building the software. Users compile the source code to create binary packages.
- **Meta-packages**: Do not contain actual software but depend on other packages for installation. They are used to install a group of related packages.

Each Linux distribution hosts its packages within repositories, which are secure locations from where packages are downloaded to your system. Repositories are signed using GPG keys to verify their authenticity and integrity. Users can configure their system to use multiple repositories, such as official distribution repositories, third-party repositories, or personal package archives (PPAs).

A significant aspect of package management involves dependency resolution. Dependencies are other packages required for the software to function. For example, installing a graphical application might require libraries for rendering graphics. The package manager handles downloading and installing these dependent packages, preventing scenarios where the software fails due to missing dependencies.

Handling dependencies efficiently can sometimes involve complex logic. For instance, consider the installation of a package that depends on multiple other packages, which in turn have their dependencies. Recursive resolution ensures all necessary components are installed correctly. Furthermore, there may be dependency conflicts where two packages require different versions of the same dependency, posing challenges for the package manager.

To demonstrate dependency management, consider installing vlc, which depends on various libraries and utilities related to media decoding and playback:

```
sudo apt-get install vlc
```

The package manager checks for vlc dependencies and installs them alongside the main application. Here is a potential output illustrating the dependencies:

```
The following additional packages will be installed:
  libvlc-bin libvlc5 libvlccore9 vlc-bin vlc-data vlc-l10n vlc-plugin-access-extra
  vlc-plugin-base vlc-plugin-notify vlc-plugin-qt vlc-plugin-samba vlc-plugin-skins2
  vlc-plugin-video-output vlc-plugin-video-splitter vlc-plugin-visualization
Suggested packages:
  vlc-plugin-fluidsynth vlc-plugin-jack vlc-plugin-svg phonon-backend-vlc
Recommended packages:
  vlc-plugin-access-extra
The following NEW packages will be installed:
  libvlc-bin libvlc5 libvlccore9 vlc vlc-bin vlc-data vlc-l10n
  vlc-plugin-access-extra vlc-plugin-base vlc-plugin-notify vlc-plugin-qt
  vlc-plugin-samba vlc-plugin-skins2 vlc-plugin-video-output
  vlc-plugin-video-splitter vlc-plugin-visualization
0 upgraded, 16 newly installed, 0 to remove and 0 not upgraded.
Need to get 40.8 MB of archives.
After this operation, 105 MB of additional disk space will be used.
Do you want to continue? [Y/n]
```

Understanding package management systems is essential for efficient system administration in Linux. Package managers automate critical tasks, ensuring software is installed correctly with the required dependencies, kept up-to-date, and securely removed when no longer needed. By mastering package management, users and administrators can maintain a stable, secure, and efficient Linux environment.

7.2 Package Management Concepts and Terms

Package management is a critical component of Linux system administration, serving as the backbone for installing, upgrading, configuring, and removing software packages. It is imperative to grasp key concepts and terms associated with package management to effectively navigate and maintain a Linux environment.

Package: A package is a compressed file containing the software program, along with metadata about the software such as its name, description, version, dependencies, and configuration details. These packages can be of different types depending on the distribution, such as '.deb' for Debian-based systems or '.rpm' for Red Hat-based systems.

Repository: A repository, often abbreviated as "repo", is a storage location from which packages can be retrieved and installed on a system. Repositories are maintained by distribution vendors or third parties, and they are essential to the package management ecosystem. They can be configured in the system's package manager to automatically download and install software.

Dependency: Dependencies are additional packages required for a specific package to run properly. The package manager ensures that all dependencies are resolved and installed along with the desired package. Proper handling of dependencies prevents incompatibilities and software malfunctions.

Metadata: Metadata in the context of package management includes information about the package such as its name, version, size, description, license, and a list of dependencies. This information is used by the package manager to handle the package effectively.

Package Manager: A package manager is a collection of tools that automate the process of managing packages. Examples of package managers include APT (Advanced Package Tool) for Debian-based systems and YUM (Yellowdog Updater, Modified) or DNF (Dandified YUM) for Red Hat-based systems. They facilitate tasks like installation, upgrades, and removal of software.

APT: APT stands for Advanced Package Tool, a package management system used by Debian-based distributions like Ubuntu. APT simplifies the process of managing software on Unix-like computer systems by automating the retrieval, configuration, and installation of software packages.

YUM: YUM, which stands for Yellowdog Updater, Modified, is an open-source command-line package management utility for computers running the Linux operating system using the RPM Package Manager.

DNF: DNF, or Dandified YUM, is the next-generation version of YUM. It has been designed to be a more efficient and cleaner replacement for YUM.

Configuration File: Configuration files maintain settings and configuration for software. Within the scope of package management, these files often reside in the '/etc' directory and help control the behavior of software and the system.

Understanding these concepts enables system administrators to manage software packages effectively, ensuring that software is up to date, properly configured, and secure. The key descriptive and functional attributes of each of these terms set the stage for advanced package management techniques, paving the way for efficient and systematic software maintenance.

Properly installed and managed software is vital for the stability and security of a Linux system. The package manager's ability to handle dependencies automatically minimizes conflicts and reduces manual overhead, allowing administrators to focus on more significant tasks. The incremental understanding of these basic concepts serves as the foundation for mastering complex package management operations within various Linux distributions.

7.3 Working with DEB Packages in Debian-Based Systems: APT and DPKG

Debian-based systems, including popular distributions like Ubuntu, use DEB packages to manage software installations. DEB packages contain compressed archives of executable files, libraries, and associated metadata necessary for software integration on the system. Two primary tools are used for working with DEB packages: APT (Advanced Package Tool) and DPKG (Debian Package).

APT (Advanced Package Tool)

APT is a powerful command-line tool used for handling packages in Debian-based systems. It simplifies the process of installing, upgrading, configuring, and removing software, by managing dependencies and package sources automatically. Some commonly used APT commands and options are discussed below.

1. Updating the Package Index

APT maintains a local database of available packages, which must be updated periodically to ensure access to the latest software versions. The command to update this package index is:

```
sudo apt update
```

This command retrieves information about available packages from the software repositories listed in /etc/apt/sources.list and updates the local index.

2. Installing Packages

To install a package, the apt install command is used, followed by the package name. For example, to install the vim text editor, the following command is executed:

```
sudo apt install vim
```

APT automatically resolves and installs any dependencies required by the specified package.

3. Upgrading Packages

Upgrading packages to the latest versions available in the repositories can be done using the apt upgrade command. This command upgrades all installed packages to their newest versions:

```
sudo apt upgrade
```

To upgrade the entire system, including handling changes to package dependencies, apt full-upgrade is used:

```
sudo apt full-upgrade
```

4. Removing Packages

APT also allows for the removal of installed software. The apt remove command is used for this purpose:

```
sudo apt remove package_name
```

If configuration files associated with the package need to be removed as well, the apt purge command can be utilized:

```
sudo apt purge package_name
```

5. Searching for Packages

To search for packages in the repository, the apt search command is employed:

```
apt search keyword
```

This command lists all packages that match the provided keyword.

DPKG (Debian Package)

DPKG is the low-level tool that handles the installation, configuration, and removal of DEB packages. It is more fundamental than APT and does not manage dependencies. DPKG commands typically work with package files directly. Some key DPKG commands are as follows:

1. Installing Packages

To install a package using DPKG, the dpkg -i command followed by the package file's name is used:

```
sudo dpkg -i package_file.deb
```

This command installs the specified DEB package.

2. Removing Packages

The dpkg -r command removes an installed package:

```
sudo dpkg -r package_name
```

To remove a package along with its configuration files, the dpkg –purge command is used:

```
sudo dpkg --purge package_name
```

3. Listing Installed Packages

To list all the installed packages on the system, the dpkg -l command is used:

```
dpkg -l
```

This command provides detailed information about each installed package.

4. Querying Package Details

To obtain detailed information about a specific installed package, the dpkg -s command is employed:

```
dpkg -s package_name
```

5. Checking File Locations

To determine which package provides a specific file, the dpkg -S command is used:

```
dpkg -S /path/to/file
```

This command outputs the package name corresponding to the provided file path.

APT vs. DPKG

While APT provides a higher level of abstraction and is generally preferred for day-to-day package management due to its simplicity and automatic dependency handling, DPKG is valuable for situations requiring direct manipulation of DEB packages. DPKG serves as the backend tool that handles the core functions of package installation and removal, whereas APT manages repository access, dependency resolution, and package indexes.

Practical Examples

Consider a practical example of installing and managing the Apache httpd server. First, update the package index:

```
sudo apt update
```

Next, install the Apache server:

```
sudo apt install apache2
```

Verify that Apache is running:

```
systemctl status apache2
```

The output confirms the status of the Apache service.

To upgrade Apache to the latest version:

```
sudo apt upgrade apache2
```

If Apache needs to be removed from the system:

```
sudo apt remove apache2
```

To purge Apache, including its configuration files:

```
sudo apt purge apache2
```

In scenarios requiring direct manipulation, such as when working with a locally downloaded DEB package or debugging dependency issues, DPKG commands may be necessary. For instance, installing a local package file:

```
sudo dpkg -i apache2_package.deb
```

Checking for missing dependencies post-installation:

```
sudo apt --fix-broken install
```

This command attempts to resolve and install any missing dependencies. Applying both APT and DPKG effectively provides robust package management capabilities in Debian-based systems, ensuring that software installations, upgrades, and removals are handled efficiently and reliably.

7.4 Managing RPM Packages in Red Hat-Based Systems: YUM and DNF

Package management in Red Hat-based systems revolves predominantly around the RPM Package Manager (RPM). This section explores the two primary package management tools used in Red Hat-based distributions: Yellowdog Updater, Modified (YUM) and Dandified YUM (DNF). Both tools serve to simplify the process of installing, updating, removing, and managing software packages.

YUM was the traditional package manager in these systems, while DNF is the more recent and advanced tool that addresses some of YUM's limitations such as performance issues and dependency resolution deficiencies. As we delve into the functionalities provided by these tools, we will understand their capabilities and commands pertinent to effective package management.

Installing Packages

To install an RPM package using YUM, the basic command is:

```
sudo yum install package_name
```

For DNF, the command is remarkably similar:

```
sudo dnf install package_name
```

Both commands will search for the package in configured repositories, handle dependency resolution, and install the necessary packages. The output of a typical 'install' command will list the package(s) to be installed, their dependencies, and a final confirmation:

```
Last metadata expiration check: 0:01:29 ago on Sun 20 Mar 2023.
Dependencies resolved.
================================================================================
 Package          Arch       Version        Repository      Size
================================================================================
Installing:
 example-package  x86_64     1.0.0-1.el8    baseos          50 k

Transaction Summary
================================================================================
Install  1 Package

Total download size: 50 k
Installed size: 123 k
Is this ok [y/N]:
```

Updating Packages

Updating a package or all packages on the system ensures software is up-to-date and secure. Using YUM:

```
sudo yum update package_name
```

To update all packages, you simply omit the package name:

```
sudo yum update
```

The analogous DNF command is:

```
sudo dnf update package_name
```

Or for all packages:

```
sudo dnf update
```

Removing Packages

Removing an installed package can free up system resources and simplify management. The YUM command to remove a package is:

```
sudo yum remove package_name
```

The corresponding DNF command is:

```
sudo dnf remove package_name
```

Both commands will prompt for confirmation and list the packages to be removed, including dependencies that are no longer needed:

```
Dependencies resolved.
================================================================================
 Package            Arch       Version          Repository            Size
================================================================================
Removing:
 example-package    x86_64     1.0.0-1.el8      @baseos                 500 k

Transaction Summary
================================================================================
Remove  1 Package

Installed size: 123 k
Is this ok [y/N]:
```

Listing and Searching Packages

Before installing or updating a package, verifying its availability in repositories is beneficial. To list available packages using YUM:

```
yum list available
```

To search for a specific package by keyword, use:

```
yum search keyword
```

With DNF, the equivalent commands are:

```
dnf list available
```

And for searching:

```
dnf search keyword
```

Repository Management

Both YUM and DNF handle repositories, which are sources for retrieving packages. Managing these repositories is crucial for controlling the software available to the system. To list configured repositories with YUM:

```
yum repolist
```

And with DNF:

```
dnf repolist
```

To add a new repository, for example in DNF, a '.repo' file is created in the '/etc/yum.repos.d/' directory:

```
sudo nano /etc/yum.repos.d/myrepo.repo
```

Inside the file, the repo configuration might look like:

```
[myrepo]
name=My Repository
baseurl=http://repo.example.com/myrepo
enabled=1
gpgcheck=1
gpgkey=http://repo.example.com/myrepo/gpgkey
```

Group Management

YUM and DNF also allow the installation of package groups, collections of packages that serve a common purpose. Listing available groups with YUM:

```
yum group list
```

To install a group:

```
sudo yum group install 'Group Name'
```

With DNF, these commands are:

```
dnf group list
```

And to install:

```
sudo dnf group install 'Group Name'
```

YUM and DNF Plugins

Both YUM and DNF support plugins—extensions that add additional features. Managing these plugins can enhance package management by providing custom behaviors. List available plugins in YUM:

```
yum list yum-plugin-*
```

For DNF:

```
dnf list dnf-plugin-*
```

Installing a plugin in YUM, for example:

```
sudo yum install yum-plugin-fastestmirror
```

And for DNF:

```
sudo dnf install dnf-plugins-core
```

Both 'yum-plugin-fastestmirror' and 'dnf-plugins-core' enhance the speed of package downloads by selecting the fastest available mirror.

Logging and History

Tracking changes made through package managers is pivotal for system auditing and troubleshooting. YUM keeps logs of transactions in '/var/log/yum.log'. View the log using:

```
cat /var/log/yum.log
```

DNF provides a more detailed history feature:

```
dnf history
```

This command lists all transactions, including installs, updates, and removals, along with the transaction ID. For viewing details of a specific transaction:

```
dnf history info transaction_id
```

This command is especially useful for identifying when and why specific packages were installed or removed, aiding in system maintenance and problem resolution.

Effective RPM package management on Red Hat-based systems involves a thorough understanding of YUM and DNF commands and features. Both tools share similar commands and capabilities, with DNF introducing improvements over YUM. Mastery of these package managers ensures efficient and secure software management on any Red Hat-based system.

7.5 Using tarballs and Source Code Installation

Tarballs, and the process of source code installation, embody the traditional method of software distribution in Unix-like systems. This method grants users the flexibility to tailor installations according to specific needs, a valuable feature in advanced scenarios such as custom configurations or when dealing with niche software. The process, though it may appear intricate, follows a structured sequence.

A tarball refers to a collection of files bundled into a single archive file using the tar command, often compressed using tools such as gzip or bzip2. Typically, software distributed as a tarball involves source code, necessitating compilation on the user's machine.

Downloading the Tarball

Developers usually host tarballs on their websites or repositories. To download a tarball, one typically uses wget or curl, depending on availability. Consider a hypothetical software hosted at http://example.com/software.tar.gz. The downloading process is executed as follows:

```
wget http://example.com/software.tar.gz
```

Ensure possessing the necessary permissions and required tools to proceed with the following stages.

Extracting the Tarball

Upon acquiring the tarball, the next phase involves its extraction. The tarball format reveals itself in its extension, guiding the decompression method. For instance, using tar.gz (gzip), the extraction command comprises:

```
tar -xvzf software.tar.gz
```

Here, -x extracts the archive, -v renders the operation verbose, -z denotes gzip compression, and -f specifies the file name.

Should the tarball be compressed using bzip2 (indicated by .tar.bz2), adjust the command:

```
tar -xvjf software.tar.bz2
```

The decompression unveils the source files in a directory, typically named after the software.

Preparing for Compilation

Navigate to the extracted directory:

```
cd software-1.0.0
```

Most source distributions contain a README or INSTALL file. These documents provide instructions tailored to the specific software, detailing prerequisites and the installation process. Compliance with these guidelines is vital for successful installation.

Dependencies pose a critical concern. Before proceeding, ensure that the system satisfies software dependencies, such as libraries and development tools. Package managers (apt, yum, dnf, or similar) facilitate the installation of these dependencies.

Configuring the Build

Configuration adapts the build process to the system environment. This step is often performed by executing the configure script:

```
./configure
```

This script verifies the environment, checks for required libraries, and provides user options like specifying installation directories:

```
./configure --prefix=/opt/software
```

Here, –prefix designates the installation directory. Failing dependencies are typically reported during this phase; resolute troubleshooting is necessary before proceeding.

Compiling the Source Code

Following a successful configuration, compile the code using:

```
make
```

The make command automates the compilation by interpreting Makefile, dynamically managing the build according to dependencies among the source files.

Installing the Software

Post compilation, elevate permissions to root (if necessary) and install the software:

```
sudo make install
```

The make install command copies the binaries, libraries, and documentation to the designated directories based on the configuration.

Verifying Installation

Validate the installation by invoking the installed software, confirming that it executes as intended. Customarily, executing the program includes accessing version information:

```
/opt/software/bin/software --version
```

Cleaning Up

After successful installation, housekeeping involves removing intermediate files generated during compilation:

```
make clean
make distclean
```

This reduces disk space usage and maintains the directory's clarity.

Handling Failures and Debugging

Compilation and installation are not infallible processes; failures may arise from missing dependencies, incompatible library versions, or overlooked instructions in the documentation. Analyzing error messages provides insights into the root causes, and leveraging the community forums and mailing lists associated with the software often aids in resolving complex issues.

By adhering to these structured steps meticulously, one gains proficiency in handling tarballs and source code installation, a skill instrumental in managing customized setups and a wide spectrum of software unavailable through traditional package managers.

7.6 Introduction to Snap Packages

The Snap package format, developed by Canonical, provides a universal approach to software deployment on Linux systems. Unlike traditional package management systems that are specific to a distribution, such as APT for Debian-based systems or YUM/DNF for Red Hat-based systems, Snap packages are designed to work across a broad range of Linux distributions. This section explores the Snap package architecture, installation process, and fundamental commands for managing Snap packages.

Snap packages, commonly referred to as snaps, are self-contained application bundles which include the binary executables, libraries, and dependencies required for the software to run. This encapsulation ensures that snaps can operate independently of the underlying system libraries and configurations, promoting cross-distribution functionality and minimizing dependency issues.

The snap ecosystem relies on two primary components: the snapd service and the Snap Store. The snapd service is a background daemon responsible for managing snap packages, including their installation, updates, and removal. It ensures that the required runtime environment is set up for each snap. The Snap Store functions as a centralized distribution platform where developers can publish snaps, and users can discover and install software.

To install snapd on a Linux system, execute the following command if it is not already installed:

```
sudo apt update
sudo apt install snapd
```

Once snapd is installed, it runs as a system service that can be controlled with standard systemd commands. For example, to start, stop, or check the status of snapd, you can use:

```
sudo systemctl start snapd
sudo systemctl stop snapd
sudo systemctl status snapd
```

After ensuring snapd is active, Snap packages can be installed from the Snap Store using the ‘snap‘ command. To find a snap, use the following command, replacing ‘package-name‘ with the desired software:

```
snap find package-name
```

This command outputs a list of available snaps matching the search term along with their descriptions and versions. Upon locating the desired snap, install it using:

```
sudo snap install package-name
```

For instance, to install the VLC media player snap, you would execute:

```
sudo snap install vlc
```

Once installed, snaps can be managed with several commands. To list all installed snaps and their versions:

```
snap list
```

To obtain detailed information about a specific snap, use:

```
snap info package-name
```

Snaps are automatically updated by default, reducing the maintenance burden on users. However, manual updates can be triggered with:

```
sudo snap refresh package-name
```

To update all installed snaps, omit the package name:

```
sudo snap refresh
```

Removing a snap from the system is straightforward:

```
sudo snap remove package-name
```

The isolation and confinement mechanisms of Snap packages provide additional security benefits. Snaps operate within a restricted environment, limiting their access to system resources unless explicitly granted permissions. This model, known as confinement, prevents malicious or flawed software from affecting the entire system. Snaps can operate in different confinement modes: strict, classic, and devmode. Strict confinement restricts snaps to their sandbox, whereas classic confinement behaves similarly to traditional packages with full system access. Devmode is used for development and testing, offering fewer restrictions.

To adjust a snap's permissions and interfaces, use:

```
sudo snap connect package-name:interface
```

And to disconnect an interface:

```
sudo snap disconnect package-name:interface
```

The Snap Store also offers a channel mechanism to manage software stability and updates. These channels include 'stable', 'candidate', 'beta', and 'edge', representing different stages of software release from production-ready to development builds. Users can specify the desired channel during installation or when refreshing snaps:

```
sudo snap install package-name --channel=channel-name
sudo snap refresh package-name --channel=channel-name
```

For example, to install the edge version of a snap:

```
sudo snap install vlc --channel=edge
```

The Snap package ecosystem thus provides a robust, cross-distribution framework for software distribution, enhancing consistency and security while simplifying the management of applications.

7.7 Flatpak and its Ecosystem

Flatpak is a relatively new framework for building, distributing, and running packaged software on Linux. It offers a single, unified system for app distribution that works across all major Linux distributions, aiming to solve the compatibility issues inherent with traditional package management systems. Flatpak packages (or flatpaks) are sandboxed, which provides enhanced security and isolation from the host system.

The sandboxing mechanism ensures that applications run in a controlled environment with minimal interaction with the core system, thus reducing the risk of system corruption or data breaches. Flatpak's core design revolves around decentralization, allowing developers and users to host their repositories, though there is a central repository as well, known as Flathub.

To illustrate the use of Flatpak, consider the command to install and manage Flatpak applications. First, it is necessary to install Flatpak itself. On a Debian-based system, this can be accomplished using the following command within the terminal:

```
sudo apt install flatpak
```

For Red Hat-based systems, the command would be:

```
sudo dnf install flatpak
```

Next, it is essential to add the Flathub repository to access a wide range of applications. This can be done with the following command:

```
sudo flatpak remote-add --if-not-exists flathub https://flathub.org/repo/flathub.
    flatpakrepo
```

With the repository added, installing an application such as GIMP from

Flathub is straightforward:

```
sudo flatpak install flathub org.gimp.GIMP
```

Once installed, the application can be run using its Flatpak identifier:

```
flatpak run org.gimp.GIMP
```

Flatpak supports various essential commands for managing installed applications. To update all installed flatpaks:

```
sudo flatpak update
```

For listing all installed flatpaks:

```
flatpak list
```

If an application needs to be uninstalled, employing Flatpak's remove command is as follows:

```
sudo flatpak uninstall org.gimp.GIMP
```

A critical aspect of Flatpak's ecosystem is its structured directory system, which ensures proper isolation and management of files. Flatpak installs packages in the location typically found under /var/lib/flatpak/. This directory contains subdirectories for apps, runtimes, and the repositories linked to the system. Additionally, each Flatpak application is confined within a namespace that limits its access to resources, providing a robust security posture.

A technological cornerstone of Flatpak is the use of **runtimes**. Runtimes are essentially shared libraries and system services that Flatpak applications depend on. They are analogous to the dependencies in traditional package management but are packaged and updated independently. For instance, GNOME and KDE are common runtimes providing the necessary environment for applications developed for their respective desktops.

Developers package their applications with minimal dependencies, significantly reducing redundancy and ensuring each application is lightweight. Users must install these runtimes separately. For example, installing the GNOME runtime can be achieved with:

```
sudo flatpak install flathub org.gnome.Platform
```

To demonstrate Flatpak's ecosystem's robustness, consider handling permissions for flatpaks. Each Flatpak can request access to OS features, including file systems and device interfaces, restricted by default. Users can manage these permissions using the command line or graphical tools like **Flatseal**. For instance, granting a Flatpak application access to USB devices can be performed via:

```
sudo flatpak override <application-id> --device=all
```

Flatpak ecosystems advocate an inspection of security measures through **bubblewrap**, a user-space sandboxing tool that creates an isolated environment using Linux's namespace features. Bubblewrap plays a pivotal role in the security architecture by ensuring that applications run with the least privilege necessary.

Lastly, Flatpak supports interactions with other package management systems, allowing for harmonious coexistence. For users and organizations looking to scale deployment, Flatpak offers commands to create local repositories, facilitating internal distribution of applications without relying on external sources. This flexibility, coupled with Flatpak's solid framework and transformative impact on Linux application distribution, solidifies its role as a critical tool in the Linux ecosystem.

7.8 Managing Software Repositories

Managing software repositories is a fundamental aspect of package management in Linux systems. Repositories are centralized storage locations from which software packages can be retrieved, installed, upgraded, and managed. Understanding how to effectively manage software repositories is crucial for maintaining a secure, up-to-date, and efficiently functioning system.

A repository typically contains a collection of software, metadata files, and package information. It is an organized directory of software binaries and their dependencies, which can be accessed via package management tools.

Types of Repositories:

- **Official Repositories:** These are maintained by the Linux distribution's maintainers or authorized contributors. They often contain thoroughly tested and stable packages.
- **Third-Party Repositories:** These are external to the official distribution repositories. They may contain additional or experimental software.

- **Personal Package Archives (PPAs):** Specific to Ubuntu and its derivatives, PPAs allow individual developers to publish software packages.

Repository Configuration Files:

In Debian-based systems, repository configuration is managed in the /etc/apt/sources.list file, as well as in separate files within the /etc/apt/sources.list.d/ directory. Each entry in these files specifies a repository location.

```
# Example of /etc/apt/sources.list entry
deb http://archive.ubuntu.com/ubuntu/ focal main restricted

# Example entry in a file within /etc/apt/sources.list.d/
deb http://ppa.launchpad.net/nilarimogard/webupd8/ubuntu focal main
```

In Red Hat-based systems, repository configurations are handled through files located in the /etc/yum.repos.d/ directory. Each repository is defined in its own .repo file.

```
# Example of a .repo file in /etc/yum.repos.d/
[base]
name=CentOS-$releasever - Base
baseurl=http://mirror.centos.org/centos/$releasever/os/$basearch/
enabled=1
gpgcheck=1
gpgkey=file:///etc/pki/rpm-gpg/RPM-GPG-KEY-CentOS-7
```

Adding Repositories:

To add a repository in Debian-based systems, you can manually edit the sources.list file or add a new file in the sources.list.d/ directory. Alternatively, the add-apt-repository command is used for PPA additions.

```
# Adding a repository manually
echo "deb http://archive.ubuntu.com/ubuntu/ focal universe" | sudo tee -a /etc/apt/
    sources.list.d/universe.list

# Using add-apt-repository for a PPA
sudo add-apt-repository ppa:graphics-drivers/ppa
```

For Red Hat-based systems, you can use the yum-config-manager command to add repositories.

```
# Adding an official repository
sudo yum-config-manager --add-repo http://www.example.com/example.repo
```

Updating Repositories:

Updating repository indices ensures that your local metadata is up-to-date with the repository server. This process is critical for accurate package management.

```
# Update repositories in a Debian-based system
sudo apt update

# Update repositories in a Red Hat-based system
sudo yum makecache
```

Removing Repositories:

Should you need to remove a repository, you can delete the corresponding entry in the configuration files. In Debian-based systems, this may involve removing a line from sources.list or deleting a file in sources.list.d/.

```
# Removing a PPA repository in Debian-based systems
sudo add-apt-repository --remove ppa:graphics-drivers/ppa
```

In Red Hat-based systems, you can disable a repository or delete the .repo file in /etc/yum.repos.d/.

```
# Disabling a repository
sudo yum-config-manager --disable example-repo
```

Repository Prioritization:

When multiple repositories provide the same package, you might want to prioritize one over the others. In Debian-based systems, the apt preferences file (/etc/apt/preferences.d/) can be used for this purpose.

```
# Example preferences file for Debian-based systems
Package: *
Pin: release a=focal
Pin-Priority: 900

Package: mypackage
Pin: version 1.0.2-1
Pin-Priority: 1001
```

In Red Hat-based systems, repository priorities can be set in the .repo files.

```
# Example configuration in a .repo file
[example-repo]
name=Example Repository
baseurl=http://example.com/repo/$releasever/$basearch/
enabled=1
gpgcheck=1
priority=1
```

Securing Repositories:

Security is critical in repository management. Always ensure that repositories are authenticated using GPG keys to verify the integrity and authenticity of the packages. Debian-based systems retrieve and store keys using the apt-key command.

```
# Adding a GPG key in Debian-based systems
wget -qO - http://archive.ubuntu.com/ubuntu/project/ubuntu-archive-keyring.gpg |
    sudo apt-key add -
```

Red Hat-based systems utilize the gpgkey directive in .repo files.

```
# Adding a GPG key in Red Hat-based systems
sudo rpm --import http://www.example.com/RPM-GPG-KEY-EXAMPLE
```

```
RPM-GPG-KEY-EXAMPLE public key imported successfully
```

Understanding the intricacies of managing software repositories enables system administrators and power users to effectively source, maintain, and secure the software ecosystem on their Linux systems. This advanced competency directly contributes to the robustness and performance of the operating environment.

7.9 Verifying Package Integrity and Authenticity

Verifying the integrity and authenticity of software packages before installation is crucial in a secure and stable Linux environment. This section delves into the methods and tools used for these verifications, focusing on digital signatures, checksums, and the handling of keyrings.

To prevent tampering and ensure the authenticity of packages, Linux distributions implement cryptographic security measures. When a package is signed digitally, a cryptographic signature is appended to it, allowing users to verify its origin and integrity using the associated public key. Similarly, checksums—hash values computed from the package contents—are used to verify that a package has not been altered during download.

Digital Signatures: A digital signature provides a way to establish both the identity of the package source and the package's integrity. It is created using a private key known only to the package distributor, and can be verified by users using the corresponding public key. On Debian-based systems, this process is managed by the Advanced Package Tool (APT), whereas on Red Hat-based systems, it is managed by the RPM Package Manager (RPM).

```
$ apt-key list # lists all public keys APT trusts
$ apt-key adv --keyserver keyserver.ubuntu.com --recv-keys <key-id> # importing a
    specific public key
```

By ensuring that a package's signature matches the corresponding public key, users can confidently ascertain the package's source and authenticity.

Checksums: Checksums involve the creation of a hash value from the contents of the package file. Common checksum algorithms include MD5, SHA1, and SHA256, with SHA256 being preferred for its stronger security properties.

```
$ sha256sum mypackage.tar.gz
```

The command returns a SHA256 hash that uniquely represents the package contents. By comparing this output against the checksum provided by the package source, users can verify that the file has not been altered.

On Debian-based systems, checksums for downloaded packages are automatically verified by APT:

```
$ sudo apt-get update
$ sudo apt-get upgrade
```

APT checks the checksums listed in the repository's Release files against the downloaded package files. If there is a mismatch, the system will alert the user and typically stop the upgrade process.

For Red Hat-based systems using YUM or DNF, checksums are handled similarly. When a package is downloaded, its checksum is automatically checked against the metadata in the repository:

```
$ sudo yum update
$ sudo dnf update
```

If discrepancies are found during these checks, the package manager stops the process and notifies the user of possible corruption or tampering.

Keyring Management: Maintaining the keyring—a database of trusted public keys—is essential for ensuring that all package verifications are reliable. Debian-based systems manage keyrings through the GnuPG system, while RPM systems handle keyrings directly with RPM commands.

For Debian-based systems:

```
$ sudo apt-key add /path/to/public.key # adding a new public key to the keyring
$ sudo apt-key del <key-id> # removing a specific public key
$ apt-key list # list all trusted keys
```

For RPM systems:

```
$ sudo rpm --import /path/to/public.key # adding a new public key to RPM database
$ sudo rpm -qa gpg-pubkey* # list all imported keys
$ sudo rpm -e gpg-pubkey-<id> # removing a specific key
```

Ensuring the keyring contains only trusted keys from verified sources is paramount to maintaining system integrity and security.

These measures—digital signatures, checksums, and keyrings—work in concert to provide robust verification mechanisms. Properly configuring and regularly updating these systems ensures that only authenticated and unaltered software is installed, significantly enhancing the security of a Linux system.

7.10 Handling Package Dependencies

Dependencies are a common aspect of package management in Linux. When installing, upgrading, or removing software packages, it is essential to understand and manage these dependencies effectively to ensure the stability and functionality of the system.

A dependency, in the context of software packages, is an external component or library required for a package to function correctly. In Linux distributions, package managers handle dependencies to prevent issues arising from missing or incompatible libraries. There are two primary types of dependencies: direct and indirect. Direct dependencies are the libraries or packages that a software package directly relies on, while indirect dependencies are the dependencies of those dependencies.

Dependency Resolution: Modern package managers like APT, YUM, and DNF have built-in mechanisms to automatically resolve dependencies. When a package is installed, the package manager searches the repositories for the required dependencies and installs them alongside the main package. The following is an example of installing a package with APT on Debian-based systems:

```
sudo apt-get install package_name
```

The package manager will then output a list of packages that will be installed to satisfy the dependencies:

```
The following additional packages will be installed:
  dependency1 dependency2 dependency3
The following NEW packages will be installed:
  package_name dependency1 dependency2 dependency3
```

In Red Hat-based systems, YUM and DNF handle dependencies similarly. For example, installing a package with DNF:

```
sudo dnf install package_name
```

The output will include a list of dependencies to be installed:

```
Dependencies resolved.
================================================================================
 Package        Arch   Version            Repository               Size
================================================================================
Installing:
 package_name   x86_64 1.2.3-1.el7         base                     5.6 M
Installing dependencies:
 dependency1    x86_64 0.1.2-1.el7         base                     1.4 M
 dependency2    x86_64 3.4.5-1.el7         base                     2.1 M
```

Dependency Conflicts: Sometimes, a situation arises where several packages require different versions of the same dependency, leading to a conflict. Most package managers are equipped to handle these conflicts and will attempt to find a solution automatically. In some scenarios, manual intervention is required.

For example, with APT, one can use the `apt-get -f install` command to fix broken dependencies:

```
sudo apt-get -f install
```

For YUM, the `yum history` command can be useful for rolling back transactions and resolving conflicts:

```
sudo yum history undo <transaction_id>
```

Dependency Management Tools: Tools such as `apt-cache` and `yum deplist` can be used to inspect a package's dependencies before installation.

With APT on Debian-based systems:

```
apt-cache depends package_name
```

This command lists all packages that `package_name` depends on.

For YUM on Red Hat-based systems:

```
yum deplist package_name
```

This command outputs the dependencies in a structured format, listing each required package and its provider.

Dealing with Circular Dependencies: A circular dependency occurs when two or more packages depend on each other, forming a loop. These situations can be particularly challenging to resolve. Most package managers attempt to handle circular dependencies during the installation process, but in complex cases, manual resolution may be necessary.

One approach to manually resolve circular dependencies involves installing the packages in stages, using the –nodeps flag to temporarily bypass dependency checks:

```
sudo rpm -ivh --nodeps package1.rpm
sudo rpm -ivh package2.rpm
sudo rpm -Uvh package1.rpm
```

While this method resolves the issue, it should be used with caution, as bypassing dependency checks can lead to system instability if not managed correctly.

Best Practices for Dependency Management: Effective dependency management relies on adhering to best practices:

- Always use the package manager's native tools for installing, upgrading, and removing packages to ensure dependencies are correctly handled.
- Regularly update the system to maintain compatibility and reduce the risk of dependency conflicts.
- Utilize virtual environments or containerization (e.g., Docker) for isolating applications and their dependencies, minimizing the impact on the primary system.
- Periodically clean up unused packages and dependencies to maintain system hygiene and reduce clutter. On Debian-based systems, the apt-get autoremove command can be used:

  ```
  sudo apt-get autoremove
  ```

  Similarly, on Red Hat-based systems, dnf autoremove serves the same purpose:

  ```
  sudo dnf autoremove
  ```

Understanding and managing package dependencies is crucial for maintaining a stable and functional Linux system. Adopting these practices ensures that the software environment remains consistent and reliable, allowing for efficient handling of software additions, upgrades, and removals.

7.11 Upgrading and Removing Packages

Upgrading and removing packages are integral tasks in package management. These tasks ensure that software remains up-to-date and that systems do not become bloated with unused or outdated packages. Efficient handling of upgrades and removals is crucial for maintaining system stability and security. In this section, we will explore the processes and commands associated with upgrading and removing packages in both Debian-based and Red Hat-based systems.

When upgrading packages, it is important to distinguish between updating the package lists and upgrading the installed packages. Updating the package lists involves fetching the latest available versions of the software repositories. This is achieved through the command:

```
sudo apt update
```

This command does not install new versions of the packages but updates the package database with the latest available versions. To upgrade the installed packages to their latest versions, the following command is used:

```
sudo apt upgrade
```

The `apt upgrade` command fetches the new versions of installed packages and installs them, preserving the current configuration of each package. The command:

```
sudo apt full-upgrade
```

is used to upgrade all installed packages, allowing the removal of obsolete packages if necessary to resolve dependency issues.

Similarly, Red Hat-based systems use:

```
sudo yum check-update
```

to check for package updates. To upgrade the packages, the command:

```
sudo yum update
```

is employed. This updates all packages to the latest version. The equivalent in DNF is:

```
sudo dnf check-update
```

and

```
sudo dnf upgrade
```

It is sometimes necessary to upgrade a specific package rather than all installed packages. This can be done using the following commands in Debian-based systems:

```
sudo apt install --only-upgrade package_name
```

Here, package_name should be replaced with the actual name of the package to be upgraded. On Red Hat-based systems, specific package upgrades can be performed using:

```
sudo yum update package_name
```

or in DNF:

```
sudo dnf upgrade package_name
```

To ensure that the system remains performant and free from unnecessary files, it is vital to remove unused packages. On Debian-based systems, the removal of a package can be done using:

```
sudo apt remove package_name
```

This command removes the package but leaves the configuration files intact. If both the package and its configuration files need to be removed, use:

```
sudo apt purge package_name
```

Red Hat-based systems use:

```
sudo yum remove package_name
```

or

```
sudo dnf remove package_name
```

to perform the package removal. It's important to clean up residual configuration files after removing packages as they can accumulate over time. In Debian-based systems, this can be executed with:

```
sudo apt autoremove
```

This command removes packages that were automatically installed to satisfy dependencies for other packages and are now no longer needed.

For Red Hat-based systems, the following command achieves similar results:

```
sudo yum autoremove
```

or in DNF:

```
sudo dnf autoremove
```

In both Debian-based and Red Hat-based systems, it is also possible to remove orphan packages (packages installed as dependencies but no longer required by any installed software). This helps maintain a cleaner system by eliminating unnecessary software.

On occasion, conflicts or issues may arise that require the forceful removal or downgrading of packages. Although these actions should be taken with caution, they can sometimes resolve critical problems. To forcefully remove a package, Debian-based systems can use:

```
sudo dpkg --remove --force-remove-reinstreq package_name
```

It is also possible to downgrade a package to an earlier version if a recent upgrade causes stability or compatibility issues. This is generally achieved by specifying the desired version in the install command:

```
sudo apt install package_name=desired_version
```

On Red Hat-based systems, the process of downgrading a package is managed by:

```
sudo yum downgrade package_name
```

or in DNF:

```
sudo dnf downgrade package_name
```

Monitoring and managing packages efficiently through upgrading and removing operations not only helps keep the system secure and optimized but also prevents potential software conflicts. Effective use of these commands ensures smooth operation and a well-maintained Linux environment.

Example outputs from these commands might look like:

```
Reading package lists... Done
Building dependency tree
Reading state information... Done

The following packages will be upgraded:
  xyz-package
1 upgraded, 0 newly installed, 0 to remove and 0 not upgraded.
Need to get 1,024 kB of archives.
After this operation, 512 kB of additional disk space will be used.
Do you want to continue? [Y/n]
```

or for a removal operation:

```
Removing xyz-package (1.0-1) ...
Purging configuration files for xyz-package (1.0-1) ...
```

These steps illustrate the systematic approach required to maintain a robust package management regime.

7.12 Automating Package Management Tasks

Automating package management tasks in Linux is a critical skill for system administrators and users who require efficient and consistent software management. Automation not only minimizes manual intervention but also ensures that systems remain up-to-date and secure with the least administrative overhead.

To automate package management, several tools and techniques can be employed, including shell scripting, cron jobs, configuration management tools like Ansible, and package management hooks. Each method offers different levels of control and flexibility, allowing you to tailor the automation to your system's specific needs.

Shell Scripting for Automation

Shell scripting is one of the most powerful and flexible ways to automate package management tasks. Scripts can execute a series of package management commands, such as updates, installations, and removals. Below is an example of a simple shell script that updates the package lists and upgrades all installed packages on a Debian-based system using APT:

```
#!/bin/bash

# Update package list
sudo apt update
```

```
# Perform upgrade
sudo apt -y upgrade

# Clean up
sudo apt -y autoremove
sudo apt -y clean

echo "Package update and upgrade completed successfully."
```

This script performs an update and upgrade while ensuring that non-essential packages and cached archives are removed. The '-y' flag is used to automatically answer 'yes' to prompts, which is essential for non-interactive script execution.

Using Cron Jobs

Cron is a time-based job scheduling tool in Unix-like operating systems. By creating cron jobs, you can schedule scripts to run at specified intervals, ensuring regular maintenance without manual intervention.

To schedule the above script to run daily, you would add an entry to the crontab file:

```
0 2 * * * /path/to/update-script.sh
```

This cron job runs the script at 2 AM every day. The syntax '0 2 * * *' specifies the minute (0), hour (2), day of the month (), month (), and day of the week ().

Configuration Management with Ansible

For more complex automation needs, configuration management tools like Ansible provide powerful capabilities to manage package installation, upgrades, and configurations across multiple servers. Ansible uses YAML-based playbooks to define automation tasks.

A simple Ansible playbook to update and upgrade packages on Debian-based systems is shown below:

```
- name: Update and upgrade APT packages
  hosts: all
  become: yes
  tasks:
    - name: Update package lists
      apt:
        update_cache: yes

    - name: Upgrade all packages
      apt:
        upgrade: dist
        force_apt_get: yes
```

This playbook will update the package lists and upgrade all packages on all hosts specified in the inventory file. The 'become: yes' directive indicates that the tasks need to be run with elevated privileges.

Utilizing Package Management Hooks

Some package managers support hooks, which are scripts or commands executed automatically at specific points during package management operations. For instance, in Debian-based systems, APT hooks can be utilized to run custom scripts before or after package operations.

To create an APT hook that runs a script after every package install, you would place a script in the '/etc/apt/apt.conf.d/' directory with the following content:

```
DPkg::Post-Invoke-Success {"exec /path/to/success-script.sh";};
```

This configuration runs '/path/to/success-script.sh' after each successful package operation. Hooks provide fine-grained control and can be extremely useful for performing tasks such as logging, custom notifications, or additional cleanup.

Automating package management tasks reduces the risk of human error, ensures consistency across different systems, and significantly saves time. Understanding and applying these automation techniques is essential for maintaining a robust and efficient Linux environment.

Chapter 8

System Monitoring and Performance

This chapter focuses on monitoring and optimizing system performance in Linux. It covers tools and methods for analyzing system logs, real-time monitoring with top and htop, and detailed monitoring of CPU, memory, disk usage, and network activity. The chapter explains the use of vmstat, iostat, and netstat, and discusses monitoring processes and system services. It addresses identifying and resolving performance bottlenecks, setting up system monitoring tools like Nagios and Zabbix, and automating performance monitoring and alerting to ensure system reliability and efficiency.

8.1 Introduction to System Monitoring

System monitoring is an essential practice in system administration, crucial for maintaining the health, performance, and reliability of Linux systems. It involves the continuous observation and analysis of system activities and resource usage to detect potential issues, optimize performance, and ensure efficient resource allocation. This section introduces the fundamental concepts of system monitoring, highlighting its importance and the basic techniques used to effectively monitor a Linux system.

System monitoring encompasses various aspects including, but not limited to, CPU usage, memory allocation and consumption, disk input/output (I/O) performance, network traffic, and the status of running processes and services. By leveraging a range of tools and methodologies, system administrators can gain insights into the operational state of their systems, enabling proactive identification and resolution of performance issues before they escalate into critical problems.

- **CPU Usage Monitoring**: This aspect of system monitoring involves tracking the utilization of the central processing unit (CPU) to ensure that its resources are being used effectively. High CPU usage can indicate processes that require optimization or potential system overload situations.
- **Memory Usage Monitoring**: Monitoring memory involves keeping track of both physical and virtual memory usage. It helps in identifying memory leaks, inefficient memory usage by applications, and overall system memory pressure.
- **Disk Usage and I/O Monitoring**: Disk monitoring focuses on the capacity and health of storage devices, as well as the read/write performance. Monitoring disk I/O operations can reveal bottlenecks that may affect system performance.
- **Network Traffic Monitoring**: Observing network activity involves tracking the volume and type of data being transmitted and received. This helps in identifying unusual traffic patterns, potential security breaches, and bottlenecks in network throughput.
- **Process and Service Monitoring**: This includes keeping tabs on the various processes and services running on the system, ensuring they are functioning correctly and efficiently.

Effective system monitoring is accomplished through a combination of manual observation and automated tools. Manual observation involves the use of command-line tools and utilities that provide real-time data and logs, which can be analyzed to understand system behavior. Here are some commonly used tools for system monitoring on Linux:

- **top** and **htop**: These utilities give an overview of the currently running processes, along with detailed statistics on CPU and memory usage.

- **vmstat**: This utility reports information about processes, memory, paging, block I/O, traps, and CPU activity.
- **iostat**: This tool provides statistics on CPU and input/output devices.
- **netstat**: This command-line tool displays network connections, routing tables, interface statistics, masquerade connections, and multicast memberships.
- **journalctl**: A utility for querying and displaying messages from the journal, such as system logs.

Automation in system monitoring is achieved through the deployment of monitoring solutions that periodically collect and analyze data, generating alerts when predefined thresholds are breached. Such tools include Nagios and Zabbix, which are robust monitoring platforms capable of overseeing large, complex environments. These platforms offer features such as alerting, dashboarding, reporting, and integration with other system management tools.

To illustrate the importance and utility of basic system monitoring tools, consider the use of the 'top' command. The 'top' command provides a dynamic real-time view of a running system, displaying a summary of the system's resource usage and a list of tasks being managed by the kernel. Below is a sample execution of the 'top' command and its output:

```
top
```

This command will produce an output similar to the following:

```
top - 10:24:15 up 24 days, 14:53,  3 users,  load average: 0.01, 0.05, 0.12
Tasks: 188 total,   1 running, 187 sleeping,   0 stopped,   0 zombie
%Cpu(s):  0.3 us,  0.1 sy,  0.0 ni, 99.5 id,  0.0 wa,  0.0 hi,  0.1 si,  0.0 st
KiB Mem :  8173148 total,  1053260 free,  2568520 used,  4551368 buff/cache
KiB Swap:  2097148 total,  2097148 free,        0 used.  5251696 avail Mem
```

The output of the 'top' command is segmented into two main parts: the summary area and the task area. The summary area provides an overview of system performance metrics such as uptime, load average, and memory usage, whereas the task area lists the running processes along with details like their CPU and memory consumption.

Understanding and utilizing system monitoring tools is foundational to maintaining the performance and reliability of Linux systems. By regularly employing these tools and analyzing their outputs, system administrators can gain the expertise required to troubleshoot and optimize their environments effectively.

8.2 Monitoring System Logs with Journalctl and Log Files

Effective system monitoring in Linux necessitates a comprehensive understanding of system logs, which are critical for diagnosing issues and understanding system behavior. This section will explore monitoring system logs using journalctl and examining traditional log files, providing practical examples and detailed explanations.

The Systemd Journal and Log Files: Systemd includes a component known as the journal, managed by the journald service, which collects and stores log data. The journal provides a centralized architecture for log management, offering several advantages over traditional log files, including structured and indexed logging for efficient querying and analysis. Traditional log files, typically located in /var/log, still play a crucial role in system logging for various applications and services not integrated with systemd.

Using journalctl: journalctl is the command-line utility for accessing and querying the journal logs. Basic usage of journalctl without any arguments displays the entire journal. To gain insight into specific portions of the log or extract relevant information, several options and filters can be applied. Here are some essential commands and their functionalities:

```
# Display the entire system journal
journalctl

# Display logs from the current boot
journalctl -b

# Display the logs of a previous boot (e.g., the second last boot)
journalctl -b -1

# Display logs for a specific time range
journalctl --since "2023-02-01 00:00:00" --until "2023-02-01 23:59:59"

# Follow real-time logging output (similar to 'tail -f')
journalctl -f
```

Filtering the logs can provide more concise and actionable insights. Below are additional filtering techniques:

```
# Filter logs by systemd unit
```

```
journalctl -u ssh.service

# Filter logs by priority (e.g., 'emerg', 'alert', 'crit', 'err', 'warning', 'notice', 'info', '
    debug')
journalctl -p err

# Filter logs by a specific process (using PID)
journalctl _PID=1234

# Combine multiple filters (e.g., by unit and priority)
journalctl -u ssh.service -p crit
```

Structured Querying and Maintenance: One of the key advantages of journalctl is the ability to perform structured queries. Users can filter logs based on numerous fields such as executable paths, message identifiers, and hardware metadata. The following commands demonstrate these capabilities:

```
# Filter logs by executable path
journalctl /usr/bin/sshd

# Filter logs by message identifier
journalctl MESSAGE_ID=<message-id>

# Filter logs by hardware metadata (e.g., by machine ID)
journalctl _MACHINE_ID=<machine-id>
```

Maintaining the journal is critical to prevent excessive disk usage. journalctl offers tools to manage log retention policies and clean up old logs:

```
# Show current disk usage and available space
journalctl --disk-usage

# Reduce journal size to a specific limit
journalctl --vacuum-size=500M

# Retain logs for a specific time period
journalctl --vacuum-time=10d
```

Traditional Log Files: Despite the advantages of journalctl, traditional log files remain important. These logs are generally located in the /var/log directory. Some common log files include:

- /var/log/syslog or /var/log/messages: Contain system log messages suitable for troubleshooting general system issues.
- /var/log/auth.log or /var/log/secure: Record authentication-related messages, essential for security audits.
- /var/log/kern.log: Capture kernel messages, useful for diagnosing kernel-level problems.

- /var/log/dmesg: Stores boot and hardware-related messages from the kernel ring buffer.

Reading and Analyzing Log Files: The tail, less, grep, and awk commands are typically used to read and analyze log files:

```
# Display the last 10 lines of a log file
tail /var/log/syslog

# Follow real-time updates to a log file
tail -f /var/log/syslog

# Search for specific keywords in log files
grep "error" /var/log/syslog

# Filter and format log file output
awk '/error/ {print $1, $2, $3, $5}' /var/log/syslog
```

Understanding these tools and techniques enhances the ability to monitor system logs effectively, identify potential issues, and ensure the smooth operation of Linux systems.

8.3 Real-time System Monitoring with Top and Htop

Real-time system monitoring is crucial in maintaining the optimal performance of a Linux system. Two widely-used tools for real-time system monitoring are top and htop. These tools allow users to observe the system's performance metrics, such as CPU usage, memory usage, and running processes, in real-time and take necessary actions to address any abnormalities.

The top command is a performance monitoring program found in Unix-like operating systems. It offers a dynamic real-time view of a running system. Here is how you can initiate top:

```
$ top
```

Upon executing the above command, the terminal displays an overview of system performance metrics. The default view comprises the following sections:

- **Summary information:** This appears at the top and includes the system uptime, number of users logged in, load averages, and usage statistics for CPU, memory, and swap space.

- **Process list:** This section lists information about active processes including their PID, user, priority, nice value, memory and CPU usage, and command name.

An example output of the top command:

```
top - 15:30:01 up  1:23,  2 users,  load average: 0.15, 0.10, 0.12
Tasks: 120 total,   1 running, 119 sleeping,   0 stopped,   0 zombie
%Cpu(s):  2.1 us,  0.7 sy,  0.0 ni, 97.0 id,  0.1 wa,  0.0 hi,  0.1 si,  0.0 st
KiB Mem :  2048000 total,   753000 free,   396000 used,   897000 buff/cache
KiB Swap:  1024000 total,   100000 free,   924000 used.  1200000 avail Mem

  PID USER      PR  NI    VIRT    RES    SHR S  %CPU %MEM     TIME+ COMMAND
 1452 root      20   0  161200  10000   4400 S   0.7  0.5   0:00.42 apache2
 1204 john      20   0  130400   8000   3200 S   0.3  0.4   0:00.15 gnome-term+
 1025 root      19  -1  157000   9000   4000 S   0.3  0.4   0:00.36 systemd-journald
```

The top command provides several interactive commands to sort and filter the process list. Some useful commands include:

- M - Sort processes by memory usage.
- P - Sort processes by CPU usage.
- T - Sort processes by running time.
- k - Kill a process by entering its PID.

Modern systems offer a more user-friendly alternative to top, called htop. To install htop, use the following command depending on your Linux distribution:

```
$ sudo apt-get install htop # For Debian-based systems
$ sudo yum install htop # For RedHat-based systems
$ sudo dnf install htop # For Fedora
$ sudo pacman -S htop # For Arch Linux
```

To launch htop, simply type:

```
$ htop
```

The htop interface is more intuitive and colorful compared to top. It provides an enhanced visual representation of system performance metrics. The primary differences between top and htop are:

- **Visual representation:** htop uses color-coded bars to represent CPU, memory, and swap usage.
- **User interface:** htop offers a more interactive text-mode interface with support for mouse interactions.

- **Features:** htop includes advanced features such as process tree visualization, easy process management (using function keys), and customizable display options.

A typical htop screen includes:

- **Header:** Displays a summary of the system's CPU, memory, and swap usage using visually appealing bars.
- **Process list:** Lists detailed information about running processes similar to top, but in a format that is easier to navigate and manage.

An example of htop in action:

```
1  [|||||||||||||           27.0%]   Tasks: 120, 1 running
2  [|||||||||||||           27.0%]   Load average: 0.15 0.10 0.12
Mem[||||||||         2048000/2048000]   Uptime: 01:23:00
Swp[||||              100000/1024000]

PID USER      PRI  NI  VIRT    RES   SHR S CPU% MEM%   TIME+  Command
1452 root      20   0 161200 10000  4400 S  0.7  0.5 0:00.42 apache2
1204 john      20   0 130400  8000  3200 S  0.3  0.4 0:00.15 gnome-terminal
1025 root      19  -1 157000  9000  4000 S  0.3  0.4 0:00.36 systemd-journald
```

Key bindings in htop include:

- F2 - Setup: Customize the htop interface, including columns, meters, and colors.
- F3 - Search: Locate a process by name.
- F4 - Filter: Filter processes by criteria.
- F5 - Tree: Toggle the process tree view.
- F6 - Sort: Change sorting order (by CPU, memory, etc.).
- F9 - Kill: Send a signal to a process to terminate it.
- F10 - Quit: Exit htop.

Both top and htop are essential tools for Linux administrators and power users. They provide vital real-time insights into system performance and process management, enabling the timely identification and resolution of performance bottlenecks. By utilizing these tools, users maintain system stability and efficiency, ensuring smooth and optimal operation.

8.4 CPU Usage and Performance Monitoring

Effective CPU usage and performance monitoring is crucial for maintaining the efficiency and reliability of a Linux-based system. Understanding how to monitor CPU metrics allows system administrators to diagnose performance issues, optimize resource allocation, and ensure that applications run smoothly.

The primary tools for monitoring CPU usage in Linux are top, htop, mpstat, and the /proc/stat file. Each of these tools provides important insights into CPU activity, such as the percentage of CPU usage, the load average, and context switching.

Using top for CPU Monitoring

The top command is a widely-used tool for real-time system monitoring. It provides a dynamic view of system processes, CPU usage, memory usage, and other critical metrics. To start top, simply open a terminal and type:

```
top
```

Once top is running, the display is updated continuously, showing the current status of the system. The CPU usage information is displayed at the top of the interface and includes:

- us: Time spent on user space processes.
- sy: Time spent on kernel space (system) processes.
- ni: Time spent on processes with altered priority (nice value).
- id: Idle time.
- wa: Time spent waiting for I/O to complete.
- hi: Time spent handling hardware interrupts.
- si: Time spent handling software interrupts.
- st: Time stolen from a virtual machine.

The following example shows the CPU usage section of the top command's output:

```
%Cpu(s):  8.8 us,  2.2 sy,  0.0 ni, 88.0 id,  1.0 wa,  0.0 hi,  0.0 si,  0.0 st
```

This output indicates that 8.8% of the CPU time is spent on user processes, 2.2% on system processes, and 88.0% of the time the CPU is idle.

Using htop for Enhanced CPU Monitoring

htop is an interactive process viewer for Unix systems and a more user-friendly and visually appealing alternative to top. It provides a color-coded representation of CPU usage, making it easier to identify which processes consume the most CPU resources. To install htop, use the following command:

```
sudo apt-get install htop
```

Run htop by executing:

```
htop
```

In htop, the CPU usage is represented by a bar graph at the top of the interface, with different colors indicating user processes, system processes, and idle time. Press F6 to sort the columns, and use arrow keys to navigate.

Monitoring CPU Usage with mpstat

The mpstat command, part of the sysstat package, provides an aggregated and detailed report of CPU utilization across all categories. To install sysstat, use the command:

```
sudo apt-get install sysstat
```

Run mpstat with:

```
mpstat
```

This will give a detailed summary of CPU activity, as shown in the sample output below:

```
Linux 5.4.0-65-generic (hostname)   02/15/2022   _x86_64_   (4 CPU)

11:20:53 AM  CPU   %usr   %nice   %sys  %iowait   %irq  %softirq  %steal   %idle
11:20:53 AM  all   5.45    0.00   2.10     0.62   0.00      0.20    0.00   91.63
```

This detailed breakdown includes user processing time (%usr), system time (%sys), I/O wait time (%iowait), and idle time (%idle), among other metrics.

Reading CPU Data from /proc/stat

The /proc/stat file contains various statistics about the system since it was last booted. This file can be read using standard text-processing tools like cat or less. The command to view this file is:

```
cat /proc/stat
```

The CPU information is presented in this format:

```
cpu  3357 0 4313 1362393 0 0 0 0 0 0
cpu0 1136 0 1405 340745 0 0 0 0 0 0
cpu1 1057 0 1411 341155 0 0 0 0 0 0
cpu2 666 0 789 339404 0 0 0 0 0 0
cpu3 497 0 707 340087 0 0 0 0 0 0
```

The columns represent total cumulative CPU time categorized as user mode, user mode with nice priority, system mode, idle task, I/O wait, hardware interrupts, software interrupts, and so forth. Each of these fields is expressed in units of jiffies (a unit of time defined by the kernel).

Monitoring CPU usage effectively using these tools enables system administrators to ensure optimal system performance, identify and rectify issues promptly, and make informed decisions regarding resource allocation and potential system upgrades.

8.5 Memory Usage and Performance Monitoring

Monitoring memory usage is crucial for maintaining optimal performance in a Linux system. Inefficient memory utilization can lead to performance degradation, slow application response times, and even system crashes. Understanding how to measure and analyze memory consumption helps in identifying potential issues and taking appropriate corrective actions.

One of the primary tools for examining memory usage in Linux is the free command. The free command provides an overview of the system's memory usage, displaying details about total, used, free, shared, buffer, and cache memory. Here is an example of how to use free:

```
free -h
```

The -h flag stands for "human-readable" and prints sizes in powers of 1024 (e.g., KiB, MiB, GiB). A typical output might look like this:

```
        total   used   free   shared  buff/cache  available
Mem:     3.8G   1.2G   548M     320M        2.1G       2.1G
Swap:    2.0G     0B   2.0G
```

In the output: - total shows the total installed memory. - used indicates the amount of memory utilized. - free denotes the unutilized memory. - shared represents memory used by the tmpfs (shared memory). - buff/cache combines memory used by kernel buffers and the page cache. - available forecasts how much memory is available for new processes.

For a more dynamic real-time view of memory usage, the vmstat command can be employed. The vmstat (virtual memory statistics) provides details about system processes, memory, paging, block IO, traps, and CPU activity. Here is an example command:

```
vmstat 1 5
```

The above line will run vmstat every second (1) for a total of five iterations (5). An example output is provided below:

```
procs -----------memory---------- ---swap-- -----io---- -system-- ------cpu-----
 r  b   swpd   free   buff  cache   si   so    bi    bo   in   cs us sy id wa st
 2  0      0 548000 420000 1480000    0    0     1     1  200  400 30  5 65  0  0
 1  0      0 548000 420000 1480000    0    0     0     2  200  400 30  5 65  0  0
 0  0      0 548000 420000 1480000    0    0     0     1  195  398 28  5 67  0  0
 0  0      0 548000 420000 1480000    0    0     0     0  190  410 27  5 68  0  0
 1  0      0 548000 420000 1480000    0    0     0     2  210  405 31  6 63  0  0
```

In vmstat's output, the memory-related columns provide the following information: - swpd shows the amount of virtual memory used. - free indicates the amount of idle memory. - buff includes memory used as buffers. - cache comprises memory used as cache.

Additionally, top and its more user-friendly cousin, htop, are indispensable tools for real-time monitoring of system performance, including memory usage. Running top provides a continuously updated listing of system processes with key metrics, including memory consumption:

```
top
```

The core metrics related to memory in top include: - %MEM: Indicates the percentage of physical memory used by each process. - RES: Represents the resident size of each process's memory. - SHR: Stands for shared memory size.

htop enhances top by offering color-coded output and an easier-to-navigate interface. It can be invoked simply by:

```
htop
```

In the htop interface, one can sort processes by memory usage by pressing F6 and selecting the %MEM column. This allows for the identification of memory-hogging processes swiftly.

To delve deeper into memory usage per process, the pmap command is useful for displaying the memory map of a process. The general syntax is:

```
pmap PID
```

For instance, investigating the memory usage of a process with a PID of 1234 would yield:

```
pmap 1234
```

The output will include detailed information about memory regions associated with the given process.

Another critical tool is smem, which provides more detailed memory usage reports classified by processes and users. The tool is not installed by default but can be added via standard package management systems, e.g., apt for Debian-based distributions:

```
sudo apt-get install smem
```

Once installed, running smem offers a comprehensive summary:

```
smem
```

A typical output includes: - PID: Process ID. - User: User owning the process. - USS: Unique Set Size (memory unique to that process). - PSS: Proportional Set Size (memory shared with other processes, distributed). - RSS: Resident Set Size (physical memory).

Analyzing these reports helps in recognizing memory-intensive applications and making informed decisions regarding resource allocation.

Swap usage monitoring is an integral part of memory management. Swap space acts as an overflow area for physical memory, allowing for the continuation of process execution when RAM is exhausted. Excessive reliance on swap space can be an indicator of inadequate physical memory. The swapon command displays swap utilization details:

```
swapon --show
```

A sample output might look like this:

```
NAME      TYPE    SIZE USED PRIO
/swapfile file    2G   0B   -2
```

Comprehensive understanding of these tools and interpreting their outputs are essential for effective memory performance monitoring. This knowledge applies to debugging performance issues, optimizing applications, and ensuring overall system stability and efficiency.

8.6 Disk Usage and I/O Monitoring

Monitoring disk usage and I/O performance is a critical aspect of system administration in Linux, as it directly affects the system's performance and responsiveness. This section delves into various tools and techniques available for monitoring disk usage and I/O activities on Linux systems. Accurate monitoring helps in identifying potential bottlenecks and ensures optimal performance.

Disk usage can be monitored using tools like df, du, and lsblk, while I/O performance can be analyzed using iostat, iotop, dstat, and blktrace. We will explore the usage of these tools with practical examples.

df - Disk Free

The df command displays the amount of disk space used and available on Linux file systems. It reports file system disk space usage, giving an overview of the total disk space, used space, free space, and the filesystem where each percentage reflects the disk utilization.

```
$ df -h
```

The -h option provides the output in human-readable format:

```
Filesystem      Size  Used Avail Use% Mounted on
/dev/sda1        50G   20G   28G  42% /
udev            3.9G     0  3.9G   0% /dev
tmpfs           799M  1.1M  798M   1% /run
```

du - Disk Usage

The du command estimates file space usage. It reports the disk space used by files and directories, which can be useful for identifying large files and directories consuming significant disk space.

To display the disk usage of a specific directory in human-readable format:

```
$ du -sh /path/to/directory
```

Where:

```
/path/to/directory    2.3G
```

lsblk - List Block Devices

The lsblk command lists information about all available or specified block devices, providing a comprehensive view of the disk structure. It is helpful for understanding disk partitions and their utilization.

```
$ lsblk
```

This command outputs:

```
NAME   MAJ:MIN RM  SIZE RO TYPE MOUNTPOINT
sda      8:0    0   50G  0 disk
 sda1    8:1    0   50G  0 part /
sdb      8:16   0  100G  0 disk
 sdb1    8:17   0  100G  0 part /mnt/data
```

iostat - Input/Output Statistics

The iostat command is part of the sysstat package and provides detailed I/O statistics for devices and partitions. It is useful for monitoring system I/O performance.

To install sysstat:

```
$ sudo apt-get install sysstat
```

Invoke iostat as follows:

```
$ iostat -x 1 10
```

The -x flag provides extended statistics. The intervals specified ('1 10') output the statistics every second for 10 seconds:

```
Device    r/s   w/s   rkB/s  wkB/s avgrq-sz avgqu-sz  await r_await w_await  svctm %util
sda       0.00  1.00  0.00   4.00   8.00    0.02   20.00   0.00  20.00   20.00  2.00
```

iotop - I/O Top

iotop is a top-like utility for monitoring disk and swap I/O usage by processes. Ensure the kernel is configured with TASK_IO_ACCT and TASK_STATS.

Install iotop:

```
$ sudo apt-get install iotop
```

Run iotop:

```
$ sudo iotop
```

Example output:

```
Total DISK READ :      0.00 B/s | Total DISK WRITE :      0.00 B/s
Actual DISK READ:      0.00 B/s | Actual DISK WRITE:      0.00 B/s
  PID  PRIO  USER    DISK READ  DISK WRITE  SWAPIN     IO>    COMMAND
 1837 be/4 root      0.00 B/s    0.00 B/s  0.00 %  0.01 %  [kworker/0:1H]
```

dstat - Versatile Resource Statistics

dstat combines the functionality of iostat, vmstat, netstat, and others, giving comprehensive real-time system resource statistics.

Install dstat:

```
$ sudo apt-get install dstat
```

To display disk metrics:

```
$ dstat -d
```

Example output:

```
----total-usage----
 read  writ
  12k   595B
  201k  881k
```

Running Blktrace and Btt for I/O Analysis

blktrace traces block I/O on Linux and is suitable for in-depth analysis of I/O patterns. btt interprets blktrace output to produce summarised data.

Install blktrace:

```
$ sudo apt-get install blktrace
```

Run a trace on a device:

```
$ sudo blktrace -d /dev/sda -o - | blkparse -i -
```

Example (partial) output:

```
8,0   1   1   0.000000001  929  Q  R 12345 + 8 [fio]
8,0   1   2   0.001000001  929  G  R
```

To summarize blktrace captures with btt:

```
$ sudo blktrace -d /dev/sda -o - | blkparse -i - -d trace.dat
$ btt -i trace.dat
```

btt then produces a summary, highlighting time spent in queues, seeks, etc.

Comprehensive disk monitoring assists in maintaining the system's health, proactively diagnosing issues, and ensuring optimal performance. Efficient use of df, du, lsblk, iostat, iotop, dstat, and blktrace can significantly aid in achieving these objectives.

8.7 Network Monitoring and Traffic Analysis

Effective network monitoring and traffic analysis are crucial for maintaining the reliability and security of a Linux system. This section delves into the tools and techniques available for analyzing network performance, identifying bottlenecks, and troubleshooting issues.

1. Introduction to Network Monitoring Tools

Several tools are available for network monitoring and traffic analysis in Linux, each providing unique functionalities. Notable tools include ifconfig, ip, netstat, ss, tcpdump, wireshark, and iftop. Each tool serves a distinct purpose, ranging from basic interface monitoring to complex packet analysis.

2. Monitoring Network Interfaces with ifconfig and ip

The ifconfig command is one of the fundamental tools for monitoring and configuring network interfaces. Though it has been largely replaced by the ip command from the iproute2 package, understanding its usage is still valuable.

```
# Display all network interfaces and their status
ifconfig -a

# Enable or disable a network interface
ifconfig eth0 up
ifconfig eth0 down
```

The ip command offers more functionalities and is currently the preferred tool for network interface management:

```
# Display network interfaces
ip addr show

# Bring an interface up or down
ip link set eth0 up
ip link set eth0 down

# Display route information
ip route show
```

3. Analyzing Network Connections with netstat and ss

The netstat command provides detailed information about network connections, routing tables, interface statistics, masquerade connections, and multicast memberships.

```
# Display all active connections
netstat -a

# Display network interface statistics
```

```
netstat -i

# Display routing table information
netstat -r
```

The ss command, part of the iproute2 package, is a modern replacement for netstat and offers more detailed and faster performance.

```
# Display all socket connections
ss -a

# Display TCP connections
ss -t

# Display UDP connections
ss -u
```

4. Packet Capture and Analysis with tcpdump **and** wireshark

tcpdump is a powerful command-line packet analyzer that allows users to capture and display network packets. It is an invaluable tool for diagnosing network issues.

```
# Capture packets on interface eth0
tcpdump -i eth0

# Capture only TCP packets
tcpdump -i eth0 tcp

# Save captured packets to a file
tcpdump -i eth0 -w capture.pcap
```

wireshark is a graphical network protocol analyzer that offers extensive filtering and deep inspection of hundreds of protocols.

```
# Start Wireshark from the command line
wireshark
```

5. Bandwidth Monitoring with iftop

iftop provides a real-time view of network bandwidth usage on an interface. It is particularly useful for identifying bandwidth hogs.

```
# Monitor bandwidth usage on eth0
iftop -i eth0
```

6. Practical Example: Debugging Network Issues

Consider a scenario where a server is experiencing slow network performance. Using the aforementioned tools, we can systematically identify the problem.

1. Check network interfaces and ensure they are up.

```
ip link show
```

2. Monitor real-time traffic to identify any unusual patterns or high bandwidth usage.

```
iftop -i eth0
```

3. Capture packets to analyze the type of traffic and identify any anomalies.

```
tcpdump -i eth0 -w traffic_analysis.pcap
```

4. Open the captured packets in wireshark for detailed analysis.

```
wireshark traffic_analysis.pcap
```

These steps collectively help in diagnosing the network issue by providing insights into interface status, bandwidth usage, and detailed packet-level information.

By utilizing these tools and techniques, Linux administrators can ensure optimal network performance and quickly address any network-related problems that may arise.

8.8 Using vmstat, iostat, and netstat

Monitoring system performance in Linux often involves utilizing specialized tools that provide detailed insights into various subsystems. Three of these essential tools are vmstat, iostat, and netstat. These utilities offer valuable metrics concerning virtual memory, I/O systems, and network statistics, respectively. Utilizing these tools can significantly aid in identifying performance issues and understanding the overall system behavior.

vmstat (Virtual Memory Statistics) provides information about system processes, memory, paging, block I/O, traps, and CPU activity. The command offers a snapshot of the performance metrics, which can be captured over specific intervals, making it useful for diagnosing intermittent performance problems.

To run vmstat, use the following command:

```
vmstat [options] [delay [count]]
```

where delay is the amount of time in seconds between updates, and count specifies the number of updates. For example, to display performance data every 2 seconds for 5 intervals, execute:

```
vmstat 2 5
```

The output provides several columns of information:

```
procs -----------memory---------- ---swap-- -----io---- -system-- ----cpu----
 r  b   swpd   free   buff  cache   si   so    bi    bo   in   cs us sy id wa st
 2  0      0 162228  45172 635216    0    0     4     9   27   30  3  1 96  0  0
```

- **procs**: Indicates the number of processes (r for runnable, b for in uninterruptible sleep).
- **memory**: Shows memory usage (swpd for swapped memory, free for free memory, buff for buffer memory, cache for cached memory).
- **swap**: Displays swap activity (si for swap in, so for swap out).
- **io**: Provides block I/O (bi for blocks received, bo for blocks sent).
- **system**: Details system activities (in for interrupts per second, cs for context switches per second).
- **cpu**: Monitors CPU activity (us for user time, sy for system time, id for idle time, wa for wait time, st for stolen time from a virtual machine).

iostat (I/O Statistics) reports on CPU statistics and input/output statistics for devices and partitions. It helps in determining I/O performance issues and identifying disks that may be experiencing bottlenecks.

To execute iostat, use:

```
iostat [options] [delay [count]]
```

For example, to get I/O statistics every 2 seconds for 3 intervals, use:

```
iostat 2 3
```

The output usually comprises CPU, device, and partition level metrics:

```
Linux 5.4.0-42-generic (hostname)     09/17/2023     _x86_64_     (4 CPU)

avg-cpu:  %user   %nice %system %iowait  %steal   %idle
           3.20    0.00    1.07    0.30    0.00   95.43

Device:            tps    kB_read/s    kB_wrtn/s    kB_read    kB_wrtn
sda               1.11        11.00        24.00      22000      48000
```

- **avg-cpu**: Indicates average CPU load (percentage of user, nice, system, iowait, steal, and idle times).
- **Device**: Shows device level statistics (tps for transactions per second, kB_read/s for kilobytes read per second, kB_wrtn/s for kilobytes written per second, kB_read for total kilobytes read, and kB_wrtn for total kilobytes written).

netstat (Network Statistics) is a versatile tool that provides various network metrics. It reports on network connections, routing tables, interface statistics, masquerade connections, and multicast memberships.

To use netstat, the general command syntax is:

```
netstat [options]
```

Some commonly used options include:

- -a: Displays all sockets (including listening ones).
- -t: Shows TCP connections.
- -u: Displays UDP connections.
- -n: Shows numerical addresses instead of resolving hostnames.
- -p: Displays the process ID and name of the program to which each socket belongs.
- -r: Prints the routing table.

For instance, to display all active TCP connections in numeric form, execute:

```
netstat -tn
```

Example output might look like:

```
Proto Recv-Q Send-Q Local Address           Foreign Address         State
tcp        0      0 192.168.1.5:22          192.168.1.2:51122       ESTABLISHED
tcp        0      0 127.0.0.1:631           0.0.0.0:*               LISTEN
```

This output indicates:

- **Proto**: The protocol used (TCP in this case).
- **Recv-Q** and **Send-Q**: Receive and send queues.

- **Local Address** and **Foreign Address**: Local and remote endpoints of the connection.
- **State**: The state of the connection (e.g., ESTABLISHED, LISTEN).

Using vmstat, iostat, and netstat, administrators can gather comprehensive data on system performance across different subsystems, which aids in thorough system analysis and troubleshooting. These tools, when used effectively, can help in maintaining optimal system performance and preemptively addressing potential issues.

8.9 Monitoring Processes and System Services

Monitoring processes and system services is crucial for maintaining the health and performance of a Linux system. Correctly identifying resource-hungry processes and failing services leads to prompt interventions that ensure system stability and efficiency. This section provides a comprehensive guide to various Linux commands and tools that facilitate effective monitoring of processes and services.

ps Command

The ‘ps‘ command is one of the oldest and most frequently used commands for process monitoring. It provides a snapshot of the current processes.

```
ps aux
```

The flags used are:

- **a**: Shows all users’ processes.
- **u**: Displays user-oriented format.
- **x**: Shows processes not attached to a terminal.

The output presents a wide range of information, including user, PID, CPU usage, memory usage, command, and more.

top Command

The ‘top‘ command goes beyond ‘ps‘ by providing a dynamic, real-time view of the running processes.

```
top
```

The default display updates every few seconds, showing processes sorted by CPU usage. Users can sort by other criteria, like memory usage, by pressing the appropriate keys (e.g., 'M' for memory).

htop Command

'htop' is an enhanced version of 'top', offering an interactive interface and better visualization. It allows users to scroll through the process list horizontally and vertically, and to perform actions such as killing processes without retrying the PID manually.

To install 'htop':

```
sudo apt-get install htop
```

To run 'htop', simply type:

```
htop
```

pidstat Command

The 'pidstat' command from the sysstat package is useful for monitoring individual processes and their usage of system resources over time.

To install sysstat:

```
sudo apt-get install sysstat
```

To use 'pidstat' to monitor CPU usage per process:

```
pidstat -u
```

Users can also monitor other metrics like I/O and memory usage with appropriate flags (e.g., '-d' for disk usage, '-r' for memory usage).

systemd and systemctl

Systemd is the modern system management daemon for initializing the system and managing services. The 'systemctl' command is used to introspect and control the state of the systemd system and service manager.

To list all active services:

```
systemctl list-units --type=service
```

Each service's status can be checked individually:

```
systemctl status <service-name>
```

Using 'systemctl', users can start, stop, restart, and reload services, facilitating granular control.

To restart Apache service:

```
sudo systemctl restart apache2
```

journalctl Command

'journalctl' is used for querying and displaying logs from journald, including logs from system services managed by systemd.

To view the logs of a specific service, such as 'apache2':

```
journalctl -u apache2
```

Logs can be filtered by time range or priority, providing detailed insights for troubleshooting.

netstat Command

While primarily a network monitoring tool, 'netstat' is invaluable for identifying services listening on network ports, helping monitor and debug networked services.

To display all listening services:

```
netstat -tuln
```

Here, '-tuln' stands for displaying TCP ('t') and UDP ('u') ports in listening ('l') state without resolving names ('n').

pgrep and pkill Commands

'pgrep' and 'pkill' are useful for finding and managing processes based on name and other attributes.

To find the PID of the 'sshd' service:

```
pgrep sshd
```

To kill all processes linked to an unidentified memory leak issue:

```
pkill -f unknown_memory_issue_script.sh
```

Accurate use of 'pgrep' and 'pkill' can empower users to automate many routine tasks.

These tools and commands, when utilized correctly, provide a solid foundation for effective monitoring and management of processes and services in a Linux system. Detailed output interpretation through command line interfaces enables users to preemptively address issues before they escalate, ensuring the system remains stable and performs optimally.

8.10 Identifying and Resolving Performance Bottlenecks

A critical aspect of managing Linux systems involves effectively identifying and resolving performance bottlenecks. Performance bottlenecks can arise from various subsystems, including CPU, memory, disk I/O, and network. This section provides a comprehensive guide on diagnosing and addressing these bottlenecks to ensure optimal system performance.

The process of identifying and resolving performance bottlenecks entails a methodological approach that includes monitoring the system, isolating the problematic component, analyzing the root cause, and implementing corrective actions. Below are detailed steps and commands used in this approach:

- **Monitor System Performance:** Utilize real-time tools such as top, htop, and atop. These tools provide a high-level overview of system resource usage and help quickly identify which subsystem is under stress.

```
top
htop
atop
```

```
top - 15:33:44 up 10 days,  8:20,  3 users,  load average: 0.00, 0.01, 0.05
Tasks: 213 total,   1 running, 212 sleeping,   0 stopped,   0 zombie
%Cpu(s):  1.0 us,  0.2 sy,  0.0 ni, 98.7 id,  0.0 wa,  0.0 hi,  0.1 si,  0.0 st
KiB Mem : 16436520 total,  2343456 free,  9452340 used,  4650124 buff/cache
KiB Swap:  8191996 total,  8191996 free,        0 used.  5571232 avail Mem
```

- **Isolate the Problematic Subsystem:** By analyzing tool output, you can often determine whether the bottleneck is CPU, memory, disk I/O, or network related.

- **CPU Bottlenecks:**

  - High system load average in top or htop.
  - A high number of processes in the 'R' (running) or 'D' (waiting for I/O) state.

To delve deeper into CPU performance, use the mpstat command which breaks down CPU usage by core.

```
mpstat -P ALL 1
```

```
11:58:56 AM  CPU   %usr   %nice   %sys  %iowait  %irq   %soft  %steal  %guest  %gnice  %idle
11:58:57 AM  all   4.00   0.00   1.00   0.00    0.00   0.00   0.00    0.00   95.00
11:58:57 AM    0   4.00   0.00   2.00   0.00    0.00   0.00   0.00    0.00   94.00
11:58:57 AM    1   5.00   0.00   2.00   0.00    0.00   0.00   0.00    0.00   93.00
```

- **Memory Bottlenecks:**
  - High memory usage reported by free or vmstat.
  - Excessive swapping, which can be indicative of insufficient physical memory.

Commands to check for memory usage:

```
free -m
vmstat 1
```

```
          total    used    free   shared  buff/cache  available
Mem:      16000   12543     340      200        3117       3024
Swap:      8191       0    8191
```

Look for high values in the 'si' (swap in) and 'so' (swap out) columns from the vmstat output.

- **Disk I/O Bottlenecks:**
  - High I/O wait time (> 10
  - Slow application response times during read/write operations.

Using iostat to analyze I/O performance:

```
iostat -dx 1
```

```
Device:  rrqm/s  wrqm/s  r/s   w/s   rkB/s  wkB/s  avgrq-sz avgqu-sz await r_await w_await svctm %util
sda       0.00    0.00   2.00  3.00  8.00   12.00   6.67     0.02    5.00   2.00    7.00   1.00  0.50
```

- **Network Bottlenecks:**
  - High network utilization reported by ifstat, netstat, or sar.

  - Packet drops or errors.

Using netstat to monitor network statistics:

```
netstat -i
```

```
Kernel Interface table
Iface     MTU   RX-OK RX-ERR RX-DRP RX-OVR    TX-OK TX-ERR TX-DRP TX-OVR Flg
eth0      1500 2643714     0      0 0     1234567      0      0      0 BMRU
```

Once the subsystem causing the bottleneck is identified, take corrective measures:

- **CPU Bottleneck Resolutions:**
  - Optimize or upgrade application code to reduce CPU usage.
  - Load balance across multiple processors or systems.
  - Upgrade CPU hardware (increase core count or CPU speed).
- **Memory Bottleneck Resolutions:**
  - Increase physical RAM.
  - Optimize memory usage within applications.
  - Tune kernel parameters to efficiently manage memory.
- **Disk I/O Bottleneck Resolutions:**
  - Use faster disks or SSDs.
  - Distribute disk I/O across multiple disks or RAID arrays.
  - Optimize file system and application access patterns.
- **Network Bottleneck Resolutions:**
  - Upgrade network hardware (higher bandwidth NICs, switches).
  - Optimize network configuration and application data handling.
  - Use traffic shaping or Quality of Service (QoS) policies.

These systematic steps and commands allow administrators to identify and resolve performance bottlenecks, maximizing the efficiency of their Linux systems.

8.11 Setting Up and Using System Monitoring Tools: Nagios, Zabbix, etc.

In this section, we will explore the setup and use of advanced system monitoring tools with a focus on Nagios and Zabbix. These tools provide comprehensive monitoring capabilities and are essential for maintaining system reliability and efficiency. Understanding their configuration and deployment will enable effective monitoring of system resources and timely alerting for potential issues.

Nagios is a powerful open-source monitoring system that enables administrators to identify and resolve IT infrastructure problems. To begin, ensure that you have a Linux environment ready to install Nagios, preferably a clean server. The following steps detail the installation and setup process for Nagios on a CentOS system, but the methodology is similar across different distributions.

Step 1: Install Required Packages

To start, install the necessary prerequisites and dependencies:

```
sudo yum install httpd php gcc glibc glibc-common gd gd-devel make net-snmp
```

Step 2: Create Nagios User and Group

Create a user and group for running Nagios:

```
sudo useradd nagios
sudo groupadd nagcmd
sudo usermod -a -G nagcmd nagios
```

Step 3: Download and Install Nagios Core

Download the latest Nagios Core package and extract it:

```
cd /tmp
wget https://assets.nagios.com/downloads/nagioscore/releases/nagios-<version>.tar.gz
tar xzf nagios-<version>.tar.gz
cd nagios-<version>
```

Compile and install Nagios:

```
./configure --with-command-group=nagcmd
make all
sudo make install
sudo make install-init
sudo make install-commandmode
sudo make install-config
```

Step 4: Install Nagios Plugins

Nagios plugins provide the various checks that Nagios performs:

```
cd /tmp
wget https://nagios-plugins.org/download/nagios-plugins-<version>.tar.gz
tar xzf nagios-plugins-<version>.tar.gz
cd nagios-plugins-<version>
./configure --with-nagios-user=nagios --with-nagios-group=nagios
make
sudo make install
```

Step 5: Configure Nagios

Set up the Nagios configuration files. The primary configuration file is /usr/local/nagios/etc/nagios.cfg. By default, sample configuration files are provided:

```
sudo cp /usr/local/nagios/etc/objects/contacts.cfg /usr/local/nagios/etc/objects/
    contacts.cfg.orig
sudo vi /usr/local/nagios/etc/objects/contacts.cfg
```

Edit the *email* address to receive notifications. Next, configure the Apache web server:

```
sudo make install-webconf
```

Create an Apache user for Nagios authentication:

```
sudo htpasswd -c /usr/local/nagios/etc/htpasswd.users nagiosadmin
```

Restart Apache and start Nagios:

```
sudo service httpd restart
sudo service nagios start
```

Now, navigate to http://server_ip/nagios and log in with the credentials created.

Zabbix Installation and Configuration

Zabbix is another powerful monitoring tool that provides similar functionalities with an intuitive web interface and robust monitoring capabilities.

Step 1: Install Zabbix Server and Web Interface

Add Zabbix repository and install the server:

```
rpm -Uvh https://repo.zabbix.com/zabbix/5.0/rhel/7/x86_64/zabbix-release-5.0-1.el7.
    noarch.rpm
yum clean all
sudo yum install zabbix-server-mysql zabbix-web-mysql zabbix-agent
```

Install the database and start database services:

```
sudo yum install mariadb-server
```

```
sudo service mariadb start
```

Secure the MariaDB installation and create the Zabbix database:

```
mysql -uroot -p
create database zabbix character set utf8 collate utf8_bin;
grant all privileges on zabbix.* to zabbix@localhost identified by 'password';
flush privileges;
exit;
```

Import the initial schema and data:

```
zcat /usr/share/doc/zabbix-server-mysql*/create.sql.gz | mysql -uzabbix -p zabbix
```

Edit Zabbix server configuration:

```
sudo vi /etc/zabbix/zabbix_server.conf
```

Set the database name, user, and password:

```
DBName=zabbix
DBUser=zabbix
DBPassword=password
```

Configure Apache for the Zabbix front end:

```
sudo vi /etc/httpd/conf.d/zabbix.conf
```

Uncomment the *php_value date.timezone* line and set your timezone. Restart the services to complete the installation:

```
sudo service zabbix-server start
sudo service zabbix-agent start
sudo service httpd restart
```

Access Zabbix at http://server_ip/zabbix and follow the setup instructions.

Both Nagios and Zabbix offer extensive capabilities for monitoring and alerting, aiding system administrators in maintaining optimal system performance and preemptively addressing potential issues. Through their detailed UIs and configuration options, they can be tailored to fit a wide range of monitoring requirements in diverse IT environments.

8.12 Automating Performance Monitoring and Alerts

Automating performance monitoring and alerts is a crucial aspect of maintaining system reliability and ensuring that any issues are promptly identified and addressed. This section discusses the principles and practices of automating these tasks using various tools and scripting techniques.

Automated monitoring involves the use of tools that continuously check the status of system components and applications. Alerts are notifications triggered when specific conditions are met, such as high CPU utilization or disk space running low. These alerts can be sent via email, SMS, or integrated into other communication channels like Slack.

Monitoring Tools

Modern monitoring tools offer extensive automation capabilities. Tools such as Nagios, Zabbix, and Prometheus provide flexible frameworks for defining performance thresholds and generating alerts.

Nagios

Nagios is a powerful monitoring system that enables organizations to identify and resolve IT infrastructure problems before they affect critical business processes.

```
# Example Nagios Service Definition
define service {
    use generic-service
    host_name server1
    service_description CPU Load
    check_command check_nrpe!check_load
    notifications_enabled 1
    contact_groups admins
}
```

In this snippet, the service checks the CPU load on server1 using the NRPE plugin. If the load exceeds predefined thresholds, an alert is sent to the administrators.

Zabbix

Zabbix provides sophisticated problem detection mechanisms and flexible notification options. A Zabbix item represents a piece of data to be monitored.

```
# Example Zabbix Item Configuration
zabbix_sender -z zabbix-server -s "server1" -k cpu.load -o 2.5
```

Here, zabbix_sender is used to manually test sending a CPU load metric to the Zabbix server.

Prometheus

Prometheus, often used in conjunction with Grafana for visualization, uses a time-series database and a sophisticated querying language (PromQL).

```
# Prometheus Alerting Rule Example
groups:
- name: example
  rules:
  - alert: HighCPUUsage
    expr: node_cpu_seconds_total{mode="idle"} < 20
    for: 5m
    labels:
      severity: critical
    annotations:
      summary: "High CPU usage detected"
```

This YAML configuration defines an alert for high CPU usage when idle CPU time falls below 20% for 5 minutes.

Notification Channels

Automated alerting requires reliable notification channels to promptly inform administrators of issues. Common channels include:

- **Email**: Standard method for delivering alerts.
- **SMS**: Provides immediate and direct notification.
- **Chat Integrations**: Tools like Slack and Microsoft Teams can be configured to receive alerts.

```
# Example Email Alert Command
echo "Subject: Alert: CPU Load High" | sendmail admin@example.com
```

Scripting for Automation

Shell scripting is a powerful way to automate monitoring tasks. Scripts can be scheduled using cron jobs to run periodically, checking system metrics and sending alerts as needed.

```
#!/bin/bash

# Check CPU Load
cpu_load=$(uptime | awk -F'[, ]+' '{print $(NF-2)}')

# Threshold for alerting
threshold=2.5

# Compare current load with threshold
if (( $(echo "$cpu_load > $threshold" |bc -l) )); then
    echo "CPU Load is high: $cpu_load" | mail -s "CPU Load Alert" admin@example.
        com
fi
```

This script fetches the current CPU load, compares it to a predefined threshold, and sends an email alert if the load is too high. It can be scheduled to run at regular intervals using cron:

```
# Cron job entry to run the script every 5 minutes
*/5 * * * * /path/to/cpu_load_check.sh
```

Centralized Logging and Alerting

Centralized logging tools like Elasticsearch, Logstash, and Kibana (ELK stack) play a significant role in automated monitoring and alerting. They aggregate logs from multiple sources, enabling comprehensive analysis and alert generation.

```
# Example Logstash Configuration for CPU Load Alerts
input {
  file {
    path => "/var/log/syslog"
  }
}

filter {
  if [message] =~ /CPU Load:/ {
    grok {
      match => { "message" => "CPU Load is high: %{NUMBER:cpu_load}" }
    }
    if [cpu_load] > 2.5 {
      mutate { add_field => { "alert" => "true" } }
    }
  }
}

output {
  if [alert] == "true" {
```

```
    email {
      to => "admin@example.com"
      subject => "High CPU Load Alert"
      body => "CPU Load is %{cpu_load}"
      via => "smtp"
      address => "smtp.example.com"
      port => 25
    }
  }
}
```

This Logstash configuration monitors /var/log/syslog for CPU load entries, checks if they exceed the threshold, and sends an email alert. The grok filter parses the log message. The mutate filter adds an alert field when the threshold is breached, which is then used to trigger the email output.

Automating performance monitoring and alerts involves setting up tools, defining appropriate monitoring expressions, and ensuring robust notification channels. By implementing these practices, administrators can effectively maintain system performance and prevent potential issues from escalating.

Chapter 9

Networking in Linux

This chapter provides a comprehensive overview of networking in Linux. It explains network interfaces and their configuration using tools like ifconfig and ip, as well as NetworkManager. The chapter covers setting up hostnames and DNS, managing network connections through the /etc/network/interfaces file, and configuring DHCP. It includes an introduction to firewalls using iptables and firewalld, network troubleshooting with tools such as ping, traceroute, and netcat, secure remote access with SSH, establishing SSL/TLS connections, and setting up and managing VPNs.

9.1 Introduction to Networking in Linux

In the dynamic realm of computing, networking is fundamental for communication between systems. Linux, being a versatile and widely-used operating system, offers robust networking capabilities. Its networking stack, including kernel features and user-space utilities, provides powerful tools for configuring and managing network connections, ensuring seamless communication across diverse network architectures.

Understanding the operational context and fundamental components of networking in Linux is critical. Linux networking encompasses both physical and logical elements. The physical side includes network interfaces, such as Ethernet cards, Wi-Fi adapters, and more specialized interfaces. Logical components involve networking protocols, IP addressing, routing mechanisms, and various configuration files.

Network Interfaces: These are the points of interaction through which Linux systems connect to networks. They can be classified into:

- *Physical Interfaces:* These include hardware components like Ethernet cards (eth0, eth1, etc.), Wi-Fi adapters (wlan0, wlan1, etc.), and more.
- *Virtual Interfaces:* These are software-defined interfaces. Examples include loopback interfaces (lo), bridge interfaces (br0), and virtual Ethernet interfaces (veth0).

Network Configuration: Configuring network settings in Linux involves manipulating various parameters, such as IP addresses, subnet masks, default gateways, DNS servers, and more. Tools like ifconfig and ip command facilitate this process.

An example of using the ifconfig command to assign an IP address and bring up a network interface is demonstrated below:

```
sudo ifconfig eth0 192.168.1.10 netmask 255.255.255.0 up
```

The ip command, which is part of the iproute2 package, provides extended capabilities over ifconfig. For instance, setting an IP address using the ip command can be done as follows:

```
sudo ip addr add 192.168.1.10/24 dev eth0
sudo ip link set eth0 up
```

NetworkManager: A more advanced utility, NetworkManager, provides dynamic and automatic configuration for both wired and wireless connections. It streamlines the process of network configuration, especially in environments where network parameters change frequently.

Hostnames and DNS: Systems on a network identify each other using hostnames, while the Domain Name System (DNS) translates these human-readable hostnames into IP addresses. Configuring /etc/hosts and /etc/resolv.conf files is integral to DNS resolution.

TCP/IP Protocol Suite: The cornerstone of network communications in Linux. It includes layers such as:

- *Link Layer:* Manages physical addressing and access to the transmission medium.
- *Internet Layer:* Responsible for logical addressing and routing through the IP protocol.

- *Transport Layer:* Ensures reliable data transmission using protocols like TCP and UDP.
- *Application Layer:* Facilitates network communication for applications, examples being HTTP and FTP.

The versatility of Linux networking is reflected in its ability to handle complex networking tasks, from simple IP address assignments to advanced firewall setups and virtual private networks (VPNs). Utilizing commands like ping for connectivity checks, traceroute for route path analysis, and netcat for debugging and testing network communication adds to the robustness of Linux networking.

Connectivity Testing with Ping: The ping command is indispensable for testing network connectivity:

```
ping 192.168.1.1
```

The output could appear as follows:

```
PING 192.168.1.1 (192.168.1.1) 56(84) bytes of data.
64 bytes from 192.168.1.1: icmp_seq=1 ttl=64 time=0.512 ms
64 bytes from 192.168.1.1: icmp_seq=2 ttl=64 time=0.607 ms
```

Networking in Linux also encompasses security elements like firewalls. Tools such as iptables and firewalld allow fine-grained traffic control, enhancing security by specifying rules for packet filtering, NAT, and more.

Understanding and leveraging these aspects, Linux users can effectively manage and secure their network environments, ensuring efficient and reliable communication across their systems.

9.2 Understanding Network Interfaces

Network interfaces are pivotal components in the Linux networking environment, functioning as the juncture where data packets transition between the host system and the network. Understanding these interfaces is essential for mastering Linux networking.

Network interfaces can be hardware-based or software-defined. Hardware interfaces include physical network adapters, such as Ethernet (e.g., ‘eth0‘, ‘eth1‘), Wi-Fi (e.g., ‘wlan0‘), and others. Software-defined interfaces, such as loopback (‘lo‘), bridge (‘br0‘), and virtual network interfaces (e.g., ‘tun0‘, ‘tap0‘), provide the flexibility to configure networking environments without requiring additional physical hardware.

To list all detected network interfaces, you can use:

```
ip link show
```

This command outputs information about each interface, including hardware address, state (up or down), and capabilities. For example:

```
1: lo: <LOOPBACK,UP,LOWER_UP> mtu 65536 qdisc noqueue state UNKNOWN mode DEFAULT group default qlen 1000
    link/loopback 00:00:00:00:00:00 brd 00:00:00:00:00:00
2: eth0: <BROADCAST,MULTICAST,UP,LOWER_UP> mtu 1500 qdisc pfifo_fast state UP mode DEFAULT group default qlen 1000
    link/ether 00:1b:21:bb:f9:dc brd ff:ff:ff:ff:ff:ff
```

To further comprehend network interfaces, one must acknowledge the structuring of the interface entries within '/proc/net/dev', which delineates communication statistics for each network interface. One can display the contents of this file using:

```
cat /proc/net/dev
```

This provides raw data, which can be parsed for various usage statistics, including bytes received and transmitted, packet errors, and more.

Configuring an interface involves two cardinal states: bringing the interface up or down. This operation can be managed using the 'ip' command. For instance, to activate an interface:

```
sudo ip link set eth0 up
```

And to deactivate:

```
sudo ip link set eth0 down
```

When detailing the configuration of an IP address to an interface, it's crucial to specify both IPv4 and IPv6 configurations. For IPv4:

```
sudo ip addr add 192.168.1.100/24 dev eth0
```

And for IPv6:

```
sudo ip -6 addr add 2001:db8::100/64 dev eth0
```

These commands statically assign IP addresses to the specified interface. Conversely, removing an assigned IP address can be executed with:

```
sudo ip addr del 192.168.1.100/24 dev eth0
```

Network interfaces' operational parameters go beyond simple addressing. They also include route specification, which directs traffic to appropriate network segments or gateways. This can be managed using the 'ip' route command, for instance:

```
sudo ip route add default via 192.168.1.1 dev eth0
```

This command sets the default route (gateway) for all outbound traffic when no specific routing path is defined.

Interface statistics and diagnostics are indispensable for network administration. ethtool enhances diagnostic capability by providing detailed statistics about the network interface card (NIC) and it can alter interface settings:

```
sudo ethtool eth0
```

Outputs detailed NIC statistics, including supported link modes, pause frame settings, and error counts.

Virtual network interfaces extend networking flexibility. For example, the 'tun' and 'tap' interfaces are widely used for VPNs and other virtual networking scenarios. Configuring these involves:

```
sudo ip tuntap add dev tun0 mode tun
sudo ip link set tun0 up
```

Bridges ('br0', 'br1', etc.) can aggregate multiple physical or virtual interfaces into a single logical interface, facilitating software-based network switches:

```
sudo brctl addbr br0
sudo brctl addif br0 eth0
sudo ip link set br0 up
```

This enables combining physical network interfaces (e.g., 'eth0') and virtual interfaces into one bridge for traffic management.

Loopback interfaces ('lo') are used for internal communication within the host, ensuring networked application compatibility even when disconnected from external networks. It is inherently configured and requires minimal administrative intervention:

```
1: lo: <LOOPBACK,UP,LOWER_UP> mtu 65536 qdisc noqueue state UNKNOWN mode DEFAULT group default qlen 1000
    link/loopback 00:00:00:00:00:00 brd 00:00:00:00:00:00
```

Understanding network interfaces necessitates proficiency in both the configuration commands and the underlying principles governing interface behavior and interactions. This knowledge is critical, forming the basis for advanced network management, troubleshooting, and performance tuning in Linux environments.

9.3 Configuring Network Interfaces with ifconfig and ip

Configuration of network interfaces is a critical task in Linux networking. Two prevalent tools for this purpose are ifconfig and ip. Although ifconfig has been traditionally used, it is now considered deprecated and replaced by the more powerful and flexible ip utility from the iproute2 suite. However, understanding both tools provides a comprehensive foundation in network interface management.

Using ifconfig

ifconfig is used for configuring, controlling, and querying TCP/IP network interface parameters.

```
sudo ifconfig
```

This command lists all the active network interfaces on the system. Each interface entry includes the interface name (e.g., eth0, lo), its MAC address (under ether), its assigned IP address (under inet), and various other data such as the MTU (Maximum Transmission Unit).

To configure an IP address for an interface:

```
sudo ifconfig eth0 192.168.1.10 netmask 255.255.255.0
```

This assigns the IP address 192.168.1.10 with a subnet mask of 255.255.255.0 to the interface eth0.

To bring an interface up or down:

```
sudo ifconfig eth0 up
sudo ifconfig eth0 down
```

The up command activates the interface, while down deactivates it. This is useful for resetting interfaces or when changes are made and need to be applied.

Using ip

The ip command is a versatile tool that not only handles configuration of network interfaces but also manages routes, ARP entries, and other network-related parameters. It provides more functionality than ifconfig and uses a different syntax.

To view all network interfaces and their configurations:

```
ip addr show
```

This command enumerates all network interfaces, their addresses, state (e.g., UP, DOWN), and additional parameters.

To assign an IP address to an interface:

```
sudo ip addr add 192.168.1.10/24 dev eth0
```

This assigns the IP address 192.168.1.10 with a prefix length of /24 (equivalent to the netmask 255.255.255.0) to the interface eth0.

To bring an interface up or down:

```
sudo ip link set eth0 up
sudo ip link set eth0 down
```

The link set command is used with the up or down argument to activate or deactivate the interface, respectively.

To delete an IP address from an interface:

```
sudo ip addr del 192.168.1.10/24 dev eth0
```

This command removes the specified IP address from the interface, which is necessary during reconfiguration or troubleshooting.

Comparative Analysis

Both tools provide fundamental capabilities for managing network interfaces but differ in scope and flexibility. While ifconfig is suitable for basic tasks and offers simplicity, ip provides robust features suitable for complex network scenarios. Given the enhanced capabilities and current usage trends, ip is the preferred tool for contemporary network management in Linux environments.

Practical use cases should consider the scenarios where each tool excels. For instance, ifconfig might be preferred in legacy systems or scripts, while ip is advantageous in modern systems with dynamic and advanced networking needs.

```
$ ip addr show dev eth0
3: eth0: <BROADCAST,MULTICAST,UP,LOWER_UP> mtu 1500 qdisc pfifo_fast state UP group default qlen 1000
    link/ether 00:15:5d:22:55:12 brd ff:ff:ff:ff:ff:ff
    inet 192.168.1.10/24 brd 192.168.1.255 scope global dynamic eth0
       valid_lft 86392sec preferred_lft 86392sec
    inet6 fe80::215:5dff:fe22:5512/64 scope link
       valid_lft forever preferred_lft forever
```

Specific fields, such as inet, link/ether, and scope, provide essential information about the interface status and configuration. One should interpret these fields to diagnose network issues or verify configurations.

Effective management of network interfaces necessitates a blend of knowledge across both ifconfig and ip utilities. Understanding the advantages and appropriate use cases for each can significantly enhance networking proficiency in Linux. This dual comprehension ensures adaptability across diverse scenarios and system environments.

9.4 Managing Network Connections with NetworkManager

NetworkManager is a powerful utility found in many Linux distributions, designed to simplify the process of managing network connections, both wired and wireless. It abstracts much of the complexity associated with network configuration, allowing users to easily switch between different network environments. NetworkManager is particularly useful for modern desktop environments and laptops, where it is necessary to switch between various networks frequently.

NetworkManager comprises two main components: the NetworkManager daemon (NetworkManager) and the graphical user interface (GUI) or command-line interface (CLI) tools used to interact with it. The daemon runs in the background, managing network connections and states, while the tools provided by NetworkManager offer user-friendly ways to configure and monitor network settings.

To utilize NetworkManager effectively, it is important to understand its core functionalities and how to operate it through different interfaces.

NetworkManager Command-Line Interface (CLI)

The most direct way to interact with NetworkManager is through its command-line tool, nmcli. This utility allows for configuration and monitoring of network connections and can be particularly useful for scripting and remote management scenarios.

Viewing Network Connections

To view all available network connections, use the following command:

```
nmcli connection show
```

This command lists all configured connections, displaying details such as the connection name, UUID, type, and device.

Bringing Up and Down Network Connections

To activate a network connection, use the command:

```
nmcli connection up <connection_name>
```

Conversely, to deactivate a network connection, the following command is used:

```
nmcli connection down <connection_name>
```

Creating a New Network Connection

Creating a new network connection can be accomplished using the nmcli tool. For example, to create a new Ethernet connection, execute:

```
nmcli connection add type ethernet ifname eth0 con-name my-eth-connection
```

This command specifies the connection type as Ethernet, assigns it to the interface eth0, and names the connection my-eth-connection.

Configuring a Wireless Network

Adding and configuring a wireless network connection involves specifying additional parameters such as the SSID and security settings. Below is an example command to connect to a WPA2-protected wireless network:

```
nmcli device wifi connect <SSID> password <password>
```

Replace <SSID> with the network's SSID and <password> with the network password.

Editing a Network Connection

To modify an existing network connection, use the command:

```
nmcli connection edit <connection_name>
```

This places you in an interactive mode where you can edit parameters of the specified connection. Use the help command within this mode to see a list of available editing commands.

Graphical User Interface (GUI) for NetworkManager

NetworkManager also provides a graphical interface, typically integrated into the system's desktop environment. Popular GUI tools for NetworkManager include nm-applet for GNOME and plasma-nm for KDE.

Accessing NetworkManager via GUI

In GNOME, the NetworkManager applet can usually be found in the system tray or top panel. Clicking on the applet icon opens a menu where you can see current connections, available networks, and network settings.

Connecting to a Network

To connect to a new network using the GUI, click on the NetworkManager icon and select the desired network from the list of available connections. For secured networks, you will be prompted to enter the necessary authentication details such as a password.

Managing Network Settings

Access the network settings through the same applet menu to manage advanced connection settings, such as configuring IP addresses (both static and DHCP), DNS servers, and proxy settings. This is often accessible via a menu option such as Edit Connections.

Adding and Editing Connections

The GUI provides straightforward options for adding and editing network connections. In GNOME, for example, navigate to Settings → Network and use the + button to add a new connection. Fill in the required details such as connection type, SSID, and security mode.

Editing an existing connection involves selecting the connection from the list and modifying its properties. This interface offers the same level of detail for network configuration as the nmcli command-line utility.

NetworkManager Service Management

NetworkManager operates as a system service managed by systemd. Common tasks include starting, stopping, and checking the status of the NetworkManager service.

Service Management Commands

To start the NetworkManager service, use:

```
sudo systemctl start NetworkManager
```

To stop the NetworkManager service:

```
sudo systemctl stop NetworkManager
```

To enable the NetworkManager service to start automatically at boot:

```
sudo systemctl enable NetworkManager
```

To check the current status of the NetworkManager service:

```
systemctl status NetworkManager
```

The output will include information about the state of the service and any active connections managed by NetworkManager.

Scripting with NetworkManager

For advanced users, scripting common network management tasks can be a significant time-saver. nmcli commands can be included in shell scripts to automate connection setup, monitoring, and troubleshooting.

Example Script

Consider the following example script to automate the connection to a specific wireless network:

```
#!/bin/bash

# Variables
SSID="MyNetwork"
PASSWORD="MyPassword"

# Connect to Wi-Fi
nmcli device wifi connect "${SSID}" password "${PASSWORD}"

# Check connection status
nmcli connection show --active
```

Save this script to a file, give it execute permissions with chmod +x <filename>, and run it to quickly connect to the specified wireless network and verify the active connections.

Incorporating NetworkManager into your network management toolkit can significantly enhance the efficiency and ease of managing Linux network connections, particularly in dynamic networking environments.

9.5 Setting Up Hostnames and DNS

Setting up hostnames and DNS (Domain Name System) in Linux is pivotal for identifying and accessing systems over a network. Hostnames provide human-readable names for devices, while DNS resolves these names to their corresponding IP addresses. Proper configuration of hostnames and DNS ensures seamless network communication and is fundamental for the stability and user-friendliness of networked systems.

Configuring Hostnames

A hostname is a unique identifier assigned to a device on a network. In Linux, setting or changing a hostname is straightforward and can be accomplished using the hostnamectl command or by editing specific file configurations.

To view the current hostname, execute the following command:

```
hostnamectl status
```

To set a new hostname, use:

```
sudo hostnamectl set-hostname new-hostname
```

Replace new-hostname with the desired hostname. This command updates the hostname immediately without requiring a system reboot.

Alternatively, you can directly edit the /etc/hostname file. Open it with a text editor, replace the existing hostname with the new one, and save the file:

```
sudo nano /etc/hostname
```

After modifying the /etc/hostname file, update the /etc/hosts file to ensure the system correctly maps the new hostname to its loopback address. Open /etc/hosts with a text editor:

```
sudo nano /etc/hosts
```

Locate the line associating the current hostname with 127.0.1.1 and update it to the new hostname:

```
127.0.0.1 localhost
127.0.1.1 new-hostname
```

This ensures the system's hostname resolution is consistent with the new settings.

Understanding DNS

DNS is a hierarchical and decentralized naming system used to resolve human-friendly domain names into IP addresses. Configuring DNS in Linux involves setting the DNS servers used by the system and ensuring correct DNS resolution.

DNS Configuration Files

The primary configuration file for DNS client settings in Linux is /etc/resolv.conf. This file contains a list of nameservers the system should query for DNS resolution. A typical /etc/resolv.conf might look like:

```
nameserver 8.8.8.8
nameserver 8.8.4.4
```

In this example, two Google public DNS servers are specified.

To manually configure DNS servers, edit the /etc/resolv.conf file with a text editor:

```
sudo nano /etc/resolv.conf
```

Make the necessary changes and save the file. Note that in some systems, NetworkManager or systemd-resolved may overwrite /etc/resolv.conf. To prevent this, you can set /etc/resolv.conf as immutable:

```
sudo chattr +i /etc/resolv.conf
```

Using NetworkManager for DNS Configuration

NetworkManager is a versatile tool for managing network settings, including DNS configurations. To set DNS servers using NetworkManager, modify the connection settings.

First, identify the connection name using:

```
nmcli connection show
```

Set the DNS servers for a specific connection:

```
sudo nmcli connection modify "connection-name" ipv4.dns "8.8.8.8 8.8.4.4"
```

Replace connection-name with the actual connection name.

Apply changes and restart the NetworkManager:

```
sudo nmcli connection down "connection-name" && sudo nmcli connection up "
    connection-name"
```

Testing DNS Configuration

To verify that DNS is correctly configured, use the nslookup or dig command. The nslookup command queries DNS and displays the results:

```
nslookup example.com
```

The dig command offers more detailed DNS query information:

```
dig example.com
```

The output should display the IP address associated with the queried domain, confirming successful DNS resolution.

Properly setting up hostnames and DNS in Linux ensures that network communications are reliable and devices can be identified and accessed efficiently. These steps are fundamental for network administrators and essential for maintaining a stable network environment.

9.6 Working with the /etc/network/interfaces File

The /etc/network/interfaces file is a fundamental component for network configuration on Debian-based Linux distributions such as Debian itself or Ubuntu. This configuration file allows system administrators to define network interfaces, specify IP addresses, gateways, and other pertinent details necessary for network communication. It is essential for scenarios where NetworkManager is not used or when one prefers a more hands-on approach to network configuration.

The file uses a straightforward syntax, composing of stanzas that define parameters for each network interface. These stanzas comprise keywords and values that dictate how each interface should behave upon system boot or when manually brought up or down.

A basic understanding of parameters and their purposes is necessary for effective configuration. The essential components typically include:

- iface: This keyword is used to define an interface and its method of obtaining an IP address.
- auto: This keyword specifies the interfaces that should be brought up automatically when the system boots.

- allow-hotplug: This keyword denotes interfaces automatically activated when detected.

Consider a simple example to statically configure an Ethernet interface eth0:

```
auto eth0
iface eth0 inet static
    address 192.168.1.100
    netmask 255.255.255.0
    gateway 192.168.1.1
```

In this configuration:

- auto eth0 specifies that the interface eth0 should be brought up automatically.
- iface eth0 inet static defines the eth0 interface and sets it to use a static IP address.
- The address 192.168.1.100 line specifies the static IP address.
- The netmask 255.255.255.0 line defines the subnet mask.
- The gateway 192.168.1.1 line sets the default gateway for the interface.

To configure eth0 with a dynamic IP address via DHCP, adjust the configuration accordingly:

```
auto eth0
iface eth0 inet dhcp
```

This sets up eth0 to obtain its IP address using DHCP each time the interface is brought up automatically.

Further customizations can be achieved by incorporating parameters such as DNS servers within the same stanza. Below is an example incorporating DNS server entries:

```
auto eth0
iface eth0 inet static
    address 192.168.1.100
    netmask 255.255.255.0
    gateway 192.168.1.1
    dns-nameservers 8.8.8.8 8.8.4.4
```

This configuration sets Google's DNS servers (8.8.8.8 and 8.8.4.4) for name resolution on the eth0 interface. Note that some systems might require additional configurations in /etc/resolv.conf to ensure DNS resolution.

Switching gears to a wireless configuration example, the configuration can involve more specific parameters, especially pointing out the SSID and WPA settings. Here's how to set up a WPA-encrypted wireless network:

```
auto wlan0
iface wlan0 inet dhcp
    wpa-ssid "your\_SSID"
    wpa-psk "your\_password"
```

In this example:

- auto wlan0 specifies the wireless interface wlan0 to be automatically brought up.
- iface wlan0 inet dhcp configures the interface to use DHCP.
- wpa-ssid "your_SSID" sets the wireless network SSID.
- wpa-psk "your_password" sets the WPA pre-shared key.

LDAP and bonding configurations can also be managed within this file. For example, a bonded interface setup can be declared as follows:

```
auto bond0
iface bond0 inet static
    address 192.168.1.50
    netmask 255.255.255.0
    gateway 192.168.1.1
    bond-slaves eth0 eth1
    bond-mode 0
    bond-miimon 100
```

This creates a bonded interface bond0 that uses eth0 and eth1 as slaves, operating in round-robin mode (bond-mode 0), with a link monitoring interval of 100 milliseconds (bond-miimon 100).

To apply changes made to the /etc/network/interfaces file without rebooting the system, utilize the following command sequence:

```
sudo ifdown eth0 && sudo ifup eth0
```

This command sequence deactivates the eth0 interface and reactivates it, thus applying the new configuration. For systems where ifup and ifdown are not sufficient, the systemctl restart networking.service command can be employed for a complete restart of networking services:

```
sudo systemctl restart networking.service
```

The /etc/network/interfaces file offers robust control over network configurations, enabling administrators to fine-tune network behaviors and address complex network requirements efficiently. The syntax remains simple yet powerful, providing a crucial skill set for adept Linux network administration.

9.7 Understanding and Configuring DHCP

Dynamic Host Configuration Protocol (DHCP) is a network management protocol used on Internet Protocol (IP) networks. In a Linux environment, DHCP allows a server to dynamically distribute IP addressing and other network configuration information to client devices on a network. This minimizes the need for manual configuration of IP addresses and greatly simplifies network management.

DHCP operates based on a client-server model and involves several key components:

- **DHCP Server**: A machine providing IP configuration information to clients.
- **DHCP Client**: Any device that requests network configuration from a server.
- **DHCP Lease**: The time-bound allocation of an IP address to a client.

The basic operation of DHCP can be summarized in four steps: Discover, Offer, Request, and Acknowledge (DORA).

Discover: When a client device connects to a network, it sends a DHCPDISCOVER message to identify available DHCP servers.

Offer: The DHCP server responds with a DHCPOFFER message, providing an available IP address and other network configuration details.

Request: The client sends a DHCPREQUEST message, indicating that it accepts the provided configuration.

Acknowledge: The server sends a DHCPACK message, finalizing the configuration and allowing the client to use the network.

To configure DHCP on a Linux system, you typically employ the isc-dhcp-server package. Installing this package and setting up the necessary configurations will enable you to run a DHCP server. Below is a step-by-step guide detailing the installation and configuration process.

Step 1: Installing the DHCP Server

First, update the package repository and install the isc-dhcp-server using the following commands:

```
sudo apt-get update
sudo apt-get install isc-dhcp-server
```

Step 2: Configuring the DHCP Server

The main configuration file for the DHCP server is located at /etc/dhcp/dhcpd.conf. This file requires editing to specify the IP address range and other network settings. An example configuration is illustrated below:

```
# Configuration file for ISC DHCP server

# Option definitions common to all supported networks
option domain-name "example.org";
option domain-name-servers ns1.example.org, ns2.example.org;

# Default lease time
default-lease-time 600;
max-lease-time 7200;

# Configuration for subnet
subnet 192.168.1.0 netmask 255.255.255.0 {
    range 192.168.1.10 192.168.1.100;
    option routers 192.168.1.1;
    option broadcast-address 192.168.1.255;
    option subnet-mask 255.255.255.0;
    option domain-name-servers 192.168.1.1, 8.8.8.8;
}
```

Key configurations within this file include:

- default-lease-time and max-lease-time: Specify the duration for which an IP address is leased to a client.
- subnet: Defines the IP address range and associated network settings.
- range: Specifies the pool of IP addresses available for lease.
- option routers: Defines the default gateway for network clients.
- option domain-name-servers: Specifies the DNS servers for network clients.

Step 3: Starting the DHCP Server

Once the configuration file is set up, the DHCP server can be started and enabled to run automatically at boot time using the following commands:

```
sudo systemctl start isc-dhcp-server
sudo systemctl enable isc-dhcp-server
```

To verify that the DHCP server is running correctly, you can check its status:

```
sudo systemctl status isc-dhcp-server
```

This command provides a status output that confirms whether the server is active and lists any errors that may exist.

Additionally, reviewing the server logs located at /var/log/syslog can aid in troubleshooting configuration issues. Below is a sample output verifying the server status and checking for DHCP operations:

```
isc-dhcp-server.service - ISC DHCP IPv4 server
  Loaded: loaded (/lib/systemd/system/isc-dhcp-server.service; enabled; vendor preset: enabled)
  Active: active (running) since Tue 2021-03-16 10:21:39 UTC; 2h 5min ago
    Docs: man:dhcpd(8)
Main PID: 1234 (dhcpd)
  Status: "Dispatching packets."
   Tasks: 1 (limit: 4915)
  Memory: 5.2M
  CGroup: /system.slice/isc-dhcp-server.service
          1234 /usr/sbin/dhcpd -4 -q -cf /etc/dhcp/dhcpd.conf
```

Step 4: Configuring DHCP Clients

To ensure that client devices can obtain IP addresses via DHCP, their network interface must be configured to use DHCP. On a typical Linux client system, this is managed through the /etc/network/interfaces file or through NetworkManager.

An example configuration in /etc/network/interfaces could look like this:

```
auto eth0
iface eth0 inet dhcp
```

Restarting the networking service on the client machine applies these changes:

```
sudo systemctl restart networking
```

Using NetworkManager, DHCP can be enabled through its graphical user interface or with nmcli, the command-line tool. For example, to configure an Ethernet connection to use DHCP with nmcli:

```
nmcli con modify eth0 ipv4.method auto
```

```
nmcli con up eth0
```

By understanding and configuring DHCP on both server and client machines, Linux administrators can efficiently manage IP addressing and network configurations, minimizing manual setup efforts and improving overall network operations. Ensuring that all parameters are correctly set up guarantees a smooth network experience, essential for both small and large networks.

9.8 Introduction to Firewalls: Iptables and Firewalld

Firewalls are vital components in network security, acting as barriers that control traffic between different network segments based on predefined security rules. In Linux-based systems, iptables and firewalld are two popular tools used to set up and manage firewall rules. This section delves into the functionalities and configurations of these tools.

iptables is a user-space utility program that allows system administrators to configure the IP packet filter rules of the Linux kernel firewall, implemented as different Netfilter modules. firewalld is a dynamic firewall management tool with support for network/firewall zones to define the trust level of network connections or interfaces.

iptables: A Closer Look

The iptables tool works with tables containing chains of rules for the treatment of network traffic. The default table used for filtering packets contains the following built-in chains:

- INPUT: Rules for incoming packets.
- FORWARD: Rules for packets routed through the system.
- OUTPUT: Rules for outbound packets.

Each of these chains can have a combination of user-defined and built-in rules to allow, block, modify, or redirect packets. Here is an example of using iptables to accept incoming HTTP connections:

```
sudo iptables -A INPUT -p tcp --dport 80 -j ACCEPT
```

This command appends (-A) a rule to the INPUT chain, specifying that incoming TCP packets (-p tcp) destined for port 80 (–dport 80) should be accepted (-j ACCEPT).

To list all current rules in the INPUT chain, use:

```
sudo iptables -L INPUT
```

Deleting a rule is done by specifying the rule number. For instance, to delete the first rule from the INPUT chain:

```
sudo iptables -D INPUT 1
```

firewalld: Dynamic Management

Unlike iptables, firewalld provides a dynamic interface, which means rules can be added or removed on the fly without needing to reload the entire firewall configuration. firewalld introduces the concept of zones, which define a set of rules for network connections:

- public: The default zone for public facing interfaces.
- home: For private networks, allowing a more liberal set of rules.
- block: All incoming connections are dropped with an ICMP host-unreachable message.

To check the firewall status, use:

```
sudo firewall-cmd --state
```

Adding a rule to allow HTTP traffic in the default zone:

```
sudo firewall-cmd --add-service=http --permanent
sudo firewall-cmd --reload
```

To list all active zones and their information:

```
sudo firewall-cmd --get-active-zones
```

To permanently assign an interface to a zone:

```
sudo firewall-cmd --zone=home --change-interface=eth0 --permanent
```

Reloading configuration ensures that these changes take effect immediately:

```
sudo firewall-cmd --reload
```

The flexibility of iptables and the dynamic abilities of firewalld provide comprehensive tools for managing network traffic and ensuring security across Linux systems. Integration with systemd further enhances these capabilities, allowing seamless operation within the broader system environment. Understanding these tools is essential for configuring effective firewall rules and maintaining secure systems.

9.9 Network Troubleshooting with Ping, Traceroute, and Netcat

Network troubleshooting is a critical skill for maintaining and optimizing communications within and between networked systems. This section delves into three essential tools commonly used for diagnosing network issues in Linux: *ping*, *traceroute*, and *netcat* (often abbreviated as *nc*).

Ping is a network utility used to test the reachability of a host on an Internet Protocol (IP) network. It measures the round-trip time for messages sent from the originating host to a destination computer.

Basic usage of the *ping* command is as follows:

```
ping <destination>
```

For example, to ping a website:

```
ping www.example.com
```

Important options for *ping*:

- -c <count>: Sends a specified number of packets and then terminates.
- -i <interval>: Sets a wait time between sending each packet.
- -s <size>: Specifies the number of data bytes to be sent.

The output is as follows:

```
PING www.example.com (93.184.216.34): 56 data bytes
64 bytes from 93.184.216.34: icmp_seq=0 ttl=58 time=8.085 ms
64 bytes from 93.184.216.34: icmp_seq=1 ttl=58 time=7.884 ms
64 bytes from 93.184.216.34: icmp_seq=2 ttl=58 time=7.984 ms

--- www.example.com ping statistics ---
3 packets transmitted, 3 packets received, 0.0% packet loss
round-trip min/avg/max/stddev = 7.884/7.984/8.085/0.082 ms
```

Traceroute helps identify the path packets take to reach a destination network. It lists all the intermediate points (routers) that data packets pass through.

Basic usage of the *traceroute* command:

```
traceroute <destination>
```

For example:

```
traceroute www.example.com
```

Important options for *traceroute*:

- -m <max_ttl>: Sets the maximum number of hops (maximum time-to-live).
- -n: Skips resolving IP addresses to hostnames for faster results.
- -q <nqueries>: Defines the number of probe packets per TTL.

The output is as follows:

```
traceroute to www.example.com (93.184.216.34), 30 hops max, 60 byte packets
 1  192.168.1.1 (192.168.1.1)  0.354 ms  0.319 ms  0.305 ms
 2  10.0.0.1 (10.0.0.1)  1.043 ms  0.933 ms  0.878 ms
 3  93.184.216.34 (93.184.216.34)  8.156 ms  8.096 ms  7.985 ms
```

Netcat is a versatile networking tool for debugging and investigating the network. It can read and write data across TCP/IP or UDP networks and is often referred to as the "Swiss army knife" of networking.

Basic usage of the *netcat* command for creating a listening TCP server on port 1234:

```
nc -l 1234
```

To connect to this server from another terminal or machine:

```
nc <hostname> 1234
```

For testing port connectivity:

```
nc -z -v <hostname> <port>
```

Where -z establishes a zero-I/O mode, -v enables verbose mode for detailed operation output.

The output upon successful connection:

```
Connection to 192.168.1.2 1234 port [tcp/*] succeeded!
```

These tools form an essential part of the network administrator's toolkit. They offer invaluable insights into network health, connectivity, and performance, facilitating the rapid identification and resolution of issues. Understanding how to use these tools effectively ensures a robust and reliable network environment.

9.10 Using SSH for Remote Access and Management

Secure Shell (SSH) is a cryptographic network protocol for operating network services securely over an unsecured network. SSH provides a secure channel over an unsecured network by using a client-server architecture, connecting an SSH client instance with an SSH server. SSH enables secure command-line login, command execution, file transfer, and tunneling.

The primary components for using SSH in Linux are the SSH client, typically included in most Linux distributions by default, and the SSH server, often found in the 'openssh-server' package.

Installation and Configuration

To install the SSH server, if it is not already installed, use the following command:

```
sudo apt-get install openssh-server
```

Once installed, the SSH server can be started and enabled to run at boot time with:

```
sudo systemctl start ssh
sudo systemctl enable ssh
```

The default configuration file for the SSH server is located at /etc/ssh/sshd_config. Key configurations within this file include specifying the port number (default is 22), which addresses to listen on, and authentication mechanisms. A common adjustment is changing the default port to improve security:

```
Port 2222
```

Basic Usage

The SSH client is commonly used to initiate a session from the terminal. The syntax to connect to a remote server is:

```
ssh username@hostname
```

For instance, to connect to a server with IP address 192.168.1.100 as the user 'alice':

```
ssh alice@192.168.1.100
```

In cases where a non-default port is used, specify it with the '-p' option:

```
ssh -p 2222 alice@192.168.1.100
```

Key-Based Authentication

For enhanced security, SSH supports key-based authentication, which uses a pair of cryptographic keys – a public key and a private key. This method eliminates the need for password-based logins, thereby reducing the risk of brute force attacks. To generate an SSH key pair, execute:

```
ssh-keygen -t rsa -b 4096
```

This command generates a key pair with RSA algorithm and 4096 bits in length. The keys are usually stored in the `~/.ssh` directory. The public key can be shared with remote servers, while the private key remains secure on the client's machine. To add the public key to a remote server, use:

```
ssh-copy-id username@hostname
```

This command appends the public key to the `~/.ssh/authorized_keys` file on the remote server.

File Transfers with SSH

SSH also supports secure file transfer via the 'scp' (Secure Copy) and 'sftp' (SSH File Transfer Protocol) commands. To copy a file from the local machine to a remote server:

```
scp /path/to/local/file username@hostname:/path/to/remote/directory
```

Similarly, to copy a file from the remote server to the local machine:

```
scp username@hostname:/path/to/remote/file /path/to/local/directory
```

For interactive file management, use 'sftp':

```
sftp username@hostname
```

Tunneling and Port Forwarding

SSH supports port forwarding, a technique that allows secure forwarding of ports over an SSH connection. This can be leveraged for securing otherwise insecure network protocols. Local port forwarding forwards data securely from an application client running on the same machine as the SSH client to an application server. To forward a local port to a port on a remote server:

```
ssh -L 8080:localhost:80 username@hostname
```

In this example, connections to port 8080 on the local machine are forwarded to port 80 on the remote server. Another variant is remote port forwarding, which allows remote servers to access resources on the local machine:

```
ssh -R 9090:localhost:80 username@hostname
```

This command forwards port 9090 on the remote server to port 80 on the local machine.

Managing SSH Sessions

For better session management, especially when dealing with multiple SSH sessions, tools like 'tmux' or 'screen' can be used. They provide session persistence, allowing users to detach and reattach to sessions, which is useful for long-running tasks or unstable connections.

To start a new 'tmux' session:

```
tmux new -s session_name
```

To detach from the session, press Ctrl+b followed by d, and to reattach:

```
tmux attach -t session_name
```

These features make SSH a versatile tool for remote access and management, providing secure and efficient ways to manage remote systems, transfer files, and tunnel network traffic.

9.11 Establishing Secure Connections with SSL/TLS

Secure Sockets Layer (SSL) and Transport Layer Security (TLS) are cryptographic protocols designed to provide secure communication over a computer network. While SSL is the older protocol, TLS is its successor, offering enhanced security features. This section delves into the implementation and management of SSL/TLS to establish secure connections in Linux environments.

To begin, a fundamental aspect of SSL/TLS involves the creation and use of certificates, which are signed by a Certificate Authority (CA). A certificate binds a public key with an entity's identity, thereby enabling secure communications. The canonical command-line tool used to manage SSL/TLS certificates in Linux is openssl.

Consider the following command sequence to generate a self-signed certificate:

```
# Generate a private key
openssl genpkey -algorithm RSA -out private.key

# Create a certificate signing request (CSR)
openssl req -new -key private.key -out request.csr

# Generate the self-signed certificate
openssl x509 -req -days 365 -in request.csr -signkey private.key -out certificate.crt
```

The above commands accomplish the following tasks: 1. The openssl genpkey command generates a new RSA private key and saves it to the file private.key. 2. The openssl req -new command uses the private key to create a new certificate signing request (CSR), capturing information about the certificate subject. 3. The openssl x509 -req command signs the CSR with the private key, generating a self-signed certificate valid for 365 days.

Certificates are more commonly signed by a CA to establish trustworthiness. Below is a typical configuration for an SSL/TLS service, such as a web server using Apache:

```
<VirtualHost *:443>
    ServerAdmin admin@example.com
    DocumentRoot /var/www/html
    ServerName www.example.com

    SSLEngine on
    SSLCertificateFile /etc/ssl/certs/certificate.crt
    SSLCertificateKeyFile /etc/ssl/private/private.key
    SSLCertificateChainFile /etc/ssl/certs/chainfile.pem
```

```
    <Directory /var/www/html>
        Options Indexes FollowSymLinks
        AllowOverride All
        Require all granted
    </Directory>

    ErrorLog ${APACHE_LOG_DIR}/error.log
    CustomLog ${APACHE_LOG_DIR}/access.log combined

</VirtualHost>
```

This configuration block for Apache enables SSL on port 443 and specifies the paths to the necessary certificate files. Specifically: - SSLEngine on enables SSL for the virtual host. - SSLCertificateFile points to the signed certificate file. - SSLCertificateKeyFile points to the private key file. - SSLCertificateChainFile (if needed) points to a file containing the intermediate CA certificates.

For a more recent, automated, and easier approach to managing SSL/TLS certificates, the Let's Encrypt service can be used. Let's Encrypt offers free certificates and an automated process, typically managed by the certbot tool.

```
# Install certbot
sudo apt-get install certbot python3-certbot-apache

# Obtain and install a certificate
sudo certbot --apache -d www.example.com
```

The certbot tool automatically configures Apache to use the newly obtained certificate. This significantly simplifies the process of setting up and maintaining SSL/TLS certificates.

Testing the SSL/TLS configuration can be done using tools like openssl and web-based services. To check the SSL connection to a server:

```
# Test SSL connection to a server
openssl s_client -connect www.example.com:443
```

The output provides details about the SSL/TLS connection, including the certificate chain, supported protocols, and cipher suites.

```
CONNECTED(00000003)
depth=2 C = US, O = Let's Encrypt, CN = Let's Encrypt Authority X3
verify return:1
depth=1 C = US, O = Let's Encrypt, CN = Let's Encrypt Authority X3
verify return:1
depth=0 CN = www.example.com
verify return:1
---
Certificate chain
 0 s:/CN=www.example.com
   i:/C=US/O=Let's Encrypt/CN=Let's Encrypt Authority X3
 1 s:/C=US/O=Let's Encrypt/CN=Let's Encrypt Authority X3
   i:/O=Digital Signature Trust Co./CN=DST Root CA X3
---
Server certificate
-----BEGIN CERTIFICATE-----
[Certificate Data]
-----END CERTIFICATE-----
---
No client certificate CA names sent
---
SSL handshake has read nnnn bytes and written nnnn bytes
Verification: OK
---
New, TLSv1.2, Cipher is ECDHE-RSA-AES128-GCM-SHA256
Server public key is 2048 bit
Secure Renegotiation IS supported
Compression: NONE
Expansion: NONE
No ALPN negotiated
SSL-Session:
    Protocol  : TLSv1.2
    Cipher    : ECDHE-RSA-AES128-GCM-SHA256
    Session-ID: [Session ID]
    Session-ID-ctx:
    Master-Key: [Master Key]
    ...
```

The details provided in the s_client output are critical for verifying the correct deployment and functionality of the SSL/TLS configuration.

By following these steps and utilizing the appropriate tools and configurations, one can effectively establish secure connections using SSL/TLS on a Linux system. Establishing such secure connections is paramount for protecting sensitive data and ensuring secure communications across networks.

9.12 Setting Up and Managing VPNs

Virtual Private Networks (VPNs) provide a secure communication channel over an untrusted network by encrypting traffic between two endpoints. This section elucidates the process of setting up and managing VPNs in a Linux environment. It encompasses key concepts such as VPN protocols, server and client configuration, and troubleshooting common issues.

The most commonly used VPN protocols include OpenVPN, IPsec, and WireGuard. Each protocol has distinct features and setup procedures, thus selecting an appropriate one depends on the specific needs and security requirements.

OpenVPN is a robust and flexible VPN solution that employs SSL/TLS for key exchange. To install OpenVPN on a Linux system, use the following command:

```
sudo apt-get install openvpn
```

Once installed, configuring the OpenVPN server involves creating server and client configuration files and generating necessary keys and certificates. The Easy-RSA package can simplify this process:

```
sudo apt-get install easy-rsa
```

Initialize the Public Key Infrastructure (PKI):

```
make-cadir ~/openvpn-ca
cd ~/openvpn-ca
source ./vars
./clean-all
./build-ca
```

Generate the server certificate and key:

```
./build-key-server server
```

Generate Diffie-Hellman parameters:

```
./build-dh
```

Copy the generated files to the OpenVPN directory:

```
sudo cp ~/openvpn-ca/keys/{server.crt,server.key,ca.crt,dh2048.pem} /etc/openvpn
```

A sample server configuration file, usually located at /etc/openvpn/server.conf, may look like this:

```
port 1194
proto udp
dev tun
ca ca.crt
cert server.crt
key server.key
dh dh2048.pem
server 10.8.0.0 255.255.255.0
ifconfig-pool-persist ipp.txt
push "redirect-gateway def1 bypass-dhcp"
push "dhcp-option DNS 208.67.222.222"
```

```
keepalive 10 120
cipher AES-256-CBC
user nobody
group nogroup
persist-key
persist-tun
status openvpn-status.log
verb 3
```

To start the OpenVPN service, use the following command:

```
sudo systemctl start openvpn@server
```

Creating a client configuration file typically involves specifying the server address and port, and including the necessary certificates. For instance, a basic client configuration file, named client.ovpn, might appear as follows:

```
client
dev tun
proto udp
remote your-server-IP 1194
resolv-retry infinite
nobind
user nobody
group nogroup
persist-key
persist-tun
ca ca.crt
cert client.crt
key client.key
remote-cert-tls server
cipher AES-256-CBC
verb 3
```

IPsec (Internet Protocol Security) is another widely used VPN protocol, often implemented via tools like Strongswan. To install Strongswan, execute:

```
sudo apt-get install strongswan
```

The main configuration file for Strongswan is /etc/ipsec.conf. An example configuration for a simple IPsec setup looks like:

```
config setup
    charondebug="ike 2, knl 2, cfg 2"

conn %default
    keyexchange=ikev2
    authby=secret
    ike=aes256-sha2_256-modp2048
    esp=aes256-sha2_256

conn home
    left=%any
    leftid=@home.example.com
```

```
    leftcert=serverCert.pem
    leftsendcert=always
    leftsubnet=0.0.0.0/0
    right=%any
    rightid=@client.example.com
    rightauth=eap-mschapv2
    rightdns=8.8.8.8, 8.8.4.4
    rightsendcert=never
    eap_identity=%identity
    auto=add
```

To start the IPsec service:

```
sudo systemctl start strongswan
```

WireGuard is a newer protocol known for its simplicity and high performance. To install WireGuard:

```
sudo apt-get install wireguard
```

Generate private and public keys for the server and client:

```
wg genkey | tee server_private.key | wg pubkey > server_public.key
wg genkey | tee client_private.key | wg pubkey > client_public.key
```

Configure the server in /etc/wireguard/wg0.conf:

```
[Interface]
PrivateKey = server_private_key_here
Address = 10.0.0.1/24
ListenPort = 51820

[Peer]
PublicKey = client_public_key_here
AllowedIPs = 10.0.0.2/32
```

Configure the client in /etc/wireguard/wg0.conf:

```
[Interface]
PrivateKey = client_private_key_here
Address = 10.0.0.2/24

[Peer]
PublicKey = server_public_key_here
Endpoint = your-server-IP:51820
AllowedIPs = 0.0.0.0/0
```

To bring up the WireGuard interface:

```
sudo wg-quick up wg0
```

Effective management of VPNs includes regularly monitoring and ensuring the security of the VPN endpoints and encrypted links. Employ system logs and monitoring tools to detect anomalies or potential breaches.

Chapter 10

Advanced Shell Scripting and Automation

This chapter delves into advanced shell scripting and automation in Linux. It covers complex variable and parameter handling, advanced conditional statements, and iterative looping constructs. The chapter explores sophisticated functions, error handling, debugging techniques, and script optimization for performance. It includes detailed instructions on interacting with system processes and daemons, using regular expressions and pattern matching, and automating tasks with cron and systemd timers. Finally, it provides best practices for creating and maintaining complex automation workflows, ensuring scripts are efficient, reliable, and maintainable.

10.1 Introduction to Advanced Shell Scripting

Shell scripting in Linux is a powerful tool that automates tasks, integrates complex workflows, and customizes the user environment. As you progress beyond the basics, understanding advanced shell scripting paradigms becomes essential for creating efficient, robust, and flexible scripts. This section discusses fundamental principles and techniques, setting the stage for more intricate topics covered in subsequent sections.

Advanced shell scripting leverages several key areas: complex variable and parameter manipulation, intricate conditional statements, sophisticated looping constructs, modular scripting with functions, detailed error handling, optimized performance, interaction with system processes, and the use of cron and systemd timers for automation. Knowledge of these areas enables the creation of sophisticated scripts that can handle a variety of tasks and conditions.

One of the core aspects of advanced shell scripting is the use of complex variables and parameters. Bash, the Bourne Again SHell, provides a rich set of features for variable manipulation, such as associative arrays and indirect expansion. Associative arrays, unlike indexed arrays, allow for the use of string keys, enabling more complex data relationships and structures.

```
declare -A user_info
user_info=( ["name"]="Alice" ["id"]=1234 ["dept"]="Engineering" )
echo "Name: ${user_info[name]}, ID: ${user_info[id]}, Department: ${user_info[dept]}
    "
```

The output is:

```
Name: Alice, ID: 1234, Department: Engineering
```

Indirect expansion offers a dynamic way to reference variables. For example, if you have a variable name stored as a string, you can access the value of the actual variable it points to.

```
varname="hello"
hello="world"
echo "${!varname}"
```

The output is:

```
world
```

Advanced conditional statements go beyond simple if-else structures, incorporating complex logical operations and pattern matching. The `case` statement is versatile, matching patterns against variables and performing corresponding actions.

```
case "$variable" in
  pattern1)
    commands for pattern1
    ;;
  pattern2)
    commands for pattern2
    ;;
  *)
    default commands
```

```
  ;;
esac
```

Pattern matching in the case statement supports wildcards and logical groupings, making it suitable for handling various input scenarios. This capability is further enhanced when combined with extended regular expressions (using tools like grep -E).

Looping constructs and iteration are crucial for processing collections of items, files, or data structures. Beyond basic for, while, and until loops, advanced scripts often utilize nested loops and conditional breaks for complex data processing.

```
for file in /path/to/directory/*; do
  if [[ -f "$file" && "$file" == *.txt ]]; then
    cat "$file"
  fi
done
```

This script iterates through all files in a directory and processes only text files, using conditional checks within the loop.

Modular scripting with functions encapsulates code blocks for reuse and maintainability. Functions can accept parameters, return values, and handle local variables, mirroring the features of conventional programming languages.

```
function greet {
  local name="$1"
  echo "Hello, $name!"
}
greet "Alice"
```

The output is:

```
Hello, Alice!
```

Understanding functions is critical for developing clearer and more manageable scripts, especially as complexity grows. They facilitate code organization and debugging.

Error handling and debugging techniques are vital for reliability and maintainability. Trap statements, conditional checks, and logging mechanisms ensure that scripts respond gracefully to unexpected conditions and facilitate diagnosis of issues.

```
trap 'echo "Error occurred at line $LINENO"; exit 1' ERR
```

The trap command captures errors and provides useful context, such as the line number where the error occurred.

Script optimization and performance tuning consider execution speed and resource usage. Techniques include minimizing subshell usage, employing built-in commands over external ones, and leveraging efficient data processing tools.

```
# Example: using a built-in command (read) instead of external (cat)
while read line; do
  echo "$line"
done < file.txt
```

Interacting with system processes and daemons such as managing background processes, signaling, and process substitution enhances a script's capability to integrate with the operating system and other running services.

```
# Example: running a command in the background
command &
pid=$!
wait $pid
```

Using regular expressions and pattern matching extends the scope of data manipulation and text processing, crucial for tasks such as parsing logs and processing user input. The combination of grep, sed, and awk commands empowers users to perform intricate pattern matches and replacements.

```
# Example: using grep with regular expressions
grep -E 'pattern' file.txt
```

Automating with cron and systemd timers schedules tasks to run at specific intervals or events, thus automating routine maintenance and monitoring tasks.

```
# Example: cron job to run every day at midnight
0 0 * * * /path/to/script.sh
```

Creating and managing complex automation workflows involves orchestrating multiple scripts and processes, ensuring they work harmoniously. Techniques include sequencing dependent tasks, handling concurrency, and implementing robust error recovery mechanisms.

Best practices for writing maintainable scripts emphasize code clarity, robust documentation, and adherence to coding standards, making scripts easier to understand, maintain, and extend over time.

These principles and techniques lay the foundation for mastering advanced shell scripting. More complex patterns, functions, and best practices are explored in-depth throughout the remainder of the chapter.

10.2 Working with Advanced Variables and Parameters

In shell scripting, variables and parameters form the backbone of complex script logic and data manipulation. Advanced handling techniques for variables and parameters can greatly enhance the flexibility and robustness of your scripts. This section covers various sophisticated methods for managing and using shell variables and parameters effectively.

1. Arrays

Bash supports arrays, which allow you to manage multiple values within a single variable. Arrays can be indexed or associative (key-value pairs).

To initialize an indexed array, you can use:

```
# Initialize an indexed array
my_array=(value1 value2 value3)
# Access elements
echo ${my_array[0]} # Outputs: value1
echo ${my_array[1]} # Outputs: value2

# Add elements to the array
my_array+=(value4)
echo ${my_array[3]} # Outputs: value4
```

To initialize an associative array, you use:

```
# Declare and initialize an associative array
declare -A my_assoc_array
my_assoc_array=([key1]=value1 [key2]=value2)

# Access elements
echo ${my_assoc_array[key1]} # Outputs: value1
echo ${my_assoc_array[key2]} # Outputs: value2
```

2. Variable Indirection

Variable indirection allows you to use the value of a variable as the name of another variable. It is particularly useful for creating dynamically named variables. To achieve variable indirection, use the `eval` command or indirect reference:

```
var_name="actual_variable"
actual_variable="Hello, World!"

# Using indirection
echo ${!var_name} # Outputs: Hello, World!
```

3. Parameter Expansion

Advanced parameter expansions provide powerful ways to manipulate variable values. Below are some common expansions:

Substring extraction:

```
str="Hello, Advanced Shell Scripting!"
# Extract substring
echo ${str:7:9} # Outputs: Advanced
```

Substring replacement:

```
str="The quick brown fox jumps over the lazy dog"
# Replace first occurrence
echo ${str/quick/slow} # Outputs: The slow brown fox jumps over the lazy dog
# Replace all occurrences
echo ${str//o/O} # Outputs: The quick brOwn fOx jumps Over the lazy dOg
```

Default values:

```
unset my_var
# Set default value if variable is unset or null
echo ${my_var:-default_value} # Outputs: default_value
```

4. Positional Parameters and Special Variables

Positional parameters represent the arguments passed to a script or a function. They are accessed using $1, $2, ..., ${10}, etc. You can also use special variables for various purposes:

- $* and $@: Both represent all positional parameters, but treat quoting differently.
- $#: Represents the number of positional parameters.
- $0: Contains the name of the script.
- $?: Contains the exit status of the last command executed.
- $$: Contains the process ID (PID) of the current shell.
- $!: Contains the PID of the last background command.

Example of using positional parameters:

```
#!/bin/bash

echo "Script name: $0"
echo "First argument: $1"
echo "Second argument: $2"
echo "All arguments (*): $*"
echo "All arguments (@): $@"
echo "Number of arguments: $#"
```

5. Advanced Use of shift

The shift command is used to shift positional parameters to the left. It is particularly useful when processing arguments in a loop:

```
#!/bin/bash

while [[ $# -gt 0 ]]
do
    echo "Current argument: $1"
    shift
done
```

6. Setting and Unsetting Readonly Variables

Readonly variables are immutable once they are set. They can be defined using the readonly command:

```
# Define a readonly variable
readonly PI=3.14159
# Attempt to modify the readonly variable (will cause an error)
# PI=3.14 # Uncommenting this line will result in an error

# Unsetting a variable
my_var="some value"
unset my_var
echo $my_var # No output, variable is unset
```

7. Local Variables in Functions

In shell scripting, variables are by default global. To limit the scope of a variable to a function, use the local keyword:

```
#!/bin/bash

global_var="I am global"

my_function() {
    local local_var="I am local"
    echo $global_var # Outputs: I am global
    echo $local_var # Outputs: I am local
}

my_function

# Accessing local variable outside the function (will be unset)
echo $local_var # No output, variable is not defined globally
```

Mastering these advanced techniques of variable and parameter handling will significantly enhance your scripting capabilities and allow for more versatile and maintainable scripts. By integrating these methods into your shell scripting practices, you can achieve more efficient data manipulation and control flow in your automated workflows.

10.3 Using Advanced Conditional Statements

Advanced conditional statements allow for more sophisticated and powerful control flow within shell scripts. These constructs enable the script to make decisions based on complex conditions, facilitating the execution of different code paths under varying situations. In this section, we will enhance our understanding of condition testing in shell scripting, including intricate comparisons, nested conditions, and the use of logical operators.

The if statement is a fundamental component of conditional processing in shell scripts. An advanced if statement can handle multiple conditions using the elif keyword and combine conditions with logical operators such as && (AND) and || (OR).

```
#!/bin/bash

# Read a number from the user
echo "Enter a number:"
read number

if [ $number -lt 10 ]; then
    echo "The number is less than 10."
elif [ $number -ge 10 ] && [ $number -lt 20 ]; then
    echo "The number is between 10 and 19."
elif [ $number -ge 20 ] && [ $number -lt 30 ]; then
    echo "The number is between 20 and 29."
else
    echo "The number is 30 or greater."
fi
```

In the example above, the script reads a number from the user and utilizes multiple elif statements to make decisions based on ranges of that number. Note the use of the && operator to combine conditions.

Another useful construct in shell scripting is the case statement, which is particularly effective when there are multiple potential values for a single variable. The case statement simplifies the logic and enhances the readability of your scripts.

```
#!/bin/bash

# Get the current day of the week
day_of_week=$(date +%A)

case $day_of_week in
    "Monday")
        echo "Start of the work week.";
        ;;
    "Tuesday" | "Wednesday" | "Thursday")
```

```
        echo "Midweek work days.";
        ;;
    "Friday")
        echo "End of the work week.";
        ;;
    "Saturday" | "Sunday")
        echo "Weekend!";
        ;;
    *)
        echo "Invalid day.";
        ;;
esac
```

In this script, the case statement determines the day of the week and prints an appropriate message. The vertical bar | is used to match multiple patterns within a single pattern list.

Advanced use of logical operators and nested conditions can also be employed to handle more intricate scenarios. Consider a script that checks for file attributes and user permissions:

```
#!/bin/bash

file_path="/path/to/file"
user=$(whoami)

if [ -e $file_path ]; then
    if [ -f $file_path ]; then
        if [ -r $file_path ] && [ -w $file_path ]; then
            echo "The file exists, is a regular file, and you have read and write
                permissions."
        else
            echo "The file exists and is a regular file, but you do not have read or write
                permissions."
        fi
    else
        echo "The path exists but is not a regular file."
    fi
else
    echo "The file does not exist."
fi
```

Here, the script first checks if the file exists using -e. Then, it further checks if the path is a regular file with -f, finally ensuring that the user has both read and write permissions through the combined use of -r and -w.

Another advanced feature is the use of the [[...]] construct, which is more powerful than the [...] test command, supporting additional operators and features.

```
#!/bin/bash

string1="hello"
string2="world"
string3="hello"
```

```
if [[ $string1 == $string3 ]]; then
    echo "string1 is equal to string3"
fi

if [[ $string1 != $string2 ]]; then
    echo "string1 is not equal to string2"
fi

if [[ $string1 == h* ]]; then
    echo "string1 starts with 'h'"
fi
```

In this example, the use of [[...]] allows for pattern matching (h*) and improved handling of strings.

Advanced conditional statements in shell scripting provide the necessary tools to create robust and efficient scripts capable of handling a wide array of scenarios. By leveraging these constructs, you can write scripts that are not only comprehensive in functionality but also clear and maintainable.

10.4 Looping Constructs and Iteration

In advanced shell scripting, looping constructs and iterative processing are essential tools for handling repetitive tasks efficiently. Mastering these constructs can significantly streamline scripts and enhance their effectiveness. Understanding the various looping mechanisms available in the shell environment, including the nuances and best use cases for each, is critical for any advanced Linux user or systems administrator.

The primary looping constructs in shell scripting are for, while, and until loops. Each of these has its specific utility and optimal use cases. Additionally, combining these constructs with other scripting capabilities, such as command substitution, arithmetic operations, and conditional statements, can lead to powerful and flexible scripts.

The for loop is used to iterate over a list of items or a range of values. The loop executes a block of code for each item in the list or each value in the range. The syntax is as follows:

```
for var in list
do
    commands
done
```

For example, iterating over a list of filenames in a directory can be accomplished as shown below:

```
#!/bin/bash
for file in /path/to/directory/*
do
    echo "Processing $file"
    # Add commands to process each file
done
```

This loop will execute the enclosed commands for every file in the specified directory. The wildcard * is used to match all files.

The while loop continues to execute a block of code as long as a specified condition is true. The syntax for a while loop is:

```
while condition
do
    commands
done
```

A practical example of using a while loop might be to read lines from a file until the end of the file is reached:

```
#!/bin/bash
while IFS= read -r line
do
    echo "Processing line: $line"
    # Add commands to process each line
done < /path/to/file
```

In this script, IFS= read -r line reads each line of the file, and the loop continues until all lines are processed. The IFS= part prevents leading/-trailing whitespace from being trimmed, and -r prevents backslashes from being interpreted as escape characters.

The until loop is similar to the while loop but continues to execute the block of code until a specified condition becomes true. Its syntax is:

```
until condition
do
    commands
done
```

An example of using an until loop is waiting for a particular service to start:

```
#!/bin/bash
until systemctl is-active --quiet your-service
do
    echo "Waiting for the service to start..."
    sleep 5
done
echo "Service is now active."
```

In this example, the loop will run until the service becomes active. The systemctl is-active –quiet your-service command checks the status of the service, and the loop waits five seconds before each check.

Nested loops are another powerful feature in shell scripting, allowing loops within loops for multi-dimensional iteration. An example of using nested for loops to create a multiplication table is:

```
#!/bin/bash
for i in {1..10}
do
    for j in {1..10}
    do
        result=$((i * j))
        echo "$i x $j = $result"
    done
done
```

In this script, the outer loop iterates over the numbers 1 to 10 (rows), and the inner loop iterates similarly (columns), calculating and displaying the result of each multiplication.

To further enhance scripts, combining loops with conditional statements can create more dynamic behavior. For example, using an if statement within a for loop to selectively process files:

```
#!/bin/bash
for file in /path/to/directory/*
do
    if [[ -f $file && $file == *.txt ]]
    then
        echo "Processing text file: $file"
        # Add commands to process text files
    fi
done
```

Here, the if statement checks if the item is a file and if it has a .txt extension before processing it.

Another advanced technique involves using loop control commands such as break and continue. These commands provide finer control over the loop execution:

break exits the loop entirely, while continue skips the remaining commands in the current iteration and moves to the next iteration of the loop.

An example using break:

```
#!/bin/bash
for i in {1..10}
do
    if [ $i -eq 5 ]
    then
```

```
        echo "Breaking the loop at $i"
        break
    fi
    echo "Iteration $i"
done
```

This loop will terminate when i equals 5.

An example using continue:

```
#!/bin/bash
for i in {1..10}
do
    if [ $(($i % 2)) -ne 0 ]
    then
        continue
    fi
    echo "Even number: $i"
done
```

In this script, only even numbers are printed, as the continue statement skips odd numbers.

Understanding and effectively using these looping constructs is vital for building robust and efficient shell scripts. Practice and experimentation with different scenarios will deepen this understanding and improve scripting proficiency. Recognizing when and how to leverage each type of loop, along with appropriate conditional and control commands, will enable the creation of complex and highly functional automation workflows.

10.5 Advanced Functions and Modular Scripts

Functions in shell scripting are essential for breaking down large scripts into more manageable, reusable, and modular blocks. This section focuses on creating advanced functions and modular scripts to streamline development and facilitate maintenance.

To define a function in a shell script, the following syntax is used:

```
function_name() {
    # Commands
}
```

Unlike basic functions, advanced functions often encompass enhanced parameter handling, scope management, and error checking. These functions are designed to be more versatile and reusable across multiple scripts.

An advanced function example with parameter handling:

```
#!/bin/bash

create_backup() {
    local source_dir=$1
    local backup_dir=$2
    local timestamp=$(date +%Y%m%d%H%M%S)
    local backup_file="${backup_dir}/backup_${timestamp}.tar.gz"

    if [[ -d $source_dir && -d $backup_dir ]]; then
        tar -czf $backup_file $source_dir
        echo "Backup created at $backup_file"
    else
        echo "Error: Invalid directory paths provided."
        return 1
    fi
}
```

In this function: - local is used to define variables with local scope, ensuring they do not interfere with variables outside the function. - The tar command archives and compresses the directory specified by source_dir into a file within backup_dir, appending a timestamp for uniqueness. - Parameter validation ensures directories exist before attempting the backup, enhancing robustness.

Calling the function:

```
create_backup "/home/user/data" "/home/user/backups"
```

Error handling within functions can be implemented using return codes. Functions can return a status code using the return command, which can be checked after the function call:

```
if create_backup "/home/user/data" "/home/user/backups"; then
    echo "Backup operation successful."
else
    echo "Backup operation failed."
fi
```

Modular scripts involve organizing shell scripts into separate files, each containing functions or logically grouped commands. This modular approach enables reuse, easier debugging, and better organization. Essential functions can be placed in libraries, which are then sourced in the main script using the source or . (dot) command.

Example of a modular approach: 1. **Library File** (backup_lib.sh):

```
#!/bin/bash

create_backup() {
    local source_dir=$1
```

```
    local backup_dir=$2
    local timestamp=$(date +%Y%m%d%H%M%S)
    local backup_file="${backup_dir}/backup_${timestamp}.tar.gz"

    if [[ -d $source_dir && -d $backup_dir ]]; then
        tar -czf $backup_file $source_dir
        echo "Backup created at $backup_file"
    else
        echo "Error: Invalid directory paths provided."
        return 1
    fi
}
```

2. **Main Script** (backup.sh):

```
#!/bin/bash

source /path/to/backup_lib.sh

SOURCE_DIR="/home/user/data"
BACKUP_DIR="/home/user/backups"

if create_backup $SOURCE_DIR $BACKUP_DIR; then
    echo "Backup operation completed successfully."
else
    echo "Backup operation failed."
fi
```

This modular approach: - Encapsulates the backup functionality in backup_lib.sh, which can be reused in other scripts. - Enhances readability and maintainability by separating logic into distinct files.

When dealing with large-scale automation, maintaining state across multiple function calls becomes crucial. Associative arrays offer a sophisticated method for managing key-value pairs, enabling more complex data manipulation.

Using associative arrays in a function:

```
declare -A config

read_config() {
    while IFS='=' read -r key value; do
        config["$key"]="$value"
    done < "$1"
}

print_config() {
    for key in "${!config[@]}"; do
        echo "$key: ${config[$key]}"
    done
}
```

This script: - Declares an associative array config. - Reads configuration file key-value pairs into the config array. - Prints all key-value pairs stored in config.

Leveraging external configuration files in conjunction with associative arrays allows more dynamic and adaptable scripts.

Example configuration file (config.txt):

```
username=admin
timeout=30
logfile=/var/log/app.log
```

Integrating the configuration in the main script:

```
#!/bin/bash

source /path/to/config_lib.sh

read_config "config.txt"
print_config
```

This comprehensive approach to advanced function creation and modular scripting fosters the development of robust, maintainable, and reusable automation solutions. Efficient structuring of scripts and functions is vital for managing complexity in large-scale scripts and achieving expert-level proficiency in Linux shell scripting.

10.6 Error Handling and Debugging Techniques

Effective error handling and debugging are critical components in the development of reliable and maintainable shell scripts. Addressing errors and unexpected behavior promptly not only ensures scripts execute as intended but also facilitates easier troubleshooting and maintenance in complex automation workflows.

Error handling in shell scripting focuses on detecting, reporting, and properly responding to errors. Bash and other shells provide several mechanisms for error control, including exit statuses, traps, and conditional constructs.

Exit Status and Error Codes

Every command executed in a shell script returns an exit status (*also known as an exit code*). By convention, an exit status of 0 indicates successful execution, while any non-zero exit status signifies an error. The special variable $? contains the exit status of the last executed command.

Example:

```
#!/bin/bash

cp source.txt destination.txt
if [ $? -ne 0 ]; then
    echo "Error: File copy failed."
    exit 1
fi
echo "File copied successfully."
```

In this example, the cp command's exit status is checked to determine if the operation was successful. If not, an error message is displayed, and the script exits with a status code of 1.

Using set for Error Handling

The set command is a built-in shell function that modifies the shell's behavior. The options -e, -u, and -o pipefail are particularly useful for enhancing error handling in scripts:

- -e: Causes the script to exit immediately when a command exits with a non-zero status.
- -u: Treats unset variables as an error and exits.
- -o pipefail: Ensures that the entire pipeline fails if any command within it fails.

Example:

```
#!/bin/bash
set -euo pipefail

cp source.txt destination.txt
echo "This message will not be printed if the copy operation fails."
```

By incorporating these options, scripts become more robust and predictable, as errors are caught instantly, preventing further execution.

The trap Command

The trap command intercepts and handles signals and other types of events. This is useful for performing cleanup tasks or custom actions when a script encounters an error or receives termination signals like SIGINT (Ctrl+C) or SIGTERM.

Example:

```
#!/bin/bash

trap 'echo "An error occurred. Cleaning up..."' ERR

echo "Executing script..."
```

```
false # This command will trigger the trap
echo "This line will not be executed."
```

In this example, the trap command specifies that if any command exits with a non-zero status (ERR), the shell will execute the embedded action to print an error message.

Implementing Custom Error Messages

Custom error messages improve the clarity of the error context, helping to swiftly identify the nature and location of issues. This can be achieved by defining a function to handle error reporting.

Example:

```
#!/bin/bash

error_handler() {
    echo "Error on line $1"
}

trap 'error_handler $LINENO' ERR

echo "Running script..."
false # This command simulates an error
echo "This line will not be executed."
```

The function error_handler() prints a message including the line number where the error occurred. The $LINENO variable provides the current line number.

Debugging Techniques

Debugging is essential to identify and fix issues within a script. Shells provide several tools and options to aid this process.

Enabling Debug Mode

Bash provides the -x option to enable debug mode, which prints each command and its arguments as they are executed. This is useful for tracking script execution and diagnosing issues.

Example:

```
#!/bin/bash
set -x

echo "This is a test message."
cp missing_file.txt /tmp/
echo "Copy operation complete."
set +x

echo "Debugging session ended."
```

Running this script will output each command with its expanded arguments, providing visibility into the script's operation.

Using the shell built-in commands set and unset breakpoints

Breakpoints are intentional stops in the script to inspect variables and environment states. The read command can act as a breakpoint by pausing script execution until the Enter key is pressed.

Example:

```
#!/bin/bash

echo "Start of the script"
read -p "Paused execution. Press Enter to continue..."
echo "Resuming execution"
```

This is particularly useful for manual inspection during step-by-step execution.

The 'echo' Command for Debugging

The echo command is a straightforward method to print variable values and messages for debugging purposes. Adding echo statements at critical points in the script can reveal the flow and state of variables.

Example:

```
#!/bin/bash

# Example function
calculate() {
    local result=$(( $1 + $2 ))
    echo "Inside function: result=$result"
}

a=5
b=10
echo "Before function call: a=$a, b=$b"
calculate $a $b
echo "After function call"
```

Running this script will print intermediate variable values, aiding the debugging process.

Using the Built-in Debugger 'bashdb'

For more sophisticated debugging, the bashdb debugger offers features such as setting breakpoints, stepping through code, and inspecting variables. Installing bashdb and running a script under its control provides an interactive debugging environment.

Example:

```
$ sudo apt-get install bashdb
$ bashdb script.sh
bashdb<1>
```

Within the bashdb session, commands such as break (set breakpoints), step (step through code), and print (inspect variables) can be used to thoroughly analyze script behavior.

10.7 Script Optimization and Performance Tuning

Optimization and performance tuning in shell scripting are crucial to ensure that scripts run efficiently and consume minimal system resources. This section examines various techniques enabling scripters to optimize their scripts for performance and reliability.

Efficient code practices are fundamental to writing optimized scripts. Minimizing the use of subshells, reducing file I/O operations, and using built-in shell features can dramatically enhance script performance. Here's a comparison showing inefficient versus efficient practices:

```
# Inefficient Code Example
FILES=$(ls /path/to/directory)
for FILE in $FILES; do
  FILESIZE=$(stat -c%s "$FILE")
  echo "$FILE is $FILESIZE bytes"
done

# Efficient Code Example
for FILE in /path/to/directory/*; do
  FILESIZE=$(stat -c%s "$FILE")
  echo "$FILE is $FILESIZE bytes"
done
```

The efficient example avoids the use of a subshell and unnecessary ls command, iterating directly over files in the directory.

Another powerful optimization technique involves using built-in shell variables and avoiding unnecessary external commands. For instance, replacing external commands like expr and bc for arithmetic operations with shell arithmetic expansion can significantly reduce script execution time. Consider the following example:

```
# Inefficient Code Example
SUM=$(expr $NUM1 + $NUM2)

# Efficient Code Example
SUM=$(($NUM1 + $NUM2))
```

Shell arithmetic expansion ($(())) is evaluated internally by the shell, making it faster than spawning a new process for arithmetic evaluation with expr.

Utilizing efficient looping constructs can markedly enhance script performance. Avoiding the use of unnecessary subshells and processes within loops can lead to noticeable performance gains. Here's an example demonstrating this:

```
# Inefficient Code Example
for i in $(seq 1 1000); do
  echo $i
done

# Efficient Code Example
for ((i=1; i<=1000; i++)); do
  echo $i
done
```

The efficient example uses the for loop with arithmetic evaluation, eliminating the seq command which creates a separate process.

Pipelining and redirection also play significant roles in script optimization. When handling large volumes of data or chaining multiple commands, efficient use of pipes can help maintain performance. Here's an example illustrating effective piping:

```
# Inefficient Code Example
cat largefile.txt | grep "search term" | sort | uniq > output.txt

# Efficient Code Example
grep "search term" largefile.txt | sort | uniq > output.txt
```

The efficient example eliminates the redundant use of cat, directly feeding the file into grep.

Additionally, controlling the scope and lifecycle of variables can prevent unnecessary memory consumption and potential conflicts. Using local variables within functions ensures that variables do not persist longer than needed:

```
# Function with Global Variable
function process_file {
  FILENAME=$1
  # processing
}

# Cleaner function with Local Variable
function process_file {
  local FILENAME=$1
  # processing
}
```

Using local not only optimizes memory use but also increases the modularity and maintainability of scripts by preventing side effects.

Lastly, profiling and benchmarking scripts are essential to measure performance improvements. Tools such as time, bash -x, and strace can help identify bottlenecks and performance issues:

```
# Simple timing with time
time ./yourscript.sh

# Detailed tracing with bash -x
bash -x yourscript.sh

# System call tracing with strace
strace -c ./yourscript.sh
```

Profiling tools provide valuable insights into the script's execution flow and resource usage, facilitating targeted optimizations.

Implementing these techniques ensures scripts are not only optimized for performance but also more robust and maintainable. This practice is crucial in complex environments where efficiency and resource management are critical.

10.8 Interacting with System Processes and Daemons

Interacting with system processes and daemons is crucial for advanced shell scripting and automation. This section will discuss how to manipulate processes, read their status, and control their behavior using shell commands and scripts.

To begin, understanding a process within the Linux environment is fundamental. A process is a running instance of a program, each identified uniquely by a Process ID (PID). The Linux kernel manages processes, and you can control them using various shell commands.

Listing Processes: To list running processes, the ps command is commonly used. The ps command comes with several options, the most commonly used being ps aux, which provides a detailed list of all running processes.

```
ps aux
```

The output might be extensive, so it is common to pipe ps aux to a pager like less for easier navigation.

```
ps aux | less
```

Filtering Processes: To filter specific processes based on certain criteria, you can use grep. For instance, to find the process ID of a running apache2 service, you can execute:

```
ps aux | grep apache2
```

Managing Processes: The kill command is used to terminate processes. It sends a signal (default is SIGTERM) to the specified process. To send a different signal, specify it explicitly. For instance, to terminate a process forcefully, one can use SIGKILL:

```
kill -9 <PID>
```

To suspend a process, you can send SIGSTOP:

```
kill -STOP <PID>
```

To resume a suspended process, send SIGCONT:

```
kill -CONT <PID>
```

Launching Processes in Background: Using the & operator, you can start a process in the background, allowing the terminal to be available for further commands:

```
./long_running_task.sh &
```

You can use the jobs command to list current jobs put into the background:

```
jobs
```

To bring a background process to the foreground, use fg followed by the job number:

```
fg %1
```

System Daemons: A daemon is a background process that runs independently of user sessions, typically providing services. Daemons can be managed using the systemctl command, which interacts with the systemd system and service manager.

To start, stop, restart, or check the status of a daemon service, you might use the following commands:

```
sudo systemctl start <service_name>
```

```
sudo systemctl stop <service_name>
sudo systemctl restart <service_name>
sudo systemctl status <service_name>
```

For example, to manage the Apache HTTP server daemon apache2:

```
sudo systemctl start apache2
sudo systemctl stop apache2
sudo systemctl restart apache2
sudo systemctl status apache2
```

Daemons that need to automatically start at boot can be enabled using:

```
sudo systemctl enable <service_name>
```

Conversely, to prevent a daemon from starting at boot, disable it:

```
sudo systemctl disable <service_name>
```

Monitoring Daemon Logs: Logging is essential for diagnosing issues. Systemd uses the journald service for logging. To view logs for a specific service, use the journalctl command:

```
sudo journalctl -u <service_name>
```

For example, to view Apache logs:

```
sudo journalctl -u apache2
```

To view real-time logs, add the –follow or -f flag:

```
sudo journalctl -u apache2 -f
```

Being familiar with these commands and their appropriate use in scripts can aid in automated management of processes and daemons, ensuring your Linux environment operates smoothly and efficiently.

10.9 Using Regular Expressions and Pattern Matching

Regular expressions (regex) are powerful tools used for pattern matching and text processing. They enable efficient parsing, searching, and replacing of text within files and streams. In shell scripting, regular expressions can enhance the capability to handle complex text processing tasks, making scripts more robust and versatile.

The syntax of regular expressions can vary between tools and programming languages, but the fundamental concepts remain consistent. This section covers basic to advanced regex syntax and demonstrates their usage in common Linux tools such as grep, sed, and awk.

A regular expression is a sequence of characters that defines a search pattern. Below are some foundational elements of regex:

- **Literals:** Matches the exact character sequence. For example, the regex abc matches the string abc.
- **Metacharacters:** Characters with special meanings, such as ., *, +, ?, [ ], ( ), \, ^, and $.
- **Character Classes:** Denoted by square brackets, they match any one of the enclosed characters. For example, [abc] matches a, b, or c.
- **Predefined Character Classes:** Shortcuts for common classes, such as \d for digits and \w for word characters.
- **Quantifiers:** Specify the number of times a character or group must appear. Common examples include * (zero or more), + (one or more), ? (zero or one), and {n,m} (between n and m times).
- **Anchors:** Used to match positions in the input. ^ matches the start and $ matches the end of a line.

Linux provides several utilities that support regular expressions for text manipulation. Below are examples of using regex with grep, sed, and awk.

Using Regular Expressions with grep

The grep command searches for patterns within files. By default, grep uses basic regular expressions; the -E option enables extended regex.

```
# Searching for lines containing 'error' in a log file
grep 'error' logfile.txt

# Searching lines that start with 'Error' and end with a digit
grep -E '^Error.*[0-9]$' logfile.txt

# Inverting the match to display lines not containing 'error'
grep -v 'error' logfile.txt
```

Using Regular Expressions with sed

The sed command is a stream editor for filtering and transforming text. Regular expressions are used to define search patterns within sed scripts.

```
# Replacing 'foo' with 'bar' globally in a file
sed 's/foo/bar/g' input.txt

# Deleting lines that match a specific pattern
sed '/^#/d' input.txt

# Replacing all digits with asterisks
sed 's/[0-9]/*/g' input.txt
```

Using Regular Expressions with awk

The awk command is a powerful text processing utility that supports complex pattern matching and text manipulation using regular expressions.

```
# Printing lines that match a pattern
awk '/error/ {print}' logfile.txt

# Splitting input based on a regex delimiter
awk -F'[,;]' '{print $1, $2}' input.txt

# Using regex in conditional expressions
awk '$1 ~ /^[0-9]+$/ {print $1 " is numeric"}' input.txt
```

Regular expressions in shell scripting extend beyond specific utilities. Bash itself offers extensive support for regex within conditional statements and parameter expansion.

```
# Checking if a variable matches a regex pattern
pattern='^[0-9]+$'
if [[ $input =~ $pattern ]]; then
    echo "Input is a number"
else
    echo "Input is not a number"
fi

# Replacing substrings using regex in parameter expansion
input="123abc456"
output=${input//[0-9]/*}
echo "$output" # Output will be '***abc***'
```

Understanding and using regular expressions effectively can significantly enhance the text processing capabilities in Linux shell scripting. Mastery of regex allows for more concise, powerful, and flexible scripts, leading to improved automation and productivity. Regular expressions can be complex, but with practice, they become an invaluable tool for any advanced Linux user.

10.10 Automating with Cron and Systemd Timers

Automating tasks in Linux is essential for maintaining efficient and reliable systems. Two of the most powerful and commonly used tools for automation are cron and systemd timers. Understanding how to effectively utilize these tools can significantly enhance system performance and reliability.

Cron: Scheduled Task Automation

cron is a time-based job scheduling daemon found in Unix-like operating systems. Users can schedule scripts or commands to run at specific times or intervals, managed by cron using crontab files.

A crontab file consists of lines specifying the tasks to be executed and the schedule for their execution. Each line follows a specific format:

```
* * * * * command to be executed
- - - - -
| | | | |
| | | | +----- day of week (0 - 7) (Sunday=0 or 7)
| | | +------- month (1 - 12)
| | +--------- day of month (1 - 31)
| +----------- hour (0 - 23)
+------------- minute (0 - 59)
```

To illustrate, consider scheduling a script backup.sh to run every day at 2 AM. The corresponding crontab entry would be:

```
0 2 * * * /path/to/backup.sh
```

Adding and Managing Crontab Entries

Crontab entries are managed with the crontab command. For a thorough understanding, here are the common operations:

```
crontab -e # Edit the current user's crontab
crontab -l # List the current user's crontab entries
crontab -r # Remove the current user's crontab
```

Special Strings in Crontab

Crontab also supports special strings for common scheduling needs. Here are a few examples:

```
@reboot    # Run when the system reboots
@yearly    # Run once a year, equivalent to "0 0 1 1 *"
@monthly   # Run once a month, equivalent to "0 0 1 * *"
@weekly    # Run once a week, equivalent to "0 0 * * 0"
@daily     # Run once a day, equivalent to "0 0 * * *"
@hourly    # Run once an hour, equivalent to "0 * * * *"
```

For example, to run a script maintenance.sh at every system reboot:

```
@reboot /path/to/maintenance.sh
```

Systemd Timers: A Modern Alternative

As systems have evolved, systemd has become the default initialization system in many Linux distributions, providing systemd timers as a more powerful and flexible alternative to cron. Systemd timers integrate tightly with other systemd components, offering advanced features such as accurate timekeeping, logging, and dependency management.

Creating a Systemd Timer

Systemd timers require two unit files: a .timer file, which defines when the task will run, and a .service file, which defines the task to be executed.

For example, to run a backup script backup.sh daily, create the following files:

- /etc/systemd/system/backup.service
- /etc/systemd/system/backup.timer

```
[Unit]
Description=Daily Backup Service

[Service]
Type=oneshot
ExecStart=/path/to/backup.sh
```

```
[Unit]
Description=Runs backup.service daily

[Timer]
OnCalendar=daily
Persistent=true

[Install]
WantedBy=timers.target
```

To activate and start the timer:

```
sudo systemctl daemon-reload
sudo systemctl enable backup.timer
sudo systemctl start backup.timer
```

Advanced Timer Configurations

Systemd provides more sophisticated scheduling using the OnCalendar directive. For instance, to schedule a task every Monday at 6 PM, use:

```
OnCalendar=Mon 18:00
```

Also, you can use OnActiveSec and OnBootSec for relative times from activation and boot, respectively:

```
OnBootSec=15min # Start 15 minutes after boot
OnUnitActiveSec=1h # Run one hour after the service was last activated
```

Monitoring and Debugging Timers

Tracking the status and logs of systemd timers is streamlined through commands:

```
systemctl status backup.timer # Status of the timer
systemctl list-timers # List all active timers
journalctl -u backup.service # Logs for the backup service
```

Systemd timers provide reliable, high-fidelity automation, integrating seamlessly with broader system management features. Efficient use of both crontab and systemd timers ensures robust, efficient task automation in Linux environments, leveraging their respective strengths for various scenarios.

10.11 Creating and Managing Complex Automation Workflows

Creating and managing complex automation workflows in Linux involves orchestrating multiple tasks, scripts, and system processes to achieve a seamless and efficient operational flow. This section will delve into the methodologies and tools available to achieve this, focusing on real-world applications and best practices.

Automation workflows can significantly reduce the potential for human error and ensure consistency in repetitive tasks. These workflows encompass various elements, such as task scheduling, dependency handling, concurrent execution, and error recovery. We will explore each of these elements in detail.

Task Scheduling

Task scheduling is a critical aspect of automation workflows. In Linux, tasks can be scheduled using cron or systemd timers. cron is a time-based job scheduler that enables scheduling tasks at specific times or intervals.

A typical crontab entry looks like this:

```
# m h dom mon dow command
0 2 * * * /path/to/backup.sh
```

In this example, the task is scheduled to run the /path/to/backup.sh script every day at 2 AM.

systemd timers provide a more modern approach to scheduling, with finer control over various timer events. A systemd timer unit file might look like this:

```
[Unit]
Description=Run backup script daily

[Timer]
OnCalendar=daily
Persistent=true

[Install]
WantedBy=timers.target
```

The corresponding service unit file:

```
[Unit]
Description=Backup script

[Service]
Type=oneshot
ExecStart=/path/to/backup.sh
```

Enable the timer with:

```
sudo systemctl enable --now backup.timer
```

Dependency Handling

Complex workflows often involve tasks that depend on the successful completion of prior tasks. Properly managing these dependencies ensures that tasks execute in the correct order. In shell scripting, this is often managed using exit statuses.

Consider the following example where Task B should only execute if Task A succeeds:

```
#!/bin/bash

/path/to/task_A.sh
```

```
if [ $? -eq 0 ]; then
    /path/to/task_B.sh
else
    echo "Task A failed. Exiting."
    exit 1
fi
```

systemd takes a more declarative approach to dependency management. Using Wants, Requires, Before, and After directives in unit files allows clear specification of dependencies.

Here is an example:

```
[Unit]
Description=Task B
Requires=task_A.service
After=task_A.service

[Service]
Type=oneshot
ExecStart=/path/to/task_B.sh
```

Concurrent Execution

To improve efficiency, some tasks can be executed concurrently. This can be achieved using background processes in shell scripts or parallel execution in the context of a job scheduler.

In shell scripts, run a task in the background using the & operator:

```
#!/bin/bash

/path/to/task1.sh &
/path/to/task2.sh &
wait
```

The wait command ensures the script waits for all background processes to complete before proceeding.

Tools like GNU parallel enable parallel execution of commands and scripts with more complex control over input sources and command arguments:

```
cat commands.txt | parallel
```

Error Recovery

Robust automation workflows require mechanisms for error detection and recovery. This can prevent partial executions and ensure the system returns to a known good state.

Implementing error handling in shell scripts using trap allows capturing specific signals and executing recovery commands:

```
#!/bin/bash

trap 'echo "An error occurred. Cleaning up..."; /path/to/cleanup.sh; exit 1' ERR

/path/to/task_A.sh
/path/to/task_B.sh
```

systemd provides Restart and OnFailure directives to handle service failures:

```
[Service]
Type=oneshot
ExecStart=/path/to/task.sh
Restart=on-failure

[Unit]
OnFailure=notify-admin.service
```

The notify-admin.service unit would handle the notification or recovery steps.

Integrating All Components

A comprehensive example integrating the discussed components could be a service that checks system health, performs backups, and notifies an administrator on failure:

```
# health-check.service
[Unit]
Description=System Health Check

[Service]
Type=oneshot
ExecStart=/path/to/health_check.sh

# backup.service
[Unit]
Description=Perform Backup
Requires=health-check.service
After=health-check.service

[Service]
Type=oneshot
ExecStart=/path/to/backup.sh
OnFailure=notify-admin.service

# notify-admin.service
[Unit]
Description=Notify Administrator

[Service]
Type=oneshot
ExecStart=/path/to/notify_admin.sh

# health-check.timer
[Unit]
Description=Run health check and backup daily
```

```
[Timer]
OnCalendar=daily
Persistent=true

[Install]
WantedBy=timers.target
```

Enable the timer to initiate the workflow:

```
sudo systemctl enable --now health-check.timer
```

Creating and managing complex automation workflows involve meticulous planning and implementation of task scheduling, dependency management, concurrent execution, and error recovery strategies. Using tools such as cron, systemd, and parallel execution utilities, Linux administrators can design robust, efficient, and maintainable automation systems.

10.12 Best Practices for Writing Maintainable Scripts

Writing maintainable scripts is essential for long-term efficiency and scalability. High-quality scripts are easier to debug, extend, and understand by other developers. Several best practices, focusing on readability, organization, and robustness, can enhance the maintainability of shell scripts.

1. Use Meaningful Variable Names

Variables should have descriptive names that convey their purpose. This eliminates confusion and makes the code more readable. For example, use file_count instead of fc.

```
# Good
file_count=$(ls | wc -l)
echo "There are $file_count files in the directory."

# Bad
fc=$(ls | wc -l)
echo "There are $fc files in the directory."
```

2. Comment Your Code

Comments explain the purpose of code blocks and any non-obvious logic. Proper commenting is crucial for scripts that are likely to be modified or reviewed by others.

```
# Check if the backup directory exists; if not, create it
if [ ! -d "/backup" ]; then
    mkdir /backup
fi
```

3. Consistent Indentation and Formatting

Consistent indentation and formatting improve code readability. Use either tabs or spaces (but not both) and align code blocks for visual clarity.

```
# Good
if [ condition ]; then
    echo "Condition is true"
else
    echo "Condition is false"
fi

# Bad
if [ condition ]; then
echo "Condition is true"
else
echo "Condition is false"
fi
```

4. Use Functions for Repeated Code

Functions encapsulate repetitive code, making it reusable and easier to manage. This also assists in isolating and fixing bugs.

```
# Function to check disk usage
check_disk_usage() {
    disk_usage=$(df -h | grep '/dev/sda1')
    echo "Disk usage: $disk_usage"
}

# Call the function
check_disk_usage
```

5. Handle Errors Appropriately

Robust error handling ensures that scripts fail gracefully and provide useful error messages. Use techniques like checking exit statuses and trapping signals.

```
# Exit on error
set -e

# Check if file exists
if [ ! -f "data.txt" ]; then
    echo "Error: data.txt not found!"
    exit 1
fi
```

Additionally, implement traps to handle unexpected interruptions:

```
# Trap CTRL+C, CTRL+Z and quit singles
trap 'echo "Script interrupted"; exit' INT TERM
```

6. Modularize Scripts

Break down large scripts into smaller, modular components. Use external files and libraries to organize related functions and logic into separate, manageable pieces.

```
# Main script
source ./functions.sh
source ./config.sh

# Call functions from external files
initialize_system
```

7. Use ShellCheck for Static Analysis

ShellCheck is a tool that provides warnings and suggestions for shell scripts, helping to identify potential issues and improve code quality.

```
$ shellcheck myscript.sh
```

8. Version Control Your Scripts

Using version control systems like Git allows multiple developers to collaborate, track changes, and revert to previous versions if necessary.

```
$ git init
$ git add myscript.sh
$ git commit -m "Initial commit"
```

9. Follow the Principle of Least Privilege

Minimize the use of superuser privileges in scripts unless absolutely necessary. This reduces security risks and potential damage from errors.

```
# Avoid this
sudo rm -rf /

# Prefer this
rm -rf ~/temp_files
```

10. Documentation

Provide comprehensive documentation for your scripts. Include usage instructions, arguments, and environment setup details. This is especially useful for complex scripts.

11. Input Validation

Validate inputs to ensure they meet expected formats or ranges. This prevents incorrect data from causing unexpected behavior.

```
read -p "Enter a number between 1 and 10: " num
if [[ "$num" =~ ^[1-9]$|^10$ ]]; then
    echo "Valid number: $num"
else
    echo "Invalid input: $num"
    exit 1
fi
```

12. Use set for Safety

Incorporate set options to control script behavior and catch errors early. Commonly used options include:

```
set -e # Exit on error
set -u # Treat unset variables as an error
set -o pipefail # Return the exit status of the last command in the pipe that failed
```

13. External Configuration Files

Store configuration details in external files that the script can source. This separates the script logic from configuration data, making it easier to manage and update.

```
# Content of config.sh
DB_HOST="localhost"
DB_USER="admin"
DB_PASS="password"
DB_NAME="mydatabase"

# Main script
source ./config.sh
echo "Connecting to database $DB_NAME at $DB_HOST"
```

Implementing these best practices in shell scripting fosters code that is not only functional but also clean, modular, and adaptable to future needs.

Made in the USA
Monee, IL
05 November 2026

67911510R00184